PRAISE FOR *THE BOYS IN BROWN*

"*The Boys in Brown* is a valuable addition to the family of football books that are about much more than football. Jon J. Kerr'  community spirit and character building that' tion as winning at Carmel Catholic High Scho
    – Neil Hayes, Author o

"It's not a sports book. It's not a civics book. It's a story about people, about modern society and ancient values of family, community and sacrifice. "
                        – Joe Aguliar, Columnist, *Daily Herald*

"Jon J. Kerr has crafted an entertaining and fast paced story with narrative zeal. Through vigorous reporting, he brings the audience into this world where football, faith and community intersect."
                        – James Powers, *Palm Springs Magazine*

"I have a son and understand the importance of mentor figures in his life. The characters in this book personify the traits of people I want coaching my son...integrity and virtue."
                        – Kevin Reiterman, *North Shore Weekend*

"*The Boys in Brown* reminds me of our program culture, of how a community's spirits can be raised when young people play the game the right way."
        – Chuck Spagnoli, Head Football Coach, Lake Forest (IL) High School

"*The Boys in Brown* is about so much more than football. It's about how the identities of young men are formed from old-fashioned midwestern principles of selflessness, honesty and putting others needs ahead of their own."
        – Bill McNamara, Head Football Coach, Stevenson (IL) High School,
                                          2014 8A State Champion

THE BOYS IN BROWN

A TEAM, A COACH, A PASSAGE TO ADULTHOOD

*To Marion, for her imperishable heart
and life lived in the pursuit of social justice.*

CONTENTS

THE BOYS IN BROWN

A TEAM, A COACH, A PASSAGE TO ADULTHOOD

JON J. KERR

THE CARMEL CORSAIRS

THE COACHES:
Andy Bitto, head coach
Ben Berg, offensive coordinator
Tom Young, running backs
Tim Schrank, wide receivers
Jerry Rejc, offensive line
Jim Rejc, assistant head coach
Dan Potempa, defensive coordinator
Mike "Fitz" Fitzgibbons, defensive line
Tom Kelly, defensive backs
Joe May, linebackers
Larry Whittier, sophomore head coach
Kevin Nylen, freshman head coach
Enzo Magrin, video coordinator

SENIORS:
Ricky Acosta, defensive back
LaRon Biere, defensive back
Jack Butler, offensive lineman

Ryan Cappis, running back and wide receiver
Matt Carr, running back and defensive back
Michael Cohen, defensive end
Sam Crowley, offensive lineman
Pat Doherty, tight end
Michael Fitzgibbons, defensive back
Jake Gaza, defensive back
Chris Georgen, defensive lineman
Connor Greene, quarterback
Eric Hessing, tight end
James Hessing, defensive back
Brad Kamins, linebacker
Jake Klahs, wide receiver
Michael Kolb, defensive lineman
Jake Larson, defensive lineman
Thomas Leahy, defensive back
Logan Lester, offensive lineman
Paul Madison, linebacker
Patrick Mulroy, tight end
Bryan Parrish, offensive lineman
Matt Principe, offensive lineman
Jeff Schroeder, defensive back
Brian Serio, quarterback
Tommy Snyder, defensive lineman
Garrett Sykora, defensive lineman
Andrew Thompson, tight end
Luke Venegoni, linebacker
Sean Wolf-Lewis, offensive lineman

JUNIORS:
Tommy Abbene, defensive lineman
Brian Brennan, running back and defensive back
Jack Brolley, defensive back

Nick Bruenning, offensive lineman

Anthony Caracciolo, defensive lineman

Jack Conarchy, manager

Kevin Cox, linebacker

Sam Duprey, defensive lineman

Michael Dyer, offensive lineman

Jordan Kos, fullback

John Krzeminski, safety

Matt Maher, running back

Morgan Mason, manager

Tyler Lees, linebacker

Mitch Nelson, linebacker

J.C. Pawlak, defensive back

Michael Panico, running back

Seamus Quilty, linebacker

Michael Riemer, defensive back

John Salvi, defensive back

Raul Santana, defensive lineman

Sean Terrett, offensive lineman

Shane Toub, offensive lineman

Luke Urbanik, running back

Mike Varney, offensive lineman

Austin Zupec, defensive back

Sophomores:

Brian Brennan, defensive back

Bill Dolan, defensive lineman

Steven O'Block, kicker

Tim Serio, fullback

PROLOGUE

THE SHOES ON THEIR FEET ARE OVERSIZED, pants sag like a teenager's on the subway. Through the masks jutting out from their crowns are the faces of freckled children, learning to play a hard, demanding team sport with boyhood in full bloom.

They go by the names Chase, Matthew, Anthony, Peter, Jack and Gomez, although those are only a few of the participants. Peter is the quarterback, his voice cracking with shrillness, and the sound of nascent puberty. He lines up under his center, Anthony. He calls the play.

"Thirty...ready, set, go!" Peter yells.

Up from their stances, the boys move. Some forward, some backward. Some to the side. And some don't move at all. A coach blows his whistle.

"Everybody listen up! We're not blocking anybody. Anthony, you're supposed to be out here."

The coach hops a few steps off the line of scrimmage.

"You see? I'm like a bunny!" he says.

"Yep. He's like a bunny," repeats Jack, the offensive tackle.

Peter lines up under center again.

"Jet right 28...ready, set, go!" he barks.

Dave, the running back, takes the hand-off from Peter and runs to the right side.

"Gomez!" the coach says. "Get your butt up higher. You'll get a better split. Slide over."

As Gomez moves over, a sound erupts from the same butt his coach was just referring to. It is a noise men of all ages recognize instantly.

"That's disgusting!" says Sean, one of the fathers who is helping out. "Ten laps for that!"

In unison, like scalawags hit by cannon fire, the boys fall to the turf, giggling.

At last, synchronicity achieved!

"Boys are pigs," says the coach. "OK, I have to go to a meeting."

Before he walks off, he pats each boy on the helmet.

"Good job. Game is Sunday. Tell your mom," he says. "And stop being jerkos."

He turns to a player in street clothes.

"Where do you live? You going to Carmel? I'm going to have to stay on top of you to make sure you're not terrorizing the teachers. Then you are really going to be a good player."

The player laughs. "OK, coach."

And then the coach is off. But he'll be back. He always comes back.

"I have to turn the lights off," he says.

CHAPTER ONE

BIRTH OF A SEASON

W HAT A RELIEF TO LET IT GO. To release the emotional weight. To tell everyone his story. He didn't know he could do it. It had been inside of him for so long. His mother. She gave him up. Why did she do that? He never understood. He still doesn't. He may never. It feels good to not think about the why for a while. Only to share that it happened. Much less complicated.

LaRon is not a pity kid. He doesn't want your sympathy. That's not why he opened up about his life. People do things, you know? Maybe she was in a bad place. Maybe the timing wasn't right. She had other children. Maybe she thought he'd be better off having someone else raise him. Somebody who had more means. Money was tight. That makes sense if you really think about it. But you know what doesn't make sense to LaRon? She didn't want him. He was just a few days old when she gave him up. Did she know something about him? Did she think he would turn out bad? That's the thought that hurts the most, what he's bottled up for so long. But for the last few days, the pain has all been tucked away, repurposed and repositioned. Now he feels compassion, empathy, even love.

God didn't make junk.

LaRon stands behind the lectern, ready to speak. His best friends are there—Ryan, Matt and Brian. They have been there for him since freshman football. He's so grateful for them. And all of these new friends! Many of whom he barely knew on Tuesday. Today is Friday. He's never told anybody the things he told them. About Marion. How they fought so much. How they used to butt heads. It wasn't always like that. When he was younger, it was different. He could tell her things. She would listen. Then it got hard. Then she got sick. It's funny how a person's perspective on life can change in just a few days. When you have time to think. To talk about stuff. And Marion's been on his mind quite a bit. He feels like he understands better. Why she did what she did. The adoption.

This is what they do at the end. Everyone together, in the church. They didn't know they would end up here, in front of all these people. It's hard to make out any faces, there are so many. There's Matt's mom and dad. And Ryan's. And Brian's. Oh, how Marion would have loved to be here. She loved the church. She wanted her son to understand God, to accept his presence. He's never been so sure. But not now. Now he feels it all around him. He feels her.

Matt calls his name.

$\sim$

There are songs that remind us of seminal moments in our lives. They provide a nostalgic sound track that can rewind our memories back to a time when a relationship was in that primordial, hypnotic, bewitched phase, or the joy of a beloved child taking his or her first steps. All it takes is a note to trigger an emotional response. The same can be said of a scent. About this place, people often say, "there's a smell to it," instantly recognizable to lifers.

This place is Carmel Catholic High School.

Its history can be traced to the 12th century. All those years ago, the Crusaders were raging in the Holy Land. Battles reached Israel, where efforts to reclaim the Holy Land fueled epic struggles that extended for centuries. Desirous for a way of life motivated by a deeper understanding of religion, those fighting stayed in the Holy Land. Many matriculated to the northwestern part of Israel, where a coastal mountain range extended from the Mediterranean Sea. The land plateaued high up top, with deep canyons on both sides. If you were to look from high above, its shape resembled that of a giant aircraft carrier.

In this stretch of land north of what is now Palestine, these fighters founded a community named Mount Carmel and devoted their lives in the spirit of a biblical prophet, Elijah. Around 800 B.C., Elijah raged fierce contests with evil forces, emotional encounters balanced by long periods of solitude and reflection. Longing to adopt Elijah's reclusive countenance after so many years of Crusader-fueled bloodshed, the 12th-century pioneers lived in tiny cells within this high ground, spending each day praying and discussing their spiritual awakenings. Before long, they called themselves the Brothers of our Lady of Mount Carmel, then later, a fraternity of Carmelites. By the early 13th century, they had drawn up their Rule of Life, about how a Carmelite should live a life in the service of God. The Rule consists of 1,600 words, divided into 24 chapters. A few chapters read as follow:

'None of the brothers must lay claim to anything as his own, but you are to possess everything in common; and each is to receive from the prior—that is from the brother he appoints for the purpose—whatever befits his age and needs.'

'Faith must be your shield on all occasions, and with it you will be able to quench all the flaming missiles of the wicked one: there can be no pleasing God without faith; [and the victory lies in this—your faith].'

'On your head set the helmet of salvation, and so be sure of deliverance by our only Saviour, who sets his own free from their sins. The sword of the spirit, the word of God, must abound in your mouths and hearts. Let all you do have the Lord's word for accompaniment.'

Also known as the "Rule of St. Albert," (named after St. Albert, a priest who scripted the chapters) The Rule was first confirmed by Pope Honorius III in 1226. Tensions forced the men to flee to Europe in the mid-13th century. In 1247, The Rule was modified by Pope Innocent IV, and the Carmelites soon went from living as hermits to becoming active members of the church.

Whether on the slopes of Mount Carmel, or in Cyprus, France, England and eventually across the Atlantic Ocean, prayer remained at the center of the Carmelite lifestyle. Words spoken by the prophet Elijah were often a guiding principle:

"God lives, in whose presence I stand."

~

It's just after 8 p.m. on June 13, 2010. On this warm summer evening, teenage boys are throwing tennis balls at each other inside a stuffy high school gymnasium in Mundelein, Illinois.

"My name is Brian."

Brian tosses the ball to one of 10 boys in a circle. The boy snatches it out of the air.

"Thanks, Brian. My name is Michael."

They cannot drop the tennis ball; otherwise the exercise starts from the beginning. All of this unfolds under the watchful eye of serious-looking men dressed in khakis and golf shirts. Except the one leading the exercise. He is wearing shorts and a gray T-shirt with "NAVY" on the front.

Quickly he throws a second round of ammunition into the game. The boys now have to track two flying objects. Balls drop to the floor. Confusion reigns. One of the stern-faced men stands alone off to the side. The top of his head is bald but for a few stray follicles that sprinkle its peak. Around his ears, his remaining hair is turning gray at the temples. He explains the point of the exercise.

"I want them to be able to work together in close quarters when the pressure is on," he says. "It's important to work through those things."

The man is Andy Bitto, the head football coach at Carmel Catholic High School. The upcoming 2010 season will be his 13th. His predecessor is the evening's activities director, Michael Fitzgibbons—Fitz to his friends—who may possess the loudest voice on the planet.

"Abject failure! That's OK!" Fitz says to a group of boys in one of his softer tones, akin to Jimmy Page playing the ukulele. "We threw six balls in there. You got better. What does this tell us about repetitions? You start listening to each other. Win together, lose together."

It's 10 weeks away from Carmel's season opener. No official practices have been held, but this night is of utmost importance to the success of the 2010 campaign. Referred to by Carmel's coaches as "Lock In," the activities are part of an all-night retreat with players from the junior and senior classes. Think indoor dude ranch meets Tony Robbins seminar, minus the livestock and walking on fire. Fitz started Lock In when he was head coach, and Coach Bitto uses it as a Pre-Cana for football players, a measuring stick for determining how his guys will get along on and off the field. Team chemistry is vital if Carmel is to reach its goal: to repeat as East Suburban Catholic Conference champions.

During one exercise, groups of ten form a human knot by clasping the hand of the person across from them. They must somehow untangle the labyrinth of arms and fingers without unclasping their grip. Coach Bitto is particularly interested in one group of snarled, twisted limbs. Within this group is senior-to-be Luke Venegoni. He stands 6-2 and wears a white T-shirt with "House of Speed" printed in front and a thin red bandana wrapped around his forehead. Luke possesses the classic tall, lean, muscular build for Carmel's speed-based defensive system. With dark, handsome features—a mix of his German mother and Italian father—Luke is straight out of football linebacker central casting, commanding a room with a luminous presence that speaks: *"Listen to me. I've been here before."*

And he has. Luke is the third Venegoni brother to play at Carmel. Showing the independent streak of a youngest child, he's the only one not to play quarterback. His brothers liked having the ball in their hands, in control of a play's outcome. As dutiful younger brothers often do, Luke tried at first to be like his older siblings. In grade school, he attempted to play quarterback. But he kept fumbling the ball when it was snapped. He soon discovered to trust his instincts and follow his heart. He liked to hit people. A perfect trait for a linebacker.

But at the moment, Venegoni's not thinking about bloodlines or shedding blockers. He's just trying to keep this creatural pretzel civilized.

"Georgan! You have to jump through here! I have to go under this and under there," he says, trying to sound authoritative in what appears to be a doomed exercise.

Also engaging limbs in the ethnological vortex is junior Jordan Kos. He's wearing a burnt-orange Texas T-shirt and a bandana wider than Venegoni's.

Brown in color, it looks like a piece of cloth stolen from the skirt of famous 18th-century Irish pirate Anne Bonny. As much as Venegoni is the perfect linebacker, Kos is the ideal fullback in Carmel's option-based offense. Standing 5-10 and weighing 190 pounds, he possesses the leg strength necessary to take hits and plow through defenders. An all-conference pick as a sophomore, he is the Corsairs' most talented offensive player. But there is concern about Kos's commitment and attitude.

While Venegoni continues to shout instructions—"Roll over! Spread out! Excellent!"—Kos stands outside, his back turned to the group, arms behind his body inside the center of the circle. Kos flashes a mischievous grin. A few seconds later, he is drawn back into the circle, lowering into a squat. As the weight of bodies shifts, one boy leans heavily on Kos, who belts, "Get off me!" Venegoni intervenes, redirecting the traffic. "What hand are you holding? Go that way!"

It's one moment in a long night of interactions, but it provides a snapshot of the retreat's intent. One leader emerges; another does nothing to diminish doubts. Coach Bitto's eyes are locked on the cluster containing Venegoni and Kos.

"You are naturally narcissistic when you are younger. It's more about me, me, me," Coach Bitto says. "We want that to shift to, 'OK, how is this process and journey going to be about us? How do we project that we can do things for other people, project this in the community? You are no longer Joe Blow at football, but Joe Blow at Carmel. It's our bone marrow."

If the mission of the school has been absorbed into the bloodstream of any man, it's Andy Bitto. He is one of twelve children, all of whom attended Carmel. One of the best running backs the school ever produced, Bitto was all-conference in 1979, his junior season. At 5-foot-10, 170 pounds, he overcame his size deficiencies with a competitiveness that bordered on insanity.

During his junior season, Carmel was set to play Warren High School, a public school in Gurnee, just north of Carmel's campus. If Bitto had gone to a public school, he would have gone to Warren. As the story goes, he had somehow gotten his hands on a stuffed mouse. Teachers remember him sticking the toy in his mouth and chewing on it while in class.

"He called it the 'Warren mouse,'" said Jerry Rejc, Bitto's geometry teacher at Carmel and an assistant football coach that season. "I kept looking at him and saying, 'Can we get this game over with?' He had so much energy. He always had energy."

By the end of the week, all that was left of the plaything was its tail. The episode became a metaphor for what happened to the poor Blue Devils that Friday night. Bitto chewed up his public school foes, rushing for more than 200 yards.

After a great junior season, Bitto decided he wanted to play in college. Ten days before his senior year, he was lifting weights in the school gym. "I was doing power cleans and slipped and fell on my back."

He dislocated nine bones in his left wrist.

"I wasn't going to the hospital. So all night long I'm rolling around in complete misery. The next morning, I finally told my mom I have to go get it checked out."

Doctors performed surgery right away. They built a cast that went all the way up his arm. "I don't know why it was that high," Bitto says. He could barely move the limb, let alone play football. But he was up against the clock, with practices for the 1980 season starting in a few days. He couldn't hold a football or work out with plaster covering up his hand and forearm. "So I took a butcher knife and cut the cast below the elbow so I could practice. I didn't miss one practice or one game. But I wasn't very good," he says. "Then I hurt my left shoulder. I was still diving into piles. The orthopedic said you wouldn't be able to move your wrist when you are 40, but I didn't care. When you are 17 you don't care about 40. It hurts me every day, but I wouldn't have it any other way."

Rejc said: "He played the year in excruciating pain. You have the utmost respect for someone who does that. He was our best player and he felt like he owed it to the team to do what he could do."

The offers didn't come. One school, Ball State University in Muncie, Indiana, told him he could walk on. If he worked hard and produced, he could earn a scholarship eventually. Bitto took it.

When he got to Ball State, he was seventh on the depth chart. "They used to post it in the locker room, 'Bitto 7th fullback.' That was a reality pill," Bitto says. But by his senior year, he had earned that scholarship. It was then he began—unofficially—his coaching career.

"There was a sophomore, Jay Neal, who was starting in front of me, an all-state wrestler who could do the splits. A stud," Bitto says. "But if you said right, he'd go left. I'd sit in the film room with him and tell him how to be a better blocker, where his head has to be. In essence, I was teaching him how to keep my job."

He did, and in the process, Neal became Bitto's first coaching pupil. "I ran into him a few years ago. He said he wasn't surprised I became a coach. He admitted I helped him out. That was nice. In turn, he was showing me what I should be doing."

And while at Ball State, Bitto began to discover what takes some men a lifetime: It was *around* the game where he felt most comfortable. It would prove to be his salvation.

In October of 1984, Bitto was a senior at Ball State. He was getting ready to head to practice. The phone rang. "It was the only time Dad ever called me," Bitto says. Mr. Bitto had news: His daughter, Andy's sister, had been in a car accident. She didn't survive. "I remember falling on the ground like my legs didn't exist." He got up and drove to the stadium for practice. It was a workday after all, and the Cardinals had a game Saturday. Bitto was putting on his uniform when he told a teammate what had happened. "He started bawling. I was still in shock. I hadn't cried yet. I told him I need to get out of here, and he was like 'Damn right. What are you doing here?'"

Bitto was home for several days. Not once did he receive a phone call from his coaches. "I'm sure they were occupied, but you couldn't take five or 10 minutes to call?" Bitto says. "They could have sent one of the coaches or a graduate assistant to represent the team. Didn't do it. Maybe it wasn't that important. I certainly didn't feel that important."

The Friday before the funeral, Carmel happened to be playing its homecoming game. Needing a break from the anguish at home, he decided to attend the pep rally. When it was over, the bleachers cleared of people, except for Bitto. Climbing up the rows to join him was one of his former football coaches. Fitz.

"I didn't know where to go," Bitto told him.

"Where else would you come?" Fitz asked Bitto.

"My college life was ending and my life was spinning out of control," Bitto recalls "I had a conversation with Fitz. I was like, 'I can get control of this. I'd rather be doing this than work in the corporate world.' I told him I need to coach." And by revealing his desires, he granted himself permission to pursue what he was always meant to do. He became an assistant coach the next year.

It's been more than 25 years since Bitto had his moment of clarity on that painful homecoming afternoon. He still mourns the loss of a beloved sister. He feels the effects of multiple concussions suffered during his ferocious playing days. "They never checked for those things in those days," Bitto says. "I can rattle off all the presidents in a row, but if I coached a kid two years ago, unless I know his face, I can't remember. It bothers me."

Tonight, at Lock In, he doesn't have to remember the evening's schedule. It's written on a sheet of paper, held by a clipboard Bitto grips with a permanently weakened left hand.

There's much to learn about the 2010 Carmel Corsairs football team. But the coach has a secure hold on his own time and place in the universe. It's right here, right now.

"I've said it before. This place smells. It smells of family. It smells like acceptance. It smells like friendship. It really smells. And God sent me to Carmel to have that smell on that day, the day before my sister's funeral. This is the job God wanted me to do. Year in year out, being here brings me closer to God."

∽

Time is up on the limb-twist contest, and Fitz gathers the boys for a post-mortem. He doubles as the school's ministry coordinator, and this season, he will be the Corsairs' defensive line coach. Fitz is as reticent about retirement as a prize fighter. After handing the head-coaching reigns over to Andy before the 1998 season, he stayed away from football until 2003, when he was on the staff of a state championship team. Shortly thereafter, he stepped away again. He's pulling a Muhammad Ali this season, back for one last round. His rationale is straight out of the father's almanac. His oldest son is a senior on the team, penciled in as a defensive starter. Keeping with an Irish Catholic tradition, he's also named Michael. Fitz wants to experience this season with Michael, not just as an observer but also as a participant.

Right now, he's fully engaged in the task at hand. So far, so good.

"There's a process to this. I noticed you started listening to each other," Fitz tells the boys. He's crouched, hands on his knees, facing them, including Michael. "You have to disregard a bad idea yet not make the person feel like a jerk."

Sitting in the front row, listening intently as Fitz bounces between professorial observations and Zig Ziglar-like motivational quotations, is senior-to-be LaRon Biere, wearing a T-shirt with Arizona State printed on the front. His dark hair and black skin make him stand out in a room filled with white kids.

CHAPTER TWO

THE HOMESTEADER

THERE'S A YOUNG MOTHER HERE AND SHE HAS A NEWBORN," the Catholic Charities caseworker told Marion Biere over the phone. "She's HIV positive and the child might be infected. The mother can't take care of him."

The woman went on to say that the mother has already lost several other children, and that she was an addict and a prostitute.

After all of those bombshells, Marion still said, "OK, let me come in and see the child."

It was May of 1993.

~

The next morning, Marion arrived at St. Therese's Hospital in Waukegan. There she saw the baby for the first time, only 72 hours old. He was tiny. So small, he looked like a preemie.

"Can you take him?" one of the nurses asked Marion. "He's in drug-induced withdrawals. He might be HIV-positive. He needs round-the-clock care."

Marion knew how critical the first few days were for a child in grave medical condition. She had spent many years as a nurse. She had a deep understanding of the health risks. Marion also understood the urgency of starting the clock on maternal-infant bonding. Children who connect with their mother soon after birth are less likely to have problems later on with substance abuse, teen pregnancy, and general juvenile delinquency. A baby born addicted to drugs compounds these potential problems. And without precious hours in a hospital room, cuddling with its mother, a baby is at higher risk, his nervous system less resilient to stress, which could lead to miscreant behavior. Marion knew all of this. Her mind was made up.

"Yes, I'll take him."

Driving home, with the tiny creature in a car seat next to her, Marion took a deep breath. For a moment, she allowed for reflection.

I just might be crazy. What will my husband think? What about my six kids? For Pete's sake, I'm a grandmother.

But through that sick little boy, there was a stronger voice speaking to the conscience of 61-year-old Marion Biere, one that she couldn't shake.

~

Marion Wegener was born in Wauconda, Illinois, on December 31, 1931. She was the first of five children of Aloys and Agnes Wegener, both Germans. From a young age she was well aware of her responsibilities as the eldest sibling. By 1940, her father had moved the family to Volo, a rural farming community 55 miles northwest of Chicago. When Marion was eight years old, Agnes became very ill, and it was Marion who took over the household until her mother recovered, cooking and cleaning and feeding the chickens. It was a heavy load, reminiscent of tales of homesteaders where the eldest daughter replaced the duties of the sick mother. Her sister, Joanne, would help as much as she could, as did her grandmother, but it was Marion who dominated the daily chores, directing her two younger siblings on how to perform theirs.

From the time Joanne could remember, Marion took to the idea of nursing as a profession. In grade school, the nuns who taught the children put on a commencement recital. There was singing, poetry reads, and other performances. It was something everyone looked forward to all year, appearing on the big stage at the local high school, Grant, in Fox Lake. Marion was in eighth grade and had the lead role in the play, "Taffy Ann." A few days before the play, she had a crushing pain in her stomach. Not wanting to disappoint her classmates and all who came from miles away to watch, she pressed on, embodying the ancient performer's creed that the show must go on. Marion would perform a scene, then find a private area behind the stage and put ice on her throbbing skin. When the play was over, she told her parents about her ailment and they took her to the hospital. The diagnosis was appendicitis. Her time in the hospital lasted a week, but she would have happily stayed longer. The nurses were so kind, so committed to her well-being, she felt at home. She was smitten.

When it was time to pick a high school, Aloys was not about to let his daughters attend the public school. He had heard rumors of the tomfoolery that went on between the public school boys and girls in the open lands near their farm. He was protective of his girls and thought they would be better influenced in a parochial environment. As for Agnes, she didn't care where her girls went to school. She never got as far as high school, and all she wanted was for them to get an education beyond what she'd experienced.

Desirous to fulfill her husband's wishes for their daughters, Agnes asked around town and learned of an all-girls Catholic school in Waukegan called Holy Child, founded in 1921 and run by the sisters from the Society of the Holy Child Jesus. But it was 25 miles away from the family farm and there was no school-provided transportation available. They would have to find a driver. So Agnes went to work, asking everyone if they knew someone who could transport Marion to Holy Child. She eventually found a man named Mr. O'Leary. He lived in Volo and worked at the Meadow Gold dairy plant not far from Holy Child. He agreed to drive Marion each morning, as long as she was dropped off at his farm, two and a half miles from the Wegeners' residence. So each day, Marion's dad drove her to Mr. O'Leary's farm. At the end of the school day, Marion would wait the hour or so it took for Mr. O'Leary to get off of work so he could drive her home. This was the routine for two years, until Mr. O'Leary had an ulcer operation. The Wegeners had to find another driver.

By then, Joanne was also at Holy Child. Their resourceful, persistent mother soon found a man who worked at Johns Mansville, a plant on the east side of Waukegan, near Lake Michigan. He lived in Lily Lake, 40 miles south of Volo. He agreed to pick the girls up in the morning as long as they were dropped off at Focil's filling station on the outskirts of town. He was a foreman at Johns Mansville Manufacturing, arriving at the plant at 6:30 a.m. This meant Marion and Joanne would have to rise before the chickens. After school, they waited hours for the man to get off his shift and take them home.

Joanne would pass the time shooting baskets with the other skirt-clad schoolgirls, while Marion would sit quietly in a vacant classroom or hallway, dutifully completing her homework. At Holy Child, Marion thrived in her studies. She was happy, making plenty of friends and forging deep relationships with the nuns who ran the school.

~

It wouldn't be out of the ordinary for girls not to go to school after eighth grade. You learned how to cook and clean and take care of the chickens. It was hard going. I remember my maternal grandmother. In order to give money to the Volo church she didn't get her new coat. Every five years she got a new coat. Her coat was worn out. She would make it last so there could be money to the church.

- Sister Joanne Wegener, Marion's sister

~

The Holy Child campus consisted of two buildings that housed a convent, dormitory for boarders, gymnasium, auditorium and classrooms. The city around it, Waukegan, was at the tail end of a population boom. As a result of both World Wars being fought in Europe, large numbers of people had immigrated to the Midwest. Before then, in the 1920s and 1930s, African-Americans migrated from the South in large numbers, looking for better

the pomposity. This was when the band would recognize its musical influences. On the album *Dead Letter Office*, R.E.M. covered the song "Pale Blue Eyes" by Velvet Underground. Before Stipe wrote about them in the album liner notes, I had no idea who Velvet Underground was. After my favorite band gave them a testimonial, I sure wanted to find out. This acknowledgment opened a window previously shut in my relationship with R.E.M. They weren't just some obtuse group of guys who invented songs out of thin air. They listened to music. They had contemporaries they admired. They were *from* somewhere.

Printed in brown paper, Carmel has its own version of an album sleeve: the team program. Handed out at each home game, the first six columns provide basic roster information found on any standard football program.

87 Patrick Mulroy SR 6'2" 205 TE

But listed in the column farthest to the right is the academic and spiritual bone marrow of each player:

St. Gilbert
St. Patrick
St. Francis
Santa Maria
St. Anastasia

There is something both germane and kindred about printing each player's grade school inside the program.

Football is a tightly uniformed sport. The body armor encourages the violent nature of the game, and its relationship with the audience can become brutishly transactional. *Wow! Did you see the hit number 56 put on that running back? Man is he a physical player. Can't wait to see whom he'll knock out next!*

What can get lost is that underneath all the armaments and protective coverings are real people who come from real places. Yes, height and body weight are important to football. It's a tough sport played by tough guys. But to see "St. Joseph's, Libertyville" listed next to the name "Tyler Lees" conjoins me with Tyler on a level more intimate than whether he can just block and tackle. Like the liner notes on an R.E.M. album, I know more about that player. I know he's from somewhere, a place revered by someone.

The 60 varsity players on this season's Carmel Corsairs come from 18 different grade schools, 16 Catholic, two public. The middle school most represented is St. Patrick's in Wadsworth, 14 miles northeast of Carmel's campus. Nine Corsairs attended St. Pat's. Eight are graduates of St. Mary's in Buffalo Grove, 10 miles south of Carmel. St. Gilbert's in Grayslake, a 13-minute drive northwest, is responsible for seven Corsairs. And St. Joseph's in Libertyville, with five football graduates, is a straight two-mile shot east of campus on Highway 176.

The rest of the names on the roster are equally spread out among grade schools: St. Francis De Sales (Lake Zurich, nine miles southwest), St. Paul (Gurnee, nine miles north), and Woodland Middle School (Gurnee). There are also representatives from Santa Maria Del Popolo (Mundelein, two miles southwest), St. Anastasia (Waukegan, 14 miles northeast), St. Bede (Ingleside), Round Lake Middle School (Round Lake), Prince of Peace (Lake Villa), Transfiguration (Waukegan) and Our Lady of Humility (Beach Park). This is a geographically, if not ethnically, diverse group of student-athletes.

Ricky Acosta, a senior defensive back, is the son of Nicaraguan immigrants. Junior defensive lineman Raul Santana, a 2008 graduate of St. Anastasia Catholic School, is Mexican. The rest of the roster is populated by white Irish lads with names lifted from the credits of a Jim Sheridan film: Brennan, Quilty, Doherty, Parrish, Cappis, Whitman, Brolley and Fitzgibbons.

Natives of the Republic of Ireland share a heritage fraught with wars, plagues, and religious prejudice. But no matter how chaotic the climate, over the centuries, the two activities most responsible for uniting a fractured people have been sport and faith. A walk around Carmel's campus is an exposure to both.

In 1915, George William Mundelein came to Chicago from New York as archbishop of the city's archdiocese. He possessed a grand vision to create a

Catholic education nerve center in Chicago. Soon after his arrival, he began to build on property in a small community known as Area, 33 miles northwest of Chicago's Loop. In 1921, he opened St. Mary's by the Lake Seminary. Five years later, half a million people traveled to what became known as Mundelein, Illinois, and St. Mary's by the Lake to attend the 28th International Eucharistic Congress.

By the 1950s, suburbanization engulfed Lake County, where Mundelein stood. A north-south tollway (Interstate 94) was built, hastening population growth. Families were escaping the city and moving to the suburbs, finding jobs with companies fortifying operation bases in Lake County. This exodus created demand for education, specifically Catholic education. Well aware of this, the Chicago Archdiocese donated 50 acres of farm land just south of St. Mary's by the Lake. For decades, the land was used to grow food and nourish the seminarians. But the Archdiocese had a grander, long-range purpose for the land—to build upon it two high schools, one for boys and one for girls. It asked two orders—the Carmelites and the Sisters of Charity of the Blessed Virgin Mary—to operate the schools.

On a rainy Monday morning, September 10, 1962, Carmel High School for Boys opened its doors. To avoid muddying up their soft-heeled loafers, the anxious young students stepped on wooden planks before entering the building. Several Carmelite priests, dressed in brown robes, used mops to dry the water-saturated floors. Later that day, the school principal, Father David Murphy, O. Carm., gathered the boys in the school's common area. Wearing a modest brown habit, he ascended a chair and spoke to the school's historic first class.

"Men, we have one objective in mind, and that is to make you gentlemen."

∽

A year later, in 1963, the Carmel School for Girls opened. The wooden planks gone, the girls walked down the freshly tiled hallways in their new brown saddle shoes. Carmel still sits on the same 50 acres of land off state

Highway 176 in Mundelein, although the school's aesthetics have changed a bit. A visitor will see athletic fields on one side of campus, to the south and east, and classrooms to the west. The property is dotted by well-manicured greenery. On early fall days, the leaves turn into a striking shade of chestnut and auburn, matching the color of the school's mahogany brick foundation. A statute of the Virgin Mary rises at each of the two entrances. Directly to the north, across Highway 176, is St. Mary's of the Lake Seminary. Single-family homes and open lands surround the area beyond the grounds.

Visitors receive brochures with mission statements that talk of "empowering students to become reflective thinkers, grateful stewards, and responsible leaders." They see evidence of state scholars and national merit finalists, and read of the college preparatory curriculum and campus ministry. Only after a dozen pages are flipped is there mention of football.

Carmel's football home, Baker Stadium, is understated in stature. On game nights, a glow emanates from the stadium lights, and it is visible for miles. But you must drive onto campus to see firsthand the 3,000-seat facility itself. Its modesty speaks to the recent rise in status of the Carmel football program.

The school fielded its first team in 1965. Over the first 20 years, the Corsairs were 68-163-3. That included a particularly ignominious six-year stretch during the 1970s, when the team's record was 13-41. Things began to turn when Mike Fitzgibbons was hired in 1986. In his third season, the Corsairs made the playoffs for the first time. Two seasons later, they won a school-record nine games. In all, Fitzgibbons-led teams earned six playoff berths during a 12-year span. When Fitzgibbons retired after the 1997 season, his defensive coordinator, Andy Bitto, was hired by then-Principal Father Bob Carroll to take over a good program and make it great. In 2000, after two losing seasons to start his tenure, Bitto and Carmel began a decade-long stretch of success never seen before. A trip to the state semifinals in 2001 was followed by a 13-win season and a Chicago city championship in 2002. The next year, the Corsairs were state champions. Three 10-win seasons followed, and in 2009, Carmel qualified for the state playoffs for the 10th straight season.

But that last effort ended with a first-round playoff loss, which would keep Carmel off the grid in 2010 preseason polls. No publication—the *Chicago Tribune, Chicago Sun-Times, Daily Herald* or *Pioneer Press*—listed the Corsairs in its Top 20.

There are good reasons for the Corsairs' lack of buzz. Aside from Lester, the offensive line has no returning starters. One of the team's running backs, junior Michael Panico, was a defensive back in 2009. Serio was a starting quarterback as a junior in 2009, but got hurt and didn't play a full season. Junior running back Matt Maher, a blocking specialist, has never played a full varsity season. On defense, Carmel is more experienced. Eight seniors— Luke Venegoni, Mike Fitzgibbons, Jake Larson, Michael Cohen, Chris Georgan, Matt Carr, Ricky Acosta and LaRon Biere—are at the top of the depth chart when the team's July team camp ends.

Essential to any successful football team is leadership. Where that will come from, especially on the offensive side, remains a question mark. During the July camp, offensive coordinator Ben Berg pulled Lester aside and made a request of his 6-1, 290-pound guard.

"We only have two returning starters on this offense that are going to be seniors: you and Serio. And we both know he is not a vocal leader. You are going to have to be a leader this year."

"Coach, I'm not exactly vocal, either," Lester said.

"You're going to have to be because he's (Serio) not going to talk," Berg said.

The most talented player on offense is junior fullback Jordan Kos. But with Kos's ability to run the football—which is at, at times, herculean— comes an intolerance for procedure. An incident during the team's July camp illuminates his disobedience and the birth of the team's of lead-by-example culture.

Carmel was conducting a non-contact drill. Throughout the drill, Kos's behavior straddled the line between indignation and lethargy. After one repetition, he was brought to the ground by Ricky Acosta, a senior defensive back. Not pleased with Acosta's aggressiveness, Kos stood up and threw the ball in his direction. Senior linebacker Luke Venegoni believed something had to be done.

"We were, like, 'Dude, what are you doing?'" Venegoni said. "He was yapping, trying to be all hotshot-like."

As soon as Venegoni got his opportunity, he struck. Kos caught a shovel pass and ran through the line. Venegoni had a clean shot at Kos and took it, sending him to the ground. Kos jumped up and again threw the football at his tackler. Both players grabbed each other's jerseys, screaming the verbal indignities typical of a live-scrimmage brouhaha. The mild fracas was quickly broken up.

Before the next play, Serio pulled Kos aside and muttered, "You need to calm down."

After the scrimmage, running backs coach Tom Young approached Venegoni. He grabbed the back of his arm, leaned in and said, "Good job." In football, self-policing is often the preferred method of justice. Leaders emerge not by making speeches, but through direct retribution. There is a hierarchical structure based on what a player earns, not on what they think they deserve.

This was an incident where one senior—Venegoni—established order. And by doing so, he sent a message to a younger, valued player that divas would not be tolerated on the 2010 Carmel Corsairs.

"I don't care what they say about it, I'm going to call you out if you are doing something wrong, if you are not doing what everybody else is doing," Venegoni said. "You don't have to open your mouth to be good. Just play."

No one heard a peep from Kos the rest of camp.

∽

Remember that old Army commercial, where after leaping out of helicopters and running a half marathon carrying 50-pound backpacks, the solider turns to his buddy and says, "We do more before 9 a.m. than most people do all day." That's how football coaches feel each fall. At the high school level, coaches have day jobs. Those jobs do not go on sabbatical from August to November. Beginning at 8 a.m., they teach five or six classes of chemistry or physics or psychology before swapping their professorial Dockers for turf-walking McGregors. At 3 p.m., they don't leave the build just change clothes.

It's not yet 8 a.m. on a Monday and Coach Andy Bitto is dik to Carmel in his Ford mini-van. He's just met with his offensive c(Bill Mack. The discussion, in a Wauconda diner, was mostly one lack dispensed advice, Coach Bitto listened. The encounter has left in- spired and haggard. "He'll ask, 'Why don't you run 31 pitch m(ar- en't you running 23 more?'" Coach Bitto says. "He gets frustra se I don't run certain plays, but we only ran 32 plays Friday night."

Carmel opened up the 2010 season in convincing fashion 56 points (allowing only seven) against an overmatched opponen rles East. The Corsairs ran for 545 yards on 27 carries, an average of per rush. Of their eight touchdowns, five were on runs of 40 yards o n a chalkboard during the offensive unit's pre-game meeting, Berg w un- der and Lightning," referring to the contrasting running styles olli- sion-happy Kos (thunder) and the wildfire blaze velocitas moti nior running back Michael Panico (lightning). Friday night, the Fig ints of St. Charles East were hit with the football equivalent of a stor and Panico combined for 439 yards and six touchdowns. The results sed how, when properly executed, the Carmel rushing attack is a form for- mance art.

"That's the way we expect it to happen. Just keep moving the own the field," offensive line coach Jerry Rejc said.

By the time football players at Carmel reach the varsity level, ey've been schooled on the system. From the first repetition on the fir ay of camp, incoming freshmen are taught system plays. Carmel is one of le few teams left in the Midwest that runs the system called the triple option, ere's how it works: When receiving the snap from center, the quarterback takes one of three actions with the football (thus the "triple option")—he hands the ball off to the fullback, keeps it, or pitches it to a running back. It sounds straightforward, but just as Beethoven wrote music in different keys and for more than one instrument, the option has numerous deviations and intri- cacies. This requires ongoing education for those who coach it, and Coach s it from outside sources. One of those sources is Mack, who was ach for 10 years at Crystal Lake High School, 20 miles away from nd then another 10 years when it became Crystal Lake Central. ed Coach Bitto since the Corsairs switched to the triple option in mel's first opponent, St. Charles East, ran a spread offensive system, sses, not runs, are the preferred method of attacking a defense. It's esis of the Corsairs' ground-based system.

n't think it's any better than anything else. It's just an offense," Mack

k speaks in a calm, scientific tone. His appearance is what you would f a semi-retired football coach who never changed his wardrobe. He hite New Balance sneakers—the kind with the velcro pull-over flap e bridge—and sports a T-shirt with Corsairs printed on it, the only on of his affiliation.

ry other offense it's 11 against 10 and the QB is doing something e ball and is not a blocker. In this case, it's 12 against 11 from the int of the quarterback is reading two people. You are taking two peo- of the defense. That's not fiction. That is really true.

t to make it happen, you have to do a lot of things right. I really be- lis. Army has gone back to triple option. The priority is not on size ating a hole, but you create space to move the ball with the nature of tense, as opposed to displacing the defense with offensive players. Now tly happens when you attack a wide field in less than a second." With that word, Mack snaps his finger to accentuate his point.

und blocking fundamentals are essential to making the triple-option offe work. That and intelligent football players who work hard. Before the first game of any season, the offensive starters will have practiced running play from the playbook 2,500 times.

"There are things you can do with the offense that if you have quick, smart, disciplined kids you can move the ball and score a lot of points," Mack said "Carmel is a great place to do it because you are going to have no one who is going to be a dummy. Everyone since the first grade on was sitting in class with book open and a pen. Everyone talks about advantages of Catholic schools with enrollment and no boundaries and some of that is true, but there is really a huge advantage from the type of family they come from, being a parochial school. So from the standpoint of having an attack that depends on discipline and intelligence first, Carmel has more of a natural environment for that."

Every Monday morning during the season, Coach Bitto and Mack meet at the same diner. By then, Mack has seen tape from Friday night's game and has formulated opinions on the team's offensive execution. His tone is both supportive and cranky; he praises play calls while equally lamenting plays that didn't work.

"In the first half they had the SAM wider, for some reason. So you could have blocked him on the 36," Mack said to Coach Bitto, sitting across the diner table. There's a long pause before Mack speaks again.

"I'll tell you, I did not see double 2's. Number 64 took the outside shoulder every time. He's definitely an 'A'-gap player as he was in a 2Y. Did any of the coaches see this?" Mack said.

"I have to ask," Coach Bitto said.

"Now this is important," Mack said.

"I'm listening," Coach Bitto said.

"I don't think 87 is a good play. They really play the wheel well. Wipe this into the wind," Mack said. "Where we really have a chance is on X right or left 83."

Mack diagramed plays on a sheet of paper as precisely as a biochemist explains how cells work. Coach Bitto listened intently, playing the role of boyish student absorbing pearls of pigskin wisdom from an aging mentor.

"All his notes are disjointed. He's 30 here, then pass here, then back to 30 again," Coach Bitto says, driving back in his Ford truck as he approaches campus. "But he knows so much. That's why you have to hang with him."

There have been dozens and dozens of early morning diner conversations. In Coach Bitto's first two seasons, 1998 and 1999, Carmel was 8-11, averaging just 15 points a game. "We were pretty good on defense, but we've always been pretty good. But we were anemic on offense. We weren't scoring enough points. So I thought we had to make things happen. Joliet Catholic was coming back on our schedule and I was thinking, 'How can we beat Joliet?'"

Shortly after the 1999 season, Coach Bitto was at home watching the 1-AA (FCS) national championship game. Running up a storm for Georgia Southern University was a 5-10 fullback named Adrian Peterson (not the superstar NFL running back, although he did play in the NFL for nine seasons).

"I was mesmerized. He was running up and down the field. That's the day I called Bill and I told him we have to meet," Coach Bitto says.

At the time, Mack was coaching at North Central College, a Division III school in Naperville. "He's got a war room in his basement," Coach Bitto says. "We talked option football for hours. I'm saying on the way home, 'I think I want to do this.'"

After initial resistance, the assistant coaches came around to the idea. The returning players were another story.

"By the summer, two starters had quit," Coach Bitto says. "Then our quarterback. Eventually 10 guys gone, all seniors."

He pulls into the parking lot, parks the car and turns off the ignition.

"This is where having mentor figures in your life helps. The president of the school at the time was Father Bob Carroll. He was the guy who hired me as head coach in 1998. He comes into the office. I said, 'I challenged the kids all summer long. If they don't love football, don't come out, as I want guys who want to play.' I tell him maybe it was the wrong thing to do as 10 seniors have quit in the last two weeks. He looked around and shut the door to make sure no one could hear.

"Father Bob said, 'To hell with them all. Coach the kids who want to play.' That was a confidence boost for me, as he sees something I don't see. I took a chance to crystallize the morale of the team. Bill (Mack) told me later, 'You have to make those decisions as a coach. I don't know if it's right, but it better be right or you'll be out of coaching.' He laid it on the line.

"That's why I have guys like Bill around."

He gets out of the car and heads inside. It's not even 9 a.m.

CHAPTER FOUR

CORSAIR CULTURE

To Carmel's coaches, the lopsided win over St. Charles East the previous week is deceiving. The one-sided result masked deficiencies, mostly in the passing game. Quarterback Brian Serio was 1-for-5 for 19 yards.

Offensive coordinator Ben Berg, who calls the plays, has a statistical ratio he'd like to see from Serio and the offense each week.

"I'd like us to run 70 plays. Ideally, 30 will be option plays, between 12 and 15 passing and we complete 7 to 9 of those throws. The other 12 to 15 plays are handoffs or specialty plays. In our state championship season, we averaged 300 yards rushing but 100 yards passing. We have to do better."

Another stat gnawing at the coaches all week—penalties. Nine of them were called against Carmel in the St. Charles East game, costing the Corsairs 85 yards. Penalties are often higher early in the season. High school teams don't get to play exhibition games and mistakes occur as a result of lack of game reps. But against good teams—and this week's opponent, Libertyville High School, is one—penalties can be devastating.

Monday practices during the season are non-contact. Players run, lift weights, then watch film. Each unit—offense and defense—watches tape from the previous game in a classroom with the coaches. Coach Bitto runs a separate film session in his office with fullback Jordan Kos and Serio.

Today, the Monday after the St. Charles East game and four days before the team plays Libertyville, Coach Bitto is ticked off at his fullback, as much as a coach can be at a player who ran for 214 yards and four touchdowns.

"Jordan, you are standing up here. That gets you a zero. You are slow there. That's a zero," Coach Bitto says while viewing plays from the game on the monitor.

The zero number references the grade given to Kos on that particular play. Coaches assign grades for each play: +1 is a positive mark, 0 is neutral and -1 is the lowest mark. The numbers are totaled up on evaluation sheets handed out each Monday.

"Why did you cut back into traffic? Get in the end zone, outrun that guy," Coach Bitto says. The play shows Kos running with the ball toward the sidelines. No defender is within five yards of him, yet rather than continue to run in the same direction, he cuts back toward the middle of the field, where defenders are trailing the play. He gets tackled after a 12-yard gain, but the Corsairs needed 15 yards for a first down. "Get us a first down or get in the end zone. Outrun that guy."

The Carmel fullback doesn't answer his coach's initial question about why he cut back into traffic. He just turns his head and stares quizzically at him.

"Listen to what I'm saying. If you want to play at the college level, you can't be slow off the ball and not get first downs. Now you can play in college, but eventually you have to poop in the kitty litter, OK?"

Kos says nothing in reply to his coach's colorful metaphor. He just waits for the next play on the screen to appear.

~

Tuesday and Wednesday of game week are what coaches call "work days." Offensive and defensive game plans for Friday's opponent are installed. Special teams—punt, punt return, kickoff and kickoff return—are a major emphasis. Starters get heavy reps. Backup players, also known as the "scout team," run the opposing team's plays. The practice session's final drill—the Team Drill—pits offense vs. defense. It's all designed to get the boys playing at peak performance by 7:30 Friday night.

Thursday is a "cleanup" day, the game plan is tightened and refined. There is less contact and a focus on practicing specialty situations, such as the two-minute offense.

The consistencies to all three days revolve around the fundamental tenants of football—blocking, tackling, reading defenses, etc. But there is another constant.

Coach Bitto talks to the boys at the end of each practice. It offers an opportunity to affirm positives from the day's session and to reinforce what remains to be done before Friday night. Before he talks, the coaches select the practice player of the day from each of the three position groups—offense, defense and special teams. The winner is given a plastic sticker colored with the shape of a brown helmet. Players attach the stickers onto their helmets as testimony of their well-earned prize. Today, junior running back Matt Maher is awarded a sticker for offense, sophomore safety Sean Brennan for defense and senior defensive lineman Chris Georgen for special teams.

Thursday is also the day the team chooses its uniform colors for the next game. The previous Friday, a home game, the Corsairs wore all brown. This decision is a democratic one, left up to the players.

"Uniforms?" Coach Bitto asks demonstratively. Everyone is gathered in the south end zone, the boys on one knee surrounding their coach. Several players yell in response, "white on brown!" It's decided—for Carmel's first road game Friday, the wardrobe will be white jerseys, brown pants.

With program business out of the way, Coach Bitto speaks.

"When you come to the school tomorrow, try and concentrate if you can. It's hard, but enjoy classes and the people around you. There's another segment of your life and that's leadership in the community. However you prepared yourself last Friday night you need to do the same every time. There are no cupcakes on the schedule. It gets harder as we get through the schedule. We have to play better than we did last week. We have to play more consistently. We are not going in there to look at the crowd. We are going there to outhit them and beat their ass. The journey is about one week at a time. Bottom line, the team that wins tomorrow is the team that executes. I don't care if it's 7-6 or 77-0. The guys in brown pants and white shirts, those are the guys that are going to win if we execute.

"Oh, one other thing. I don't like guys walking around school tomorrow with ties unbuttoned. If you can't button your tie, then buy a bigger shirt. I don't want you walking around and people saying, 'He looks like Salvo the Clown.' It's important to understand we are leaders in the school. We need to be thankful for the opportunity. If you eat a french fry the wrong way or leave your table dirty, I'm going to hear about it. It doesn't mean you are a dirt bag, it doesn't mean you are going to jail. It's not any of that. It's because you are a Carmel football player and we expect higher standards from you. If you put yourself in the limelight and you perform great on the field, they expect the same at the mall, at a restaurant, and in the classroom. You are going to behave, and know what to do and when to do it. The atmosphere in school is the way you guys handle it. Stress the importance of leadership, scholarship, fellowship and godliness.

"OK, let's get a cheer."

And with that, practice is over for the day.

~

The habit of athletes "carbing up" before a sporting event goes back generations. "Carbing up" is when athletes inhale mountains of pasta and other carbohydrate-heavy foods the night before a game.

The science is simple—the human digestive system changes carbohydrates into glucose, or blood sugar. The body uses that sugar to fuel cells, tissues and organs. All are needed to pass, punt, kick, run and tackle.

It's Thursday night. In less than 24 hours, Carmel plays rival Libertyville High School. Senior linebacker Luke Venegoni hosts this week's pre-game meal. If a statistic existed for pound of meat served per pound of flesh, Luke's mom, Claudia, would be a first-ballot hall-of-famer.

Rib-eye steaks. Hot beef sandwiches. Barbeque pork. These comestibles are paired with an endless parade of sidedish provisions—pastas, salads, sandwiches, sloppy joe's, cakes, and cookies. This is grub with grit, foodstuff that feeds hungry footballers.

Luke is the last of four Venegonis who have gone through Carmel, starting with the oldest, Mark, who entered the school in 2000. Jenna started in 2002, David in 2004, and now Luke, who first enrolled in 2007 and graduates in 2011. All played football, baseball, or track and field. Too numerous to count are the number of team parties hosted by the Venegonis. There are two simple rules for occupants: You either create or you consume. Tonight, Claudia and Betsy Larson, mother of senior defensive lineman Jake Larson, are the creators. More than happy are the rest of the guests to exercise consumption committee memberships. After all, players on winning teams know their roles.

"My other boys were quarterbacks," Claudia says. "I would have the entire offensive line over every Thursday. Just the starters. Then each week they would invite one player who had done well the week before on offense or defense. Every week. Rib eyes were their favorite. Those offensive linemen could really eat."

Claudia is referring to the 2003 state title team. That team was quarterbacked by her son.

"They could eat what we're eating tonight with 11 or 12 guys. Drew Cairo-Gross was on that team. The rib eyes were at least a pound and he had three. Drew Osterhout ate like half a pound. It was interesting to see who was a big eater. Mark's line averaged 265."

Copious amounts of energy and focus are spent preparing for Friday nights. But much of the program's culture is forged here, in suburban kitchens, where mothers feed the boys who in 24 hours, will play in front of thousands of adoring fans.

"It wouldn't work if it wasn't for the moms, because there's not going to be a team dad. It's not going to happen," Claudia says while putting another tray of cookies into the oven. "I've been a team mom in baseball, basketball, soccer. Moms are the ones who do it. I think Andy [Bitto] knows you better be thinking about the moms. Carmel's different, as there is so much parental involvement. Some schools, they don't have that."

Betsy Larson says: "It's not that they don't have it, it's that they don't encourage it. My kids went to Woodland Middle School in Gurnee. We went through public school where some teachers were very happy to have you involved. But some school buildings you walked into and they were like, 'Oh, you're a parent. You must be here because you are upset about something.' Those were the conclusions they jumped to before they even got to know you. Carmel is not like that. A real good example is we had our junior meeting with Jake. We went in and we were walking through the hallway. It was Mark [Betsy's husband and Jake's father] and I. We met Jake in the counselor's office and all these kids were saying 'hi' to us. We saw some people we knew, some parents that we knew. Then we got to the parking lot and Mark was like, 'OK, now I get it. Now I understand the difference between here and there.'"

"It's like going to a party," Claudia says. "If I'm driving, I go see the parents at the front door. They just know. Don't even ask, I'm going to the door."

"Yes," Betsy says. "It's expected that if you have people over and they've never been to your house, that you call or they call. It's expected, and that's not the way it was in public school."

Two players, linebacker Tyler Lees and running back Michael Panico, enter the kitchen from the basement where they've been eating.

"You don't want any more cookies?" Claudia asks.

"No, thank you Mrs. Venegoni. We appreciate it. We're going to head home," Panico says.

Claudia removes another batch of cookies from the oven. Another whiff and Lees and Panico may change their minds.

"My philosophy is school should feel like a family, should feel safe," Claudia says. "I didn't think Warren [High School] or Woodland provided that. My kids went to St. Gilbert's [for middle school]. For all of them, half of their graduation classes went to Carmel. That's another big difference. I'm used to knowing every kid in the grade. My kids were on the bus at the same time. They all came home together and went to school together, which is an altogether different experience."

Betsy says good night and heads out the door. Within a few minutes, most of the boys have left. Claudia strolls into a back room and returns with a photo album. The book is an archive to her children's athletic achievements. With each page flip, the progression of the Venegoni family bloodline is revealed in pictures. There's "little" Luke (as his older brother Mark likes to call him) in youth football, Little League baseball, middle school and Carmel athletic uniforms (football and baseball). This is the same for Mark, David and Jenna. The experience is akin to viewing a Bruce Springsteen concert picture album, beginning with his early Asbury Park days through the Boss's most recent shows at Madison Square Garden.

Claudia reminisces over her boys' Carmel football experiences. "Andy [Bitto] told me freshman year, 'Your son [Mark] is going to be quarterback of the varsity and they are going to win state.' He knew. That group, the difference between them and David's group was Mark's team always played like a team. You didn't have guys complaining about who got the ball like David's junior year [2006]. The poor kid. They would yell at David if they didn't get the ball! I mean, he has to make the right reads otherwise he gets in trouble. That's not team playing. That's not how you win the game. You win by teamwork. And Mark's team played together, from freshman year they did."

The year Mark's team won the state title, Luke was an impressionable adolescent. Following in his older brother's footsteps as a Carmel football player was never a question. He staked his independence elsewhere.

"He just wrote a paper about that for school. 'I hated my brothers because they always told me how good their teams were.' Obviously, there was brother stuff. My team's better, blah, blah, blah. He never wanted to be a quarterback. He wanted to hit people. He played his first varsity game when he was 14. He said he was so nervous. 'Mom, I don't even know where I was.' David was the quarterback. Those were the only games they played together," Claudia says.

Claudia has probably shown the album to numerous people over the years. There is a timbre of discovery in her voice ("This was right around the time David had his braces taken out") that would make any visitor believe she is leafing through it for the first time. Her praise of Carmel is unshakable.

"The one thing about Carmel, everybody knows what everybody does," she says. "Mark, his senior year, he had his friends come over to the house. If someone sees you at a party and someone sees you drinking at the party and tells Andy, that's all it takes. So, Mark really had to make sure. Because he knew. Mark checks Luke's Facebook to make sure no one is on there. Luke says, 'It's like having another father. He's like my dad. He keeps checking my stuff.' He wants Luke to do as well and have the same opportunities he did. He wants him to go to state."

She puts the picture book away. On a mantel in the front hallway is a picture frame, which contains a newspaper article. It's a story on linebacker LaRon Biere. Claudia cut the article out and had it framed. She says she plans to give it to Biere next time she's at school. Which will be in less than 24 hours.

"We have to be at Carmel by mid-afternoon," she says. "We have to feed the boys before the game."

The work of a team mom never ends. And there can never be enough food.

~

Most sports teams have captains. They are the embodiment of a program's culture, leaders by action and example. Often, these captains are chosen early and remain in the position throughout a season.

But not at Carmel.

"Every week, we rotate our captains. We have five new ones every week," Coach Bitto says.

The weekly captains only have one requirement—they must be seniors. Playing time is not a prerequisite to captaincy. "We have no [roster] cuts," Coach Bitto says. "So if we can provide an environment where the kids who don't play still learn leadership, this can be a learning ground."

There are 31 seniors on this season's roster, meaning each will be captain for at least one game of the nine-game regular season. If the Corsairs make the playoffs and win a few games, most seniors will be two-time captains.

It's Friday afternoon, a few minutes before 4 o'clock. Kickoff against Libertyville is not for three and a half hours. Carmel has just wrapped its special-teams meeting, held in the school's South Conference Center. Coach

Bitto calls a meeting with the day's captains before everyone heads to the cafeteria for the pre-game meal. The environment is relaxed.

Coach Bitto outlines the captain's duties—observe behavior, be alert of player conduct, deem its appropriateness for the time of day. "Normally some guys freak out early, and that's wasted energy. Your job is to keep people aligned, and we need their concentration. If someone is distracting other people, that's the time to step and control it. Don't be a jerk about it. I don't expect that to be happening, but you need to control it."

A captain also has to recite the pre-meal prayer.

"Speak loudly, thank the parents for the food and the great opportunity," Coach Bitto says. "One thing we don't pray for is to win, because God will run us over and chop our brains out."

He shares a story to illustrate his vivid metaphor.

"One year [1999] the kid giving the prayer that day said, 'Let's pray we beat Gordon Tech tonight.' So we're down 17-10 with 50 seconds left. We get the ball back and score a touchdown. Our kicker shanks the extra point and we lose 17-16. I think that was God chopping us up a bit. I don't think that is the purpose of playing football.

"Our job is to play the best we can and for each other. This is a good group that kind of gets it. Some years are different, but I already have this sense. But the more we emphasize that throughout the year, that we need to bring emotion and how we are going to play for each other, I think we'll do OK."

Minutes later, the prayer is spoken. God is kept out of it. There will be no brains being chopped out tonight.

∼

One traffic light, 1.3 miles. That is all that separates Carmel and Libertyville High School. One is public, one private. One pulls students from a defined district, the other has no borders. One plays in the East Suburban Catholic Conference, the other in the North Suburban Conference. One wears brown and white, the other orange and black. One mascot is a species of cat that roams three continents. The other is a pirate, which rambled along the Mediterranean seas centuries ago. One time of year these separate communities assemble around a like-minded passion. Tonight, September 3, 2010, for a football game, is that time.

It is the fourth and final scheduled meeting between the regional rivals. The previous three were won by Carmel.

"I don't think they want to play us anymore," Coach Bitto says. "It's hard to blame them."

Just minutes before the 7:30 p.m. kickoff, a common area behind the south end zone of Libertyville's football stadium is a sea of white. That's where much of the visiting student body has camped on this pleasant late-summer night. Hundreds walked the short distance down Route 176 from Carmel's campus to Libertyville's carrying posters and thunder sticks. As they await the entrance of their uniform-clad classmates, they manically smack the plastic slats in a unified state of hysteria.

On the stadium's west side rest the home bleachers. Named the "X-Factor," students dress almost all in black. The sound of kazoos and hip-hop music reverberate throughout the stadium, presenting an atmosphere in stark contrast to the washed out, gleeful appearance of the opposing student body. In conjunction, the climate is college-like, more fitting of a Michigan-Notre Dame contest than two high schools with a combined enrollment of a little more than 3,000.

The Corsairs gather on bended knee on a patch of grass behind the west bleachers. Coach Bitto begins to speak.

"God, for whatever reason, has put all of us together at this moment at this time to play Libertyville, in front of our whole community and their whole community on a glorious night in September. Not many guys get the opportunity to play in front of 10,000 people as a high school player. You do. You have that right. You've earned that right.

"How you perform is the next challenge. The challenge in the performance is, will I perform for you? Will you perform for the guy next to you? Will you represent our community? What does our community mean? Carmel has a different way. We have a different way of going about things. It's about caring for one another. It's about doing the extra stuff and not expecting anything in return! It's about playing hard not for myself! It's about playing hard to represent the greatest high school in the country! Let's go do it!"

~

Libertyville is determined not to lose to Carmel for the fourth straight year. To take better advantage of the talents of versatile senior quarterback A.J. Schurr, longtime coach Randy Kuceyeski has switched to a spread offense. On the game's first drive, the Wildcats catch the Corsairs on their heels, marching 62 yards in a drive that culminates in a 19-yard touchdown pass from Schurr to senior Jeremy Birck in the back of the end zone. The seven plays took a tidy 1:34 off the clock. On Carmel's first possession, it goes 80 yards, ending in a one-yard run by quarterback Brian Serio. Only six minutes have lapsed. This promises to be an offensive shootout worthy of the frenetic ambience.

~

"Coach Berg, can you hear me!" Coach Bitto shouts into his headphones.

It's midway through the third quarter, and Libertyville has just tied the game at 27 on a blocked punt return for a touchdown.

Coach Bitto is trying to resume communication with offensive coordinator Ben Berg, stationed in the press box across the field from the Carmel sidelines. But he can't. The line is dead. The coaches' headsets are non-functional. Coach Bitto will have to call the plays.

With 6:12 remaining in the third quarter, Carmel takes over on its 20-yard line. All game, the Corsairs have moved the ball on the ground with their triple-headed attack of Serio, fullback Jordan Kos, and running back Michael Panico, who had a 74-yard touchdown run earlier in the quarter. On this drive's first snap from center, Serio moves one step to his right, then jams the ball into the belly of Kos. But he pulls it back, cradling it with both hands and sprinting into an open alley on the right side. Twenty-eight yards later, he's finally dragged down.

The triple-option system is about deception. It's about making a defender think you are doing one thing with the ball, then, like a Las Vegas stage magician—voila!—doing something different. The play is the perfect example of how crafty deception leads to big plays.

Trailing on the play, senior left tackle Sean Wolf-Lewis raises both arms in the air at the 50-yard line. "That's it!" he screams. "That's Carmel football!"

Four plays later, Carmel faces a 2nd and 5 from the Libertyville 13-yard line. Serio fakes a hand-off to Kos, then steps back to pass. Senior tight end Patrick Mulroy, lined up on the right side, sprints toward the end zone. Libertyville defenders hedge toward the line of scrimmage ever so slightly, expecting another running play. The hesitation leaves Mulroy plenty of open space, and Serio lofts a perfectly thrown ball that the 6-2 tight end snatches out of the air before a Wildcats defender can catch up. The 13-yard touchdown caps a six-play, 80-yard touchdown drive and puts Carmel back on top 34-27 with 4:28 left in the third quarter.

From the press box, Berg yells into his still non-functioning headgear. "I still can't hear anything out of these headphones. But that was a great call on the touchdown, coach!"

On the ensuing possession, Libertyville takes over on its 16-yard line. On the first play, Schurr is hit hard behind the line of scrimmage by defensive end Jake Larson. The ball is jarred loose and rolls into the end zone, and linebacker LaRon Biere falls on it for another Carmel touchdown. That's two scores in 11 seconds, and what had been a close game is now a 41-27 Carmel lead.

Just as Coach Bitto stressed pre-game, the Corsairs are playing with emotion. But they are the more composed team, repurposing the crowd's heightened energy into robust on-field execution.

"For high school football, you can't tell me this is great? Our whole school, their whole school," senior defensive end Michael Cohen says aloud after Serio scampers into the end zone from 12 yards out to give Carmel a 48-27 lead with 8:43 left in the game. "Our level of confidence is growing. We are good at handling adversity."

Junior Matt Maher caps the scoring with a seven-yard touchdown with 2:32 left. The final score of 55-27 is by no means a perfect outcome (Carmel had a blocked punt for a touchdown and a fumble lost) but it's pretty darn good. The offense piles up 477 yards of total offense (410 on the ground). Serio was fantastic, rushing for 127 yards on 11 carries with two touchdowns. The defense shows signs it might be one of the school's best units in several years.

"Our strength is running guys down and making them go to the sidelines," defensive coordinator Dan Potempa says. "We brought pressure and when you do that, a quarterback has to think fast. That's what you want."

~

This is one bus ride home from a game Carmel wishes was longer.

"Get out of my way...I'm bigger than you!" yells the team bus driver to the cars below as she maneuvers her way out of the cramped Libertyville High School parking lot.

In the seats behind the vociferous driver, the Corsairs celebrate with the zeal of pirates just having found a lost treasure.

Post-game traffic has cars crawling down Route 176. But with only 7,000 feet to travel, the victorious Corsairs are back on campus within minutes.

In the coaches' room, everyone is appropriately cheerful. The team blocked and tackled well tonight, certainly in the second half.

"Matt Maher is the best blocker since Serio," Coach Bitto says.

He's referring to Mike Serio, a running back on the 2003 state title team and Brian Serio's older brother. "Maher was beating the crap out of a kid and Panico just..."

He claps his hands together to emphasize Panico's breakaway speed.

"Coach," Berg says to Coach Bitto. "You should reward yourself a sticker for that drive."

Berg is referring to when the headsets mysteriously went out in the third quarter, forcing Coach Bitto to call the plays during the go-ahead drive.

"I was making things up and everything was working," Coach Bitto says.

Kos walks into the room. "I can't find my iPod," he says. Then he finds his music player resting on a side table against the wall. Kos had a good night—75 yards on 16 carries with a touchdown.

Coach Bitto turns around in his chair.

"Am I going to have to buy ice cream again?" he says to his fullback.

In preseason, Coach Bitto told the offense that any time they scored 40 or more points, he would buy everyone (defensive players, too) ice cream to be consumed after Saturday's practice.

"They went through six gallons last week," Coach Bitto says.

"You may want to start making (the minimum score) 50 or 55," Kos says with a mischievous grin. "Everyone's talking about the ice cream in the locker room."

"OK, you guys earned it," Coach Bitto says. "See you in the morning."

～

Tom Biere takes a right turn off Route 176 onto Route 60. His father, Jim, sits in the passenger seat. They are heading home after the game, to Ingleside. It's late, both are tired and just about talked out. Except for football. They can always talk about football. And LaRon.

Jim turns to Tom. "Can you believe how quick LaRon jumped on that ball in the end zone?"

"Yeah, he got there pretty quick," Tom says. "I thought he played pretty well. He's not afraid to make hits."

"Oh, no. He's definitely not scared to clobber somebody," Jim says.

"You're right about that, Dad," Tom says.

"I didn't know how this defense thing would work out, but he looks like he knows what he's doing out there. I'm proud of him," Jim says.

"So am I," Tom says. He stares straight ahead, both he and his father's thoughts wander off into the dark skies of the rapidly cooling September evening.

CHAPTER FIVE

THE GIRLS OF HOLY CHILD

IT WAS NO SURPRISE TO ANYONE when Marion Wegener decided to go to nurse's school. If a woman wanted a career in 1950, teaching was the only other option. Marion knew that being in a classroom all day with children was not her cup of tea. She remembered how the nuns treated her when she had her appendix removed in the eighth grade. How they helped make her well, doing so with such dignity and grace. She wanted to do the same for others.

So she enrolled in nursing school at St. Therese's Hospital, just down the road from Holy Child. The nuns who ran the school were from the Holy Ghost convent in Techny, Illinois. All they asked from students was a $60 entrance fee. They could pay the tuition back—$320 for three years—once they graduated and had secured a job. And the nuns didn't charge any interest over the three years. They wouldn't think of it. They were on this earth to be merchants of God. And by helping those who want to help the sick, they were serving Him.

Still, scraping the $60 entrance fee together was no simple task for some. There was one young woman from just over the border in Wisconsin. Her father had died, leaving her mother with a farm and three children to raise. Her mother sold one of their two cows so her daughter could go to school. These stories were not unusual.

There were 26 girls in Marion's freshman class. Her roommate was Nadine Sedar, who was friends with Marion's cousin, Agnes. Before school started, Marion and Nadine went on a trip to get to know each other. They and Nadine's parents went to the North Bay in Canada. None of them had been to that part of the world before. They visited the home of the Dionne sisters, the first natural quintuplets ever to survive well past childbirth. One night, they were at a supper club and the band played "God Save the Queen." All of the American vacationers in the room stood up to sing along, believing it to be "My Country 'Tis of Thee," as the melodies sound exactly alike. Marion and Nadine looked at each other in total bewilderment. "Why would Americans stand for the British national song?" they asked each other.

My how small the world must have seemed to these two young women from rural Illinois about to embark on a nursing career.

~

The dormitory for the nursing students was on the top floor of St. Therese's. There were three wings divided by third-year students, second-year and freshman students on the floor, each with a bathroom. There was a rec room, where the girls could hang out, talk and smoke. There was a small television, the first most of them had ever seen. Marion didn't like to smoke but she did like to talk. When they weren't working, she, Nadine, Marilyn Biere, Joan Zupec and the other girls in their class would go to Sander's, a hamburger joint on Washington Street in Waukegan. They would sit outside, eat their burgers and fries, and fend off the advances of boys who would pull up in their dark blue Ford sedans, pressing the gas pedal to show off the sweet sound of their V-8 engines. They would shop during the day down Genesee Street, then at night stop at the American Legion Hall, where there was live music on Friday nights. They would sip on cheap Morgan David wine—how sweet it was!—and dance the evening away. Sometimes Marion would go out dancing with the girls. Most often, she would go home to visit her family when she had a day off from school. And those days were rare, as the girls worked extremely hard, six days a week. There was bookwork during the day, then patient work at night. The nuns would rotate the education—six weeks in the lab, six weeks in dietary—so they would be comfortable with the different disciplines. Eventually the girls would pick a specialty: pediatrics, medical or surgery. Marion chose surgery, which had the sickest patients. The night before surgery, patients would check in and Marion would scrub and prep them. After surgery, Marion would help them recover, giving them backrubs in the afternoon, then bed baths at night. It was far from glamorous work, but Marion embraced the menial tasks, developing a rapport with patients unmatched by the other students.

The floor the girls worked on at St. Therese's was small, with room for only 30 patients. Often there were beds in the hallways, because there wasn't enough space. This was because the nuns—Sister Madeline in obstetrics, Sister Augustella in medical and especially Sister Depacis Becker, the head of nursing—never turned anyone away, even if they had no means to pay. Things were a lot different in those days. There was less paperwork and bureaucracy in nursing, leaving time for the girls to develop relationships with the patients. They could talk to them, get them to relax and reassure them they were in good hands, and help relieve the tension they were feeling and sense of isolation.

By the second and third years, the original class of 26 had whittled down to 20, and they were especially close, sometimes to the exasperation of the nuns. They were prone to spells of goofy behavior, as 18-to-20-year-olds are when in tight proximity for so long. Some nights, the girls would stay up late in the rec room making noise, waking Sister Depacis, who lived across the hall from their rooms. They would hear her stirring, putting on her habit before leaving her room to administer a scolding. The girls would run to their rooms and hop into bed, pretending to be asleep. When Sister Depacis flipped on the light switch, she could hear the girls giggling underneath the sheets.

Sr. Depacis worked the girls very hard, expecting more at times than they felt they could give. But in return, she gave devotion, often shown in non-traditional ways. There was the time Marilyn was running a fever. Sister Depacis told her she was going to give her a potion that would cure her, something she had learned from her childhood in Germany. She gave Marilyn hot lemonade and whiskey, then covered her in blankets. Marilyn sweated till her fever broke.

Because of the unwavering commitment the nuns showed to them, the girls were grateful, but most important, dutiful. They did not want to let the sisters down. How could they when so many of them were attending school for free? How could they when they were healing the sick and the poor? When one of the nuns told them to do something, they did it out of obligation.

In the summer of 1952, just before their final year of schooling, Marilyn's mother was diagnosed with cancer. Marilyn didn't know what to do, so she sought the counsel of Sister Depacis, who told Marilyn she had a responsibility to be at home, with her mother. She could always come back and finish her training. So that's what she did. She moved back into the family home in Long Grove, 21 miles away from her classmates and her best friends. Then Marion came to visit. She knew Marilyn was hurting, quarantined from her nursing life. Marion helped her friend with her mother, but what she provided most was friendship.

During one of their many chats over this period, Marilyn mentioned she had a brother. Jim Biere was in the service, fighting in the Korean War. Marion saw a picture of this man, with a strong jawline and square face that highlighted attractive bloodline features on his father's side (Irish) and his mother's side (French). She found him quite handsome. Marilyn wrote a letter to Jim, telling him about this nice, sweet girl she knew in nurse's training named Marion. Granted emergency leave to visit his ailing mother, Jim left Korea and came home to Long Grove. One day, Marion stopped by. There was an immediate attraction. That night, as he sat by his mother's bedside, he excitedly told her about this pretty friend of Marilyn's he had just met.

After a few dates with her nursing classmate, Marilyn asked her brother a question: "You're not getting serious, are you?"

Jim flashed a playful grin, and said, "She's quite a gal."

Before he left for Korea, he and Marion were engaged to be married.

～

Back then, the nuns never had a day off. The ones on the floor were on call 24 hours a day. Sometimes they'd be on the floor and they'd go to chapel and to dinner and come back in the evening. I think they earned about $18 a month. It wasn't until Vatican II when things changed, so you can understand why they'd be crabby, but they were all so very nice.

– Joan Zupec

You had to be a compassionate and caring person to be in nursing. It was very unusual, but I would say 100 percent of the girls that I graduated with all continued to work afterwards, even after they got married. And we worked for many, many years. I was always impressed with that group.

– Marilyn Adams

When I started teaching at St. Veronica's [a grade school in Chicago, 1955] we got $10 a month and worked 15 hours a day. You have to understand we grew up with women who donated their lives. It wasn't just our parents and grandparents but it was all these other influences which formed the culture, the bedrock. In those days that influenced values, understanding, perception. You want to call it a philosophy of life, a spirituality such it was back then. All of these things form the way we see, the way we understand. It is our psyche.

– Sister Joanne Biere

～

Inside the school cafeteria, the boys stand. Their faces wear skepticism. Empty tables surround them. If not for the sound of nervous, shuffling feet, the room would be completely silent.

Above them, men in cloaks wander the hallways. A strong wind rattles the building's bones.

A candle is lit.

Ad initium.

~

Since he's been at Carmel, LaRon has heard about these few days. Whispers in the classroom. Idle chatter at lunch or in the locker room. A limited narrative spun in mythological text. Remember the movie *Fight Club*?

The first rule of fight club is nobody talks about fight club.

Now he's here. His stomach is in knots. He texts a friend.

"I don't know why we are here. At least I have Brian, Ryan, and Matt."

Yes, LaRon does have Brian, Ryan and Matt. And Ricky. Since freshman year, that first summer, during football. That's how they met. Matt and LaRon were standing in line during drills. LaRon was in the wrong line and Matt yelled to him, "Hey, man, you are in the wrong line!" LaRon fired back, "I'll do what I want!" No one tells LaRon where he should be, or what to do. He could see Matt laughing through his facemask at his teammate's defiance. A friendship was born.

That season, 2007, LaRon started for the Carmel freshman team at running back. Of course he was a running back. His hero, Walter Payton, was a running back. His parents would show videos of Payton and buy books about Payton. LaRon mimicked Payton's style—running one way, then changing direction and going the other way. Somehow he'd get 10 yards, just as Payton did. LaRon didn't always listen and follow the plays. He just ran where he felt like going. That frustrated the coaches. But LaRon always prefers options. He doesn't like to feel boxed in.

He never felt that way around his new Carmel friends.

LaRon began to hang out at Matt's house in Long Grove. Ryan was there, too. One day, after practice, Matt introduced LaRon to Ricky. Then Brian started to show up.

The five of them were soon inseparable—lifting weights together, then to practice, then to Matt's house. Repeat. They spent so much time together,

LaRon's mom would have to call and tell him it was time to come home. But LaRon didn't always want to go. He felt safe around his buddies.

The summer before sophomore year, Matt's parents, Scott and Beth, hosted a picnic. Everyone was having a great time. As often happens at the Carrs', the day turned into night, then early morning. Beth assumed LaRon would stay the night, as he often did. Instead, he asked if his parents could join the party.

"My parents are coming to pick me up but I want to stay awhile. Can you talk to them?" LaRon asked Mrs. C, as he called her.

"Why don't you just sleep over?" Beth said. It was a reasonable question to ask. The clock read well past midnight. It was a long drive from Ingleside, where Jim and Marion Biere lived.

"No, they don't want me to sleep over. They are going to come get me," LaRon said. "So when they get here, my dad likes beer and my mom sweet white wine."

"OK, I got you covered," Beth said.

And they came. On the back porch of the Carrs' house, Jim sipped on a Budweiser and Marion a Riesling. Marion talked about how her life changed the moment she walked into that hospital room at St. Therese's 15 years before and laid eyes on that sick black child. Yes, LaRon could be a handful at times. What teenager isn't? But his presence gave her purpose. She was grateful for the friends he had made, for the nourishing environment Carmel was supplying.

Behind the deck, on the Carrs' spacious lawn, a bonfire glowed under a star-kissed early morning sky. LaRon laughed with his friends and out of the corner of his eye, watched his mom and dad mingle with the other parents. So this is what normal feels like? If so, he hoped he could feel this way all the time.

~

In this drafty, white-walled room, LaRon is not sure what to think. No one has told him anything. Brian and Ryan stand on either side of him.

A candle burns. The room is flush with shadowy light. Whatever this is, it's begun.

They were given instructions before they came. They'd have to write stuff down. They'd have to listen, then talk. Reveal.

What was something given to them they cherish?

LaRon loved to snowboard. Anything with a board. He was always a bit of a daredevil. There was the time he was skateboarding in middle school. He tried to do a trick and fell awkwardly on his leg, breaking a bone. Then last winter, snow had fallen the night before. It was 7 a.m. Everyone showed up—Matt, Ryan, Ricky, Brian—boards in tow. Marion wasn't so sure this was a good idea.

It wasn't two hours before LaRon came home with a broken bone in his shoulder.

How LaRon enjoyed being outside, especially with his buddies. They'd go up to Wilmot Mountain in Wisconsin, laughing the whole way, in anticipation of a day to be spent together riding their boards in the snow.

Now, in a quiet, minimalist room containing just a table and chairs, he's thinking more about those times. About relationships and acceptance. And how love can come in small doses.

He'd saved a lift ticket from Wilmot. When asked to present a physical item that has meaning, that is what he shows.

CHAPTER SIX

THE WAY IT WAS

To the vagabond hearts and nomadic souls of the world, this fact may not appeal to your sensibilities: Of the 10 varsity football assistants at Carmel, six graduated from the school. Of the four who didn't graduate, two—Mike Fitzgibbons and defensive backs coach Tom Kelly—have children enrolled at Carmel.

Fitzgibbons, the defensive line coach, and assistant head coach Jim Rejc were once head coaches at the school, only to return as assistants.

This speaks to the environment's persuasive dogma; whatever disagreements may arise between competitive grown men over decades of service time—and there are plenty—they are subjugated by an unwavering love for their school. This emotion is the connective tissue that unites and binds them together, and for these men, it's for life.

Ben Berg, the offensive line coach and coordinator, first coached under Fitz in 1988. Berg speaks in a measured cadence, yet has a forceful tenor to his voice easily heard amid the chaos of football. He teaches AP Psychology and believes football is much a mastery of the brain as the body. At times, he will refer to himself in the third person as "Benfucius," a tongue-in-cheek word play after the ancient Chinese philosopher Confucius. Berg scripts the first 15 plays before each game. Below the play list is often a pearl of wisdom such as, "It isn't the plays or the system that gets the job done. It's the quality of the people in the system."

Joe May is one of nine of Charles and Margaret May's 15 children to have graduated from Carmel. He was a fullback but possessed an arm more suited for throwing a baseball than a football. After graduating in 1978, he moved south to play college ball for former major leaguer Eddie Stanky at South Alabama.

"I was on the radar to play pro ball. I had all the natural talent in the world but didn't work hard enough to grow it into more of a talent. I pissed it away," May said.

After a career selling newspaper ads, May came back to Carmel (if they leave, they often come back) to coach and teach in 2003. He now coaches linebackers. Players love him for the reasons so many love their coaches at this place: He is right where he wants to be, doing exactly what he wants to do.

Tim Schrank is the Corsairs' wide receivers coach. He graduated from the school in 1991 but never played a down of football. His only exposure to football was as Fitz's stat man his senior year. Schrank ran track and played basketball though. His father was a coach and as the youngest of three boys, "I was always being coached no matter what," he said. He returned to coach in 2000 and is a teacher at a nearby middle school. Schrank projects a big brother-type vibe, a coach who eases player anxiety after a missed assignment or block with a pat on the shoulder pad. "My style fits in well. I do more one-on-one," he said. He calls the two hours on the practice field "the favorite part of my day."

Even the unofficial video coordinator goes way back with the school. Enzo Magrin was a freshman at Carmel in 1966. The admissions board accepted his application despite his checkered history. "In those days, you could go into the seminary after junior high," Magrin said. He possesses haggard physical features that defy an otherwise warm interpersonal disposition. He smiles often. "I graduated from Sacred Heart in Melrose Park and went right in. We had a dorm of 30 kids. But I was kicked out.

"I had these horrible cramps in the middle of the night. I started screaming and yelling because it hurt. There's supposed to be silence between 8 p.m. and 8 a.m. I guess I didn't take pain very well."

There was more.

"Another time I had a Latin test for declensions. I was having trouble remembering them so one night I went in the closet and closed the door. It was one of these rollback closets and I had a flashlight underneath all the blankets, studying my declensions. You were supposed to be in bed by 10. There was this guy. He was a Sicilian from Italy. He was a year older. He was the monitor. He opens the door and sees the light and thinks it's a ghost, so he screams bloody murder. I got caught. Little things like that accumulated. So they kicked me out. They said I was too immature.

"Then I came here."

Magrin's tenure at Carmel—1966-70—came at a time of great cultural unrest in our country, but within the school walls at 999 E. McKinley, structure and discipline reigned.

"At the time, we had two schools, Carmel High School for Boys and Girls. You were never allowed on the girls' side unless you had a class, and there were very few of those classes. In the middle of the school you had the cafeteria. You could eat or be at the library with the girls. But the nuns would come by with rulers and they would measure. You had to be 18 inches apart otherwise they would smack the guys. If they thought you were too close, they would check."

While young Enzo never felt the sting of the Almighty for sitting too close to a girl, he did get in trouble a few times for tardiness. His punishment was the 1960s Catholic school version of detention, known as JUG, or "Justice Under God." Often this meant sitting in a classroom chair, hands folded, back straight, head up while staring at the clock for an hour. Other times, offenders were made to do traditional chores like sweeping the hallways or fertilizing the football field. For more serious or repeat offenses, harsher punishment was rendered.

"The priests had the paddle," Magrin said. "You had to earn that,"

He remembers one particular case very well: A student who had a choice to either do JUG or take the paddle. "He didn't want to stay for an hour so he took the paddle." After school, the student came to the office of Father Peter to receive his punishment. An assistant in the discipline office, Magrin witnessed the exchange. "Father Peter swats him and he goes flying through the door. He comes back, tears streaming down his face, and Father Peter said, 'Let that be a lesson to you.' He had eight more to do, but Father Peter let him go. Father Peter hated doing it. You could see it on his face."

These are stories from a bygone era. JUG and paddle-wielding priests are no more at Carmel. That is just fine with Magrin, as his nostalgia is not reserved for archaic punishments. But Magrin does worry about the lack of figures like Father Peter. There have been no priests on staff since 2008. There is one nun—Sister Mary Sattgast, the school's registrar, who has worked at the school in various capacities since the girls' school opened in 1963.

The scarcity of priests and nuns roaming the halls of catholic schools is not uncommon these days. Catholic school enrollment peaked in the decade of Carmel's birth, when there were 5.2 million students in almost 13,000 schools across the country. By 1990, the enrollment dipped by more than half, to 2.5 million students attending 8,719 schools. That decade 573 more schools closed. Since 2000, Catholic schools have folded at a rate of 117 per year. Combined enrollment for primary and secondary schools has fallen 22 percent. The reasons for these statistics are numerous, ranging from economic to sociological. But at the core is a shift away from religion's influence within our nation's culture.

From the turn of the 20th century, when the Catholic Church supported 3,500 schools run by local parishes, through the 1960s, much of a household's identity was rooted in its geography as it related to a parish.

"Back in those days, when you asked someone where they lived, they would say, even if they weren't Catholic, 'Oh, I live by St. Henry's.' Because everyone knew where the parishes were. They had a lot of churches, a lot of ethnic churches. It was part of the makeup of Chicago," said Father Frank Franzmann, a chaplain at St. Mary's of the Lake Seminary in Mundelein. "Now when someone asks where they live, they might say, 'Oh, West Rogers Park.'"

Growing up by St. Henry's Parish on Chicago's North Side (in Rogers Park by modern geographical standards), Franzmann knew he wanted to be a priest at an early age. As all aspiring clerics in Chicago did in the 1960s,

Franzmann began his education as a high school student at the Quigley Preparatory Seminary in Chicago. But before acceptance, there was a recommendation that all friar wannabes had to secure.

"There were some guys in my class who said, 'I'd like to go to Quigley,'" Franzmann said. "One of the nuns at St. Henry's said, 'Over my dead body. I'm not recommending you, as you are too much of a cut-up. You won't make it academically.' There was a Catholic ethos."

Father Bob Carroll was Carmel's principal from 1994-2008 and held the same position at Carmelite sister Mount Carmel from 1980-1990. He was Carmel's very last priest on staff.

"Years ago, everything was ordained by your parents, your church or other things," Carroll said. "You had constant contact with your spirituality. You didn't get away from that realm. There were prayers, there was church attendance, church realities, there were celebrations and feast days and movements of sacraments. For a number of people, that's becoming passé."

The decline of religion's importance in the American household makes parochial education an afterthought, he said.

"You can see it. The grandparents' faith was very strong, and the parents' faith becomes more dissipated just because of the sheer number of activities involved. Then it comes down to the third generation. They are told to practice soccer on Sunday mornings. So there is no time for church. It becomes something that has happened. Sociologically, it's become a pattern of American culture."

Between stints at Mount Carmel and Carmel, Carroll worked as a manager of several schools (Dunbar, Amundsen, Schurz) within the Chicago Public School system. He saw up close the sometimes-hollow process of educating kids in an urban setting. "It devolved into how a teacher presents material. If a student can learn it, education takes place. If the student can't or doesn't want to learn it, you don't care, as you can't stop. You can put the material out there, but you cannot be concerned if the student has learned it."

He said the dynamic is much different at Catholic schools.

"They have the attitude, 'I want you to know this and learn this because it's important for you' or 'you don't have to know this that well as it's not that important.' Then it begins to make sense," Carroll said. "[Students] have a sense about that you are worth the challenge no matter who you are. You are worth it. [Teachers] have dedicated their lives to this so there must be something about me that makes these people run around and think I'm important."

These days, the teachers are college graduates (often with master's degrees) who speak from their classroom pulpit wearing dress shirts or slipovers rather than the cloth of a clergyman or canoness. They are the everyday modern face of parochial education. To them, the departure of priests and nuns from the classroom is simply the natural order of things.

"Their job was to inspire a community, to continue that mission," said Jeff Ptacek, a history teacher at Carmel. "Every religious community, to a sense, is humble enough and aware enough to say, 'We are not going to be around forever.' Our goal is to not be a permanent fixture here. Our goal, our mission, is to instill within a community a sense of the significance of Catholic education. Once that baton has been passed on to laypeople like myself, we become the people who carry on the mission of the church."

At Carmel, that mission was established by two orders—the Sisters of Charity of the Blessed Virgin Mary and the Carmelites. Both orders still run the school, with oversight from the Archdiocese of Chicago. The BVM's, as they are referred to, and Carmelites make up the school's board of corporators, serving in an advisory capacity. They are rarely seen, but their vocation carries on.

"We've become the new BVM's and Carmelites. We are the presence of that mission," Ptacek said. "I don't need a habit to live the spirituality of the school. I know the faith, I know the tradition."

~

For an old-timer like Magrin, maintaining a filament of the orthodoxy spoken of by Father Franzmann, Father Carroll and Ptacek—one of traditional Catholicism—is a mission that still ties him to the school.

For nearly two decades, it certainly wasn't football.

"We went through 17 years of one winning season. I was very frustrated and every year I said, 'I'm not coming back.' But I would," Magrin said. "I felt my mission was not necessarily to win football games but to bring people to Jesus."

Magrin does this through prayer.

"I pray for the kids. I worry about their health. How are they doing as people? That is what it is all about. I think when you pray you are more disciplined. When you have more prayer, God disciplines you more. To know the Lord you have to work at it and be open to him, which is not necessarily what you want. Like a football team. They want to do what they want, but they have to do what the coach wants, so they are working as a team to accomplish the objective. For religion, it's heaven. For football, it's winning the game."

In the 44 years since he first set foot on the school grounds, he's missed just nine home games. He had a good excuse for those absences. "My mom was sick," Magrin said.

Those ill-begotten seasons in the 1970s and '80s are now reaping championships. No one is more tickled than Magrin by the Corsairs' decade-plus run of football success. But to him, the game is an exercise in personal and spiritual growth, allowing him to reach a higher level of understanding about his own place and worth in the universe. That belief remains inextinguishable, as is his desire to pay it forward.

"Basically I feel that Carmel is a religious school in the sense that it is trying to follow God's will. Do we do a perfect job bringing people to Jesus? No, not even close. But we're trying. It would help if we had some priests and nuns. It's not going to happen, unfortunately. That's the case with every school.

"Because we're trying, I'm going to support the school as much as I can. It all centers around Jesus. As long as we try and do what He wants, it's a great school.

"If we went the other way, my devotion would quickly fade."

CHAPTER SEVEN

CATHOLIC LEAGUE

CARMEL'S HEAD FOOTBALL COACH SITS BEHIND A DESK, his head turned to a black 13-inch monitor. Conservative radio station WIND 560-AM plays over an office radio. Host Michael Savage is breaking down the pros and cons (mostly cons) of Obamacare. He's also lamenting President Obama's appearance on David Letterman almost a year ago.

The coach agrees with Savage. "Our president shouldn't be going on Letterman. It's unpresidential."

"Obama is not your father's President," says a visitor.

"He should be," the coach replies. "Of course, I didn't like my father's president, either."

"Who was that?"

"FDR."

Andy Bitto is a fan of the History Channel, admirer of many presidents not named Franklin Delano Roosevelt (George Washington, Abraham Lincoln, and Ronald Reagan are favorites) and obscure 1970s pop culture. He often refers to sophomore kicker Steven O'Block as "Gus the kicking mule." This is a reference to the 1976 Don Knotts movie *Gus* about a Yugoslavian mule that can kick a football 100 yards. But today, Monday, he's not viewing reruns of *Three's Company* or reading transcriptions of Reagan's speeches. There are more pressing concerns.

"I like our backfield. Kos needs to be better without the ball. He hit two holes, fumbled, and besides that, he doesn't block or fake as well ask I'd like," Coach Bitto says, without looking away from the monitor. "Our defense is playing great. More of a challenge this week. A different animal."

The Corsairs are 3-0 on the season after destroying St. Viator 39-0 on Friday night, the first conference game. Starting the season 1-0 in the knock-down, drag-out East Suburban Catholic is always preferred for any team with championship aspirations. But beating the Lions is gratifying on its own: They are not well-thought of around these brown hallways. Located in Arlington Heights, St. Viator is the closest Catholic high school to Carmel (14 miles). Bitto is quick to dismiss any narrative equating geographic proximity to chummy relations.

"Some schools have a way of presenting themselves in a certain fashion and others don't," Coach Bitto says, finally stopping the tape.

His desk is buried underneath a sea of brochures, papers, and boxes. If Vince Lombardi lost his whistle, this would be the last place to look. "They present themselves sportsmanship-wise in ways I would never accept. Their acceptability is different than ours. I just don't appreciate some of the things the kids do representing their school. I would be embarrassed and I would address it."

There are numerous incidents the coaches refer to when discussing St. Viator. The earliest occurred in the late 1980s. Before entering the field for the second half, offensive coordinator Ben Berg was pushed in the back by a St. Viator player. The Lions player took the field for the second half unpunished. "If that stuff happened here, they would be tossed off the team," Berg said. In a home game in 1994, Carmel had gone ahead by four touchdowns in the fourth quarter. Fitz, the head coach at the time, pulled his starters from the game. Against Carmel's second-team defense, the Lions scored two touchdowns. The Corsairs put their starting offense back on the field. "I'm watching this like it's a movie," said Berg, who was not coaching but sitting in the stands. "One of their coaches calls a time-out. He comes out to talk to his kids and he's screaming at our quarterback [Nick Yeager]. I don't know what he's saying but he's screaming at him." Jim Rejc, who was coaching for the Corsairs that night, said: "The St. Viator coach was screaming not only at Yeager but at his players to get Yeager."

After the time-out, Carmel called a simple dive play to run the clock down, hoping the runner would fall forward. Instead, "The kid breaks it for a touchdown," Berg said. "Our receiver was blocking one of their kids on their side of the field. I don't know if he said something but he gets in a melee with that kid and their bench jumps on our kid."

Nine of Carmel's offensive players rush to help their teammate. A brawl ensues. "All nine of our kids got suspended the following week," Berg said. "They had 30 suspended and had to forfeit their next game."

There have been other incidents, albeit of a more non-violent nature, and over time, memories of games fade. But not all memories.

"And that's what bothers me. It's a great school academically, I'm sure. But they let their kids play a little looser than I would," Coach Bitto says.

Some of the looseness he refers to was on display late in Friday's game.

"They were cussing at our guys in the pile."

Football is a physically demanding sport where brawn is often rewarded over brains. Intellect is necessary, but not at the expense of toughness. Yet Coach Bitto is a firm believer that muscularity must be performed with dignity. They are not separate acts but equal temperaments. For a teenager to play for him, this sensibility must be understood.

He mentions a phone call after the St. Charles East game a couple of weeks ago, won by Carmel 56-7.

"A St. Charles parent called me the next day and said, 'You played with a lot of class.' He was very complimentary toward our kids," Coach Bitto says. "That's getting someone on our side although we thrashed them. If we win and we act like buffoons when we walk off the field and they say, 'Hey those Carmel guys are jokes.' It doesn't matter. I don't care if we go 1-8. You have to get people on your side."

Just as Coach Bitto finishes his point, there's a knock on the door. It's a player with a question for his coach.

"Coach Bitto, can I get a new practice uniform?"

"Why?"

"I can't find it. My mom lost it and.."

"Your mom? What does your mom have to do with anything?" Coach Bitto interrupts. "It's your responsibility."

The boy looks down at his shoes, embarrassed by his absent-mindedness. He's wearing a powder-blue polo shirt, khaki pants and slip on loafers.

Carmel has an earnest dress code easy to be charmed by.

Coach Bitto has just changed out of his day-job outfit—shirt, tie and khakis—and into his coach's ensemble of a gray T-shirt with Carmel Corsairs lettering in front, khaki shorts, brown and yellow shoes and brown ball cap. It's early September and the temperature outside is in the low 70s. His cheekbones still show a hint of late-summer color.

"Do you know who Coach Young is?" Coach Bitto asks the boy, a junior.

"Yes."

"Check the equipment room."

"Thanks," says the boy, grabbing his backpack and opening the door to leave. Before the door closes, it is opened again by another lost soul.

"Coach Bitto?"

"What?"

"'I'm not feeling well. I told the nurse.."

"What's wrong?"

"I don't know. I've been dizzy and my stomach. It's not.."

"So you want to take a day off?"

"No, but my mom.."

"Your mom? OK. We'll just have to play Joliet Catholic without you."

"Well, no. I'll be fine. It's just.."

The door opens again. Another player enters. He leans against the wall to the right of Bitto's desk.

"Twenty questions in here," Coach Bitto says. "One at a time."

"Can I go?" asks the sick one.

"Go. I can give you some Pepto Bismol. That might fix your stomach."

"I don't know if." the boy says.

"It's OK. Go home and get well."

"Coach Bitto, did you get my email?" asks the new entrant, a sophomore. "My dad is sick."

"Yes, I forwarded it over to Coach Whittier," Coach Bitto says, referring to Larry Whittier, the sophomore coach.

For a second, the room is silent.

"Go take care of your dad. Let me know if there's anything you need. Or if you need to punch me in the face. But don't take that literally. You're too big."

The boy laughs, probably for the first time all day. He picks up his backpack, turns and walks out.

Coach Bitto leans on his desk, his forearms supporting his weight.

"His dad has some physical issues," he says, his voice now a monotone. "We need to support him. I know what that's like. It's no fun."

He leans back into his chair.

"The mom excuses are the worst. 'My mom didn't wake me up, that's why I'm late for school?' What do you mean your mom? Have you ever heard of an alarm clock?"

~

Before the Southern states erected coliseums where, by the hundreds of thousands, its legions of fan boys and debutante dress-wearing gals could watch the grand American game of football, the sport had the Chicago Catholic League. In 1927, the first city championship pitted the winners of the CCL and the Chicago Public League. The game between Carl Schurz High School and Mount Carmel drew 50,000 fans to Soldier Field. At the time, it was the largest crowd ever to watch a high school football game. A three-yard fourth-quarter touchdown run by Mel Brosseau gave the Caravan an unlikely 6-0 victory over Schurz, which was ten times the size of Mt. Carmel. News accounts of the game said Mount Carmel declared itself the "undisputed" champion and "the most powerful and best team in Chicago prep history." Schurz, on the other hand, failed to publicly acknowledge the game's outcome and promoted itself as city champion.

In the ensuing decades, the CCL was as sure a bet to have a team in the state title game. From 1976 until 2009, the conference accounted for 29 different state champions in seven separate classes. Five times during that stretch it had multiple title winners in the same year. To say the conference is in its own class is like saying the 1927 Yankees could swing the bats a little. Eight schools (St. Lawrence, Bishop McNamara, St. Rita, Providence Catholic, Loyola Academy, Brother Rice, Gordon Tech and Mount Carmel) have won state titles, proving the league is not top-heavy. It has tradition (first formed in 1912), great teams, and the Chicago Archdiocese on its side.

In the 1950s, as parents of baby boomers began to move their families north and west of Chicago, settling in towns such as LaGrange, Schaumburg, Kankakee and Mundelein, high schools began to crop up all over what before had been open land. In 1966, four years after Carmel opened its doors, it joined the Suburban Catholic Conference. By 1974, it had been renamed the East Suburban Catholic Conference. Joliet Catholic was also a member. A year later, the Hilltoppers won the conference's first state title. It was the first of four in a row and 13 in 23 years. Although not necessarily a causation for football greatness, JCA has groomed several notable alumni—former DePaul basketball player George Mikan, actress Melissa McCarthy and several Major League Baseball players, most notably Bill Gullickson, who won 20 games for the Detroit Tigers in 1991. Yet the most well-known graduate might be Rudy Ruettiger, who was once told by an irascible college football coach that he was "a hundred and nothin'" and would amount to nothing" and somehow parlayed that insult into a hit movie about his life and nationwide fame. The film is called, "Rudy."

In Carmel's first 40 years of existence, it had beaten Joliet Catholic once. That was in 1972. Jake Ciccone coached the Corsairs at the time. After a successful coaching run in Michigan, Ciccone was hired to rebuild the Carmel program, which was floundering, having won eight games the previous four seasons. Ciccone was a believer in stripping down the playbook. He ran two plays—trap right and misdirection left—and on one mild Saturday afternoon that year, those two plays were enough to beat the mighty Hilltoppers and legendary coach Gordie Gillespie, 12-6.

Between 1973-2002, The Corsairs played the Hilltoppers 17 times. They lost all 17 games. The 2003 victory by Carmel was momentous, coming at the end of the regular season and propelling the Corsairs to what would be their only state title. Carmel has since beaten Joliet Catholic twice, in 2006 and 2008, and while it no longer feels inferior, it hasn't quite shed a little brother complex.

"They've [Joliet Catholic] had tradition since the '40s and '50s," Coach Bitto says. "Mount Carmel since the '20s. We are a Carmelite school, just like they are. We are trying to develop that tradition. We are in the infancy stage of our development."

He stands on the Carmel field, holding practice charts on note cards attached to a clipboard. On the cards are sketches of plays from Friday night's opponent, Joliet Catholic Academy. The cards could just as easily be from 1975, when the Hilltoppers won their first state title. They are historically a power running team, with physical, downhill running backs and big, strong, offensive linemen. The scheme mirrors the economic footprint of the school's student population.

"I think they are more around the blue-collar side," Coach Bitto says. "We are a little different, as we have a mix of different socio-economic scenarios. We have some really wealthy kids, some that are struggling and in-between. I know Coach Sharp handles his kids like they are his own kids and expects them to behave like champions everywhere they go. Those are the similarities we have."

The Corsairs arrive for the day's practice. It's Tuesday, 3:20 p.m., time for stretching and calisthenics. Coach Bitto wanders up and down the rows of players, giving instructions. He likes this time of day. He can visit with the boys, talk to them informally before the business of practice begins. "Hey, it's Justin Bieber!" he yells in the direction of Michael Panico, who is just arriving.

Coach Bitto has letters addressed to Panico from Notre Dame and Northwestern, to name a few of the high-profile schools recruiting the 5-8, 170-pound running back. Through the first three games, he is the team's rushing leader with 445 yards. Panico is as *indifferent* to Carmel's rule on hair length (cut above the ears) as he is to oncoming tacklers. This is why Coach Bitto has begun referring to his star running back as Justin Bieber, the teen idol with the mop-top.

It's catching on.

"Hey, Justin!" yell a few of the players in unison.

Before he begins calisthenics, Panico quickly pulls his head back, giving his just-above-the-ears shag a slight flip in mock affirmation. A few team-mates laugh. A slight grin crosses his lips. He wants everyone to know he's in on the joke.

~

Coach Bitto and the assistant coaches believe they can throw the football on Joliet Catholic. "It's going to come down to three plays probably, one way or another," he says. "We have to make two of them. I think we can do it through the air."

Serio has played well at quarterback the first three games, having run for 239 yards and three touchdowns. But there are still concerns about his passing. After an excellent performance against Libertyville in Week Two, he regressed against St. Viator. In that game, he underthrew Panico on what would have been a sure touchdown. Berg has been putting passing plays into the offense to take advantage of the mismatch Panico creates against the defense. All Serio has to do is loft the ball high in the air, and the speedy Panico will run under it. Instead, Serio's throws have been low liners, forcing receivers to stop their routes and turn back to catch the ball. Against Joliet Catholic, it's important the quarterback is on target.

"I'm tired of being nice," Coach Bitto says. "I need to get him out to prac-tice and throw. If it takes until the cows come home, we'll do it."

During the first few drills Wednesday, a poor throw rolls off Serio's right hand, bouncing on the turf well short of the intended receiver. Coach Bitto doesn't waste time.

"Brian, you are level-oneing it again," he says, describing a throw that is straight on a line. "If the guy is underneath, throw it over the top! Chuck it and let him run and get it."

On the next play, Serio underthrows another pass.

"I never see you follow through, Brian! I never see you follow through. Never. That's why the ball is short all the time. Let's go!" Coach Bitto says.

After another low ball, and now Serio is the one barking. "Goddammit! Huddle up!" he says to the offensive unit.

Coach Bitto doesn't like his quarterback's response or tone. "Are you going to stop getting down on yourself?"

Next is a non-rhetorical question directed to Serio: "Brian, can I throw the ball?"

"No," Serio says.

"Am I 17 (years old)?" Coach Bitto asks.

"No."

"You are the guy who has to do it. Poop it out of your butt and let's go. I'm not going to drive up to Antioch [where Serio lives] and buy you an ice cream at the Tastee Freez or whatever they have up there off I-173. Besides, I don't like maraschino cherries."

The few players observing this exchange laugh. "Tastee Freez is awesome!" one says.

"I love Tastee Freez," says another.

All the ice cream chatter has lightened the mood. Serio overthrows Panico on the next play, but Coach Bitto is pleased. "At least you threw it. That's better."

Serio's case of the throwing yips notwithstanding, coaches are confident the Corsairs can score points Friday night. This is not one of JCA's better defensive teams. It figures to be a high-scoring contest as the Hilltoppers feature running back Josh Ferguson, who is already committed to play college ball at Illinois. Numerous Big Ten schools are recruiting another, Malin Jones, a junior.

The man in charge of creating Carmel's defensive game plan is first-year defensive coordinator Dan Potempa. A former linebacker at Carmel, he was coached by Bitto, then the defensive coordinator.

"I remember one time talking to him before I graduated," Potempa says. "I said when I got out of college I was going to hang out and live on the beach in California. He said, 'Dan, you are full of crap. You are going to come back to Carmel and be my defensive coordinator.' I remember thinking, 'No way. I'm not coming back here.' Lo and behind, somehow someway."

Potempa played college football for a short time at Iowa State, finishing at Kaneland College in Wisconsin. As Coach Bitto predicted, he returned to Carmel to coach and teach. The 31-year old Potempa is an ambitious game-planner whose coaching style—a mix of cerebral bookishness and obsessive diligence—pushes the limits of what high school players can do both physically and intellectually.

Most of Carmel's conference competitors run a version of the trendy spread offense that uses four or five receivers and the whole field.

To counter this attack, the Corsairs will run a 3-3-5 defensive scheme, with three down linemen, three linebackers, and five defensive backs. Carmel is not big, but they are fast, with linebackers and defensive backs who can run receivers down in open space. This was evident in the Libertyville game. This week's version will be what the coaches call their "Joliet Catholic" defense.

"We don't want them to run right in the seam. We want to get everything to bounce out," linebackers coach Joe May says.

∽

Fans of Chicago-area high school football would have to have their heads stuck in a challis to not know it was Carmel-Joliet Catholic week. Both teams are 3-0. Both have cracked the *Chicago Tribune's* Top 10. Amplifying the weighty atmosphere is the fact Carmel-Joliet Catholic is the only Friday night game in the area. Lake and northern Cook counties contain a large Jewish population and Rosh Hashanah is this week. All other games are moved to Thursday or Saturday to honor the holiday. If you want your Friday-night lights, you'll have to come to 1 Carmel Parkway in Mundelein. This is not just another game.

Before Wednesday's practice ends, a quick sideline poll of a few other players confirms the Corsairs are confident they can beat their Carmelite brothers.

"They always have good talent. I respect them in that matter. I don't respect them when I play them," says Luke Venegoni, Carmel's middle linebacker. Potempa's decision to play Venegoni inside—a more physically demanding position than outside—has proved brilliant. Venegoni is the unquestioned leader of the defense, embodying the strong/silent -type needed on any winning team. He prefers to let his play do the talking and, for the first three games, it's working. Venegoni has 28 tackles and one sack.

Senior defensive lineman Jake Larson offers up more analysis on how Carmel can win: "We're pretty much trying to create a pile at the line so they have to run outside. This is not one of the games you get your name in the paper."

Someone who must play well Friday night is LaRon Biere. He has emerged from the first three games as one of the team's best defensive players. A ferocious hitter, he has a tough assignment against the Hilltoppers: Hold the line of scrimmage and don't let Ferguson or Jones bounce outside.

"I can do it," Biere says. "I just have to execute what the coaches tell me to do."

Standing on the practice field away from the rest of the loose, chatty Corsairs is safety Michael Fitzgibbons. Tall and freakishly skinny, like an altitudinous bass player in a rock band, he's wearing a pad on his right forearm. It's to protect the bone bruised in the team's win over Libertyville. It won't keep him out the game. A young man with a cockamamie sense of humor, Fitzgibbons is all business when it comes to football and Joliet Catholic.

"Viator is a hatred. Joliet is more of respect," Fitzgibbons says. "Even if we are not vying for the championship, we are neck and neck, so every time we play them it's respect, as we know they are always good and so are we."

Fitzgibbons was on last year's team that lost to the Hilltoppers 17-16 on a last-second field goal. The sting still resonates. Payback is a motivator.

"Oh, yeah, especially for kids that played last year," Fitzgibbons says.

The night before, a group of players went to the funeral of the mother of a teammate who graduated last year. It was in the south suburbs, close to Nazareth Academy, a school located in LaGrange that is in Carmel's conference. A long hike on a school night, but this was a buddy who just lost his mother. To them the trip was not burdensome, but obligatory. "A couple of us went to the funeral. They were talking about the game," Fitzgibbons says. "These were parents and they were asking, 'Are we ready?' It hit me. We are well known. People down there know about the game."

Fitzgibbons' stony practice-field persona contrasts with the other, less callous side of his personality. During a scorching hot August practice, he was taking a water break. The coach nearest him muttered something about the importance of sharing the plastic bottle he was drinking from with a teammate standing nearby. Fitzgibbons turned to the teammate and said about the coach, "Don't listen to him. That's the pregnancy talking." Then turning to the coach who dared request his charity, he said, "When is the baby due?"

Under normal circumstances, a player commenting on the girth of his adult coach would warrant disciplinary action. But there is nothing common about this player-coach relationship. Fitzgibbons's barb was directed at Coach Mike Fitzgibbons, his father. Fitz has a private counseling practice in addition to his day job as school ministry director and part-time coaching gig, not leaving much time for exercise. The pregnancy comment could be construed as a flippant—Fitz himself admits he's a tad overweight—observation from a disrespectful son. In truth, the more time any observer spends around the two Michaels, it's obvious the witty banter is not dysfunctional diatribe but affectionate conjecture.

"When did you say the baby was due?" Junior again asks. "Aren't you in the third trimester by now?"

"Stop it. You're terrible," Senior responds with a chuckle.

Although Senior is running himself ragged—working his day job at Carmel, his night job as counselor—the two hours he shares each day on a football field with his quipster of a son is the gift that keeps on giving.

"How can I not sit back and ride the dream? What parent gets to do this?"

~

After a two-and-a-half hour practice, Serio hoists his reward over his left shoulder. Per program tradition, quarterbacks stuff practice footballs into a large backpack and carry them back to the coach's office. "It's not that bad," he says.

Serio is another legacy Corsair. His older brother, Mike, was a running back on the 2003 state championship team. When big brother first came home with a Carmel football uniform, Serio knew he wanted to be just like him.

"That's what made me fall in love with Carmel football," Serio says. "I guess it was the camaraderie with the teammates, the celebration afterwards and really wanting to be a part of it. Sitting in those stands and dancing after touchdowns with my parents. Then we'd always go to someone's house and eat food, then go home. It was a lot of fun.

"Mike would talk all the time about football. He was the hardest working kid I ever met. That got into me."

Recently graduated from college and living in New York, Mike Serio is in regular contact with his younger brother. Especially during football season.

"We always talk about the team and Carmel football. He calls me up after games," Serio says. He looks down, flashing a wide, playful grin, an expression not seen during the recently completed hard practice. "That's a huge deal to live in his footsteps, but I think it helps me. I like the pressure. I like when there's thousands of fans. It makes the game like it's more intense. There's a little pressure to not disappoint, to live up to my name. So I'm going to try and do everything I can to win a state championship just like he did."

There are current examples in the NFL game of successful quarterbacks who are fussy, demanding, alpha males (Peyton Manning, Tom Brady, Drew Brees). In contrast, there are examples of Super Bowl-winning teams led by compliant, tolerant non-alphas like Eli Manning or Kurt Warner. Serio would fall into the non-alpha category, a genuinely kind, earnest young man who prefers to let his play do the talking. Not once this season has any-one seen him yell at a teammate or, outside of calling a play, raise his voice. The boys up front who block for him swear by his humility, balanced with a tough-as-nails running style that often sets a savage tone during games.

"He always does the right thing. Never takes the credit," senior offensive lineman Logan Lester said. "Inside the 5-yard line, some quarterbacks keep the ball. With Serio, it doesn't matter to him. He's going to give the ball or pitch the ball."

"I get to my guy, Logan hits his guy, Brian pulls and hits the hole so hard. And he never comes out," senior offensive lineman Sean Wolf-Lewis said. "Sure, he's quiet and doesn't say much, but there's no other quarterback we want. He leads by how hard he plays."

"I just really respect Serio. The way he lowers his head and shoulder into guys. He just has no regard for his body," Jordan Kos, the fullback, said.

Serio walks the hallway just outside the locker room. He opens the door to the coaches' office and drops the footballs. A little less than an hour ago, he had gotten an earful from the coach. Now he just wants to take a shower, eat a hot meal, and tackle the evening's academic homework. But before he heads home, he reveals a competitive streak, the one his teammates swear is inside him.

"I don't know. I want to get better. I'm trying," Serio says. "With Coach Bitto getting in my face, it pisses me off. It makes me want to do better on the next play. If a coach just lets you make mistakes and you don't correct them, how does that help?"

He walks ponderously through the locker room door. Just one more practice left before Friday night and the Corsairs' biggest game of the season so far.

~

Thursday goes as scheduled. It's a lighter day than Tuesday and Wednesday, when the offense and defensive game plans are installed. The climate is a mix of steadfast purpose and energetic jocularity.

"You look a little pretty today," Coach Fitzgibbons says to Coach Bitto between drills.

"What about you? What are those, cargo shorts?" Coach Bitto says back to Fitz, who has eschewed pants on a warm September afternoon. "And what's that shirt?"

"It's my father-in-law's," Fitz says.

"Why are you wearing a dead man's clothes?" Coach Bitto says.

This is the type of spontaneous, good-spirited exchange you would expect between two men who have known each other for almost 35 years. And while Coach Bitto, the 10th of 12 Bitto children to attend Carmel, became a football star and scholarship college player before coming back to teach and coach, Fitz's passage to 1 Carmel Parkway was considerably less preordained.

He started at Carmel as a teacher in 1976, one year before Coach Bitto enrolled as a freshman.

"I went to Chicago State, got out in three years with a degree in English and wanted to goof off for a year. I ended up interviewing here, and they offered me the job," Fitz says. "In order to take the job, I had to teach football and wrestling. The only time I had ever snapped a helmet on my head before I became a coach was when I wore one at a Halloween party."

Back in those days, there were seven coaches for all three levels—freshman, sophomore, and varsity. "They had a math teacher who was helping out the freshmen, but they super-glued his briefcase to the floor," Fitz says. "So that didn't work out."

He worked his way up to defensive coordinator on the varsity. "I really didn't know what the hell I was doing. You figure it out after a while," Fitz says. "To me, football was like English. You treat kids with some dignity. You learn it, you teach it, you rep it. 'OK, this makes sense to me. It's just like a classroom.'"

He taught, coached, and volunteered at school retreats. He soon realized another area of need at the school—ministry. "I was doing it in my doorway from my classroom. I would work retreats, and kids would have issues that came out and would want to talk to me."

While an assistant coach, Fitz got to know coaches from other schools in the conference. He was interested in how they were integrating faith components into football. Some of the coaches conducted game day-chapel services. So when Fitz became head coach in 1986, he started doing the same thing.

"All of the math teachers are supposed to pray in class. All of the English teachers pray before play performances. You recognize the fact it is all- encompassing and you are helping to instill the same set of values," Fitz says. "As campus minister, it was a natural to extend it to football. I think I was the only campus minister who was also head football coach."

And so the Carmel football team prayed. A lot. Priests would conduct services, often lasting 20 minutes. The boys sat in silence. Fitz soon got his master's in counseling and pastoral studies. He began to lead game-day prayer services. Gradually, the boys became more expressive.

"When you see high school boys do the sign of peace before a game, that is the most intense sign of peace you can ever imagine," Fitz says. "Those are real hugs. You are building a team. One time a kid got up his senior year. No one knew why he didn't play his junior year. He got up homecoming week and started crying. He had testicular cancer. Went down to Mexico for treatment. He was sobbing in front of the whole team. We won the game and carried him off the field."

And soon there was a lot more winning. In 1989, Carmel made it to the state quarterfinals. The defensive coordinator that season was a tireless young coach named Andy Bitto. When he became athletic director in 1992, the relationship between football and the athletic department became more cohesive. Coaches were hired to handle the increasing number of kids participating at all levels. Weight training became the bedrock of program culture. Players were bigger, stronger and smarter, athletically and spiritually.

In 1995, Carmel played Notre Dame School for Boys in its final game of the year. The Corsairs were led that season by quarterback Nick Yeager. "He was the best player on the team. Whatever he did, the kids followed," Fitz said. Late in the game, Yeager threw an eight-yard touchdown pass, and Carmel went on to beat the Dons 36-35. After the mandatory post-game handshake with opposing players and coaches, the Corsairs gathered by the south end zone. "I'm talking to reporters, and the coaches are jacked up," Fitz says. "I didn't know what they were doing."

What the players did, led by Yeager, was get down on one knee and recite, in chorus, the Lord's Prayer. "We always prayed inside," Fitz says. "I was always worried about what might happen [outside], especially after a loss."

There was no cause for concern that night for Fitz. Only pangs of gratitude.

Then in 1997, Morris thrashed Carmel 41-0 in the quarterfinals. Fitz knew it was his last game as head coach. Before the game was played, he had told no one of his plans except the principal, his assistants and his wife. As was now tradition, after the post-game handshakes, players gathered in the end zone to say the Lord's Prayer. Only this time, the student body joined them.

"The very first time the student body runs onto the field, it's my last home game and they are praying together. That moment is frozen in time, it's perfect," Fitz says. "It's perfect because my goal was to have all of that come together. If there was something I'd want to do with a football team that never won was I'd want to win, and I'd want to be sure God was there and I'd want to build community. And it was clear it was all happening in that one moment, and so it was OK to leave."

The next year, Bitto took over as head coach. The winning continued, as did the expressions of faith.

"Andy's carried a lot of that stuff over," Fitz says. "He's a better football coach than I was. More organized. He has a great vision. Everything is a program decision. He's constantly thinking about that. I don't remember if I was doing that, maybe later. I just know he's doing it."

Back after his two previous retirements, Fitz is still ministering, leading the team's game day chapel services. In introspective moments, he can't help but think about how unlikely his life's story is. To him, God truly had a plan.

"A guy from the South Side of Chicago decides to teach English and they tell him he has to coach football and wrestling and he's never done it before and throws his heart and soul into the school and 10 years later he becomes head football coach and campus minister and his goal is to win and bring God back into it all and make sure the spiritual aspects of athletics is important. And then the moment occurs.

"I suppose I do what I do because those moments are so perfect. They are unmistakable. They can't be read any other way. That's why this place is so special, because there's no other way to read those moments."

CHAPTER EIGHT

CARMELITES VS. CARMELITES

It's 4:50 p.m. Friday, September 20. Dressed in shirts and ties, Corsair football players are lined up in two long rows inside Titus Brandsma Chapel on Carmel's campus. Michael Fitzgibbons stands behind a lectern in front of varicolored stained glass. He looks down, and then raises his head to speak.

"So, we gather together in the name of the Father, Son and Holy Spirit. Let us prepare ourselves. A reading from the Gospel according to Mark…"

'What shall we say the kingdom of God is like, asked Jesus? What parable should we use to explain it? It is like this. A man takes a mustard seed, the smallest seed in the world, and plants it in the ground. After a while it grows up and becomes the biggest of all plants. It puts out such large braces that the birds come and make their nests in its shade. This is the gospel of the Lord.'

"So why the mustard seed?" Fitzgibbons asks. "It occurred to me earlier in the week that it fits perfectly when you watch a group of guys like you develop into what you are becoming. A number of people said it a number of times, and it was said after the game in the locker room by one of the coaches that something special is happening, something special is here. And it's true as Coach Bitto reminds you every day of all of your hard work and how special you are. What he said after practice ran true to me. Then I read an article in line at the Walgreen's about Brian Serio talking about when his brother played here.

"The seed wasn't sown when you joined football, was it? The seed of this might have been sown when your brother played football. The seed of this might have been sown when you started playing football when you were seven years old in one of the towns here in Lake County or in another state. And like all great things, great miracles, great wonders, you all collided here. And look what it's become. That small seed is becoming something great. A mustard seed is the smallest seed, and it grows to be the biggest you can possibly see. That's what is happening here. What a great time to reflect on that. Today. Today. A great rivalry and a great, great, great big game. How exciting is that? To think about that opportunity, today.

"So, we bring our needs and requests before God. You know how we do this. Our tradition is start in one corner and say what's on your mind and what or who you'd like to pray for."

Silence fills the air. To the right of where Fitzgibbons stands, the first boy speaks.

"My parents," he says.

Each boy in the chapel follows.

"My team."

"My sister."

"My mom."

"My brothers."

"My dad and my grandmother."

"This team."

"My brothers."

"My sister. My dad. My stepdad."

"My family and this team."

"All the injured players on this team."

"My wife and kids."

They finish.

Fitzgibbons reads another passage. He then asks everyone to stand. They recite the Lord's Prayer.

"Now offer each other the sign of peace," Fitzgibbons says.

The boys take turns embracing. The sound of strong hands softly tapping sturdy backs reverberates throughout the chapel.

All in the chapel receive Communion. Tranquility commands the room. Coach Bitto speaks.

"I want you to take a few minutes and reflect and realize how positively this group has affected our whole community. Our student body, our faculty, our alumni. Especially, our families, of course, but the players who played before you. I'm telling you of guys that played all the way back in the mid-'60s to last year are watching. Realize how God has given you the opportunity and knowledge to work hard enough and long enough to get people on your side. The more people you have on your side in a positive way, the more successful you will be.

"You are lucky people. You can express your luck and your love for one another through the game of football. That is a gift. Take a moment to reflect on that gift and what it means to you."

A few of the boys lean forward, their heads in their hands. Some lie on the floor. Others stare intensely into the eyes of a teammate next to them. No words are spoken.

~

"The game is what everybody celebrates, but it is so tiny, so tiny to the overall experience," Fitzgibbons said later. "When we have pre-game chapel, some things happen that are unbelievable. Whatever we feel is transferred in some way.

"I believe in all that stuff, the movement of the spirit."

~

Coach Bitto talks frequently to his players how football is a game of emotion. All of Friday's pre-game activities are a buildup to the opening kickoff. But he can't do it all. Players shoulder responsibility for their own state of mind. And he encourages them to lean on peers to help shepherd them toward optimal mindfulness.

It's 7:30 p.m., the exact capstone time of the week's preparations. Players, coaches and officials are on the field. Fans fill the bleachers.

The defensive unit is near the north end zone. Clustered like a brown-stained mob, they swerve in unison from side to side. In the center, leading the horde, is Luke Venegoni.

"We have to focus! We have to kick their asses! Their running back... who cares where he's going to college! We have to take out his legs!" he screams through his dungeonus facemask. The players reply to each edict with a forceful "YEAH!" This exhibition of raw, tribal exuberance has become a weekly pre-game routine.

Just as the linemen, linebackers, cornerbacks and safeties hear their leader loud and clear, Venegoni also hears the shouts, the bluster. They may not think he can hear them, but he can. The bombast, the do-this, the do-that.

Shouting from the Carmel stands during games are Venegoni's older brother, Mark, and father, John.

"Thirty-seven, you've got to pick it up! You have to step it up!" Mark yells.

"Get to the ball faster!" John howls.

Mark is the loudest and the most frequent, but he knows his little brother. He knows he plays better angry. He knows the screaming pisses Luke off, and when Luke is pissed off, he plays like an animal. And that's when Luke can't be blocked, can't be stopped. When he's angry. That's the way Luke wants his brother and dad to see him play. He wants to please them, he wants to be the player deserved of their attention. Mark has his championship ring, from 2003. Sometimes, he'll show it off. Not to brag, but to let him know he has one. And Luke wants his own. What little brother doesn't want what his big brother has?

In minutes, Luke will take the field for the biggest game of his life. As he hollers to his encircled teammates, his eyes bulge from their sockets like a prizefighter's moments before the opening bell. He's ready to give everyone watching something to talk about.

~

At 7:35 p.m., Joliet Catholic kicks off. The ball is caught by Jordan Kos at the 15-yard line and returned to Carmel's 37.

On the first play (31 pitch right), Michael Panico corrals the pitch from Brian Serio in the left flat and gallops 25 yards. Five plays later, Kos takes a hand-off from Serio and sprints 25 yards for a touchdown. It's just the start Carmel wanted. Four players carry the ball, and the offensive line creates big holes. On that drive, the Corsairs act very much like the swift, bounty-seeking pirates their nickname defines.

Before the offense can revel in their early success, the Hilltoppers strike back. Starting at their own 20, Josh Ferguson, the Illinois recruit, takes a handoff and darts through the hole between the right tackle and guard, and that's all he needs. Ferguson is gone for 80 yards. Touchdown Hilltoppers. It's 7-7.

Carmel starts the next drive on its 23-yard line. After a methodical series of pitches, dives and keeps—this is option football—the Corsairs are at their own 46-yard line, ready for 2nd down and 7.

On film, Carmel coaches saw how Joliet Catholic's defensive backs played just off the line of scrimmage. This strategy is designed to stop Carmel's productive running game. This "stack-the-box" scheme is often used against the Corsairs. Also on film, coaches observed how Hilltopper safeties focus on the run and don't provide help down the field. This leaves open spaces for wide receivers to roam. It's the perfect time to call the game's first pass.

Coach Berg calls the play into the headset ("89 ends right"). Serio runs toward the sidelines to get the play from Coach Bitto. He makes the call in the huddle, then the Corsairs hustle to the line of scrimmage. Serio fakes a handoff to Kos, who dips his shoulders slightly. On the right flat, just by the yardage makers, senior receiver Ryan Cappis takes the first steps of a streak route. Serio backpedals five more yards in the perfectly aligned pocket and launches a deep ball. The Joliet Catholic cornerback bites ever so slightly on Serio's ball fake, as does the safety playing seven yards off the line of scrimmage. The hesitation allows Cappis to gain a step. At the Hilltoppers' 26-yard line, Cappis catches the pass in stride and sprints untouched the rest of the way for a 54-yard score.

Serio just pooped out a touchdown pass.

With 5:19 left in the first quarter, Carmel regains the lead, 14-7.

 On the sidelines, adrenaline flows like hot brown lava.

"They can't stop us!" senior offensive guard Logan Lester screams.

"That was awesome!" Cappis yells at Serio as they approach the team bench.

Before Carmel players can finish a swig from their water bottles, the Hilltoppers counter punch again. Taking an inside handoff from Carmel's 23-yard line, running back Malin Jones finds a seam between the hash marks and in seconds, gallops into the Corsairs' end zone for a touchdown. It's 14-14, and there is still 5:03 left in the first quarter.

The pace of this game is like a Six Flags roller coaster. Adjustments will be made. It has to slow down. Then it's a matter of basic football—who will block and tackle better than the other team?

Right after the Hilltoppers' extra point, Coach Bitto turns to defensive coordinator Dan Potempa and calmly asks what everyone would like to know: "What is going on?"

Potempa's response: "We've got it."

∼

Sitting high in the stands, among the thousands of brown-and-gold-peppered fans, are a father and son. Jim Biere is there to watch his adopted son, LaRon. His youngest natural son, Tom, sits to his left.

 "This is quite a ball game so far," Jim says.

"No way they can keep this up," Tom says. "We may get to 100 points by halftime!"

"LaRon's hardly been on the field," Jim says.

"He hasn't had a chance to. Both teams are scoring so quick."

A few plays later, LaRon sheds a block and breaks into the Joliet Catholic backfield. He crashes into Jones, who spins away, taking a few steps before crumpling to the turf. He's a few feet short of a first down. The Hilltoppers will have to punt.

LaRon sprints off the field. He reaches the sidelines, stopping near one of the benches. A water bottle is in his left hand. He clutches the facemask of his now-removed helmet with his right. His hard hat is gold colored, the letter "C" painted on it in brown, the same letter "C" is in white on his uniform shoulder. On his brown jersey, he wears the number 25, printed in white. His brown pants extend just below his knee. White socks rise from his ankles up his leg, leaving a small gap above his calf. His cleats are also white, pinned to his feet by heavy layers of tape. Engraved in black on each shoe by his left and right ankles are two tiny letters:

"MB."

~

LL Cool J once rapped about not believing the hype. This is a rare contest worth the build-up. A true *magnum opus*.

The first quarter ends on a 94-yard kickoff return for a touchdown by Ferguson. On the possession before Carmel kicked it back to Joliet Catholic, Serio threw his second touchdown pass of the quarter, this one for 19 yards to tight end Pat Doherty. For five seconds of regulation time, the Corsairs led 21-14. But Ferguson's touchdown gallop makes the score 21-21. For the first 12 minutes, we have a basketball game on turf. But, predictably, beginning with the second quarter, the pace slows. Carmel makes an elementary defensive adjustment. "We just need to calm down and stop over-pursuing. Execute our stuff," Potempa says.

For the most part, the defense shuts down Ferguson and Jones over the Hilltoppers' next few possessions. Likewise, Joliet Catholic starts tackling better and not letting receivers run wide open. The second quarter is scoreless, as is most of the third. Serio ends the drought when he scampers 12 yards for a touchdown to make it 28-21 with 4:45 left in the third quarter.

Later in the quarter, sophomore kicker Steven O'Block drills a 44-yard field goal to give the Corsairs a 10-point margin.

Late in the fourth quarter, Jones breaks off a 55-yard run. It's the first time since the opening drives that Joliet Catholic has made a big play. Making the tackle on Jones is Tommy Snyder, a senior defensive lineman. After the play, Snyder doesn't get up. Coach Bitto and Carmel's trainer, Dan Henrichs, run out to check on Snyder, who is on all fours, his head facing down. He doesn't appear to be seriously injured, maybe just needing to catch his breath after the last play. Before Henrichs and Coach Bitto can get there, Snyder opens his mouth and engages in some exercise-induced hurling.

Henrichs and Coach Bitto arrive on the scene just as the vomit hits the turf.

"Someone has to clean it up," says a referee in a matter-of-fact tone.

"OK, I'll..." Henrichs says.

"No, give me the towel," Coach Bitto says. He grabs it from Henrich's shoulder, jumps to his knees and wipes up the gelatinous remnants from Snyder's pre-game meal. Coach Bitto hands the bile-stained towel back to Tessa Lester, one of the student trainers. Tessa wears an understandable "What? I didn't sign up for this!" look on her face as she walks back to the sidelines.

Snyder regains his bearings and stands up. He has a question for his coach.

"Can I go back in the game?"

"No, you have to come out."

They all walk off the field and play resumes. The thousands-deep home crowd applauds Snyder's courage, unaware of barf-gate's details.

∾

Seconds later, Ferguson scores on a 1-yard touchdown plunge with 2:06 remaining to make the score 31-28. The Hilltoppers have only one timeout, and are forced to try an onside kick. Carmel recovers and is able to run the clock out.

At 10:12 p.m., the final horn blasts through Baker Stadium. The scoreboard reads Carmel 31, Joliet Catholic 28. From the south end zone, students dressed as hillbillies (the dress theme of the game) storm the field, waving brown flags, thrilled to share the momentous victory.

Shaking hands with Hilltoppers coach Dan Sharp, Coach Bitto wears a grin shaped more by relief than revelry. Sharp smiles back through gritted teeth.

"A heckuva game, coach!" Sharp says.

"That's a great team you have," Coach Bitto replies. "We were lucky to win."

Serio chats happily with reporters at midfield. The Carmel quarterback threw only two passes all night, both for touchdowns. There's Fitz, standing in the north end zone, staring back at the opposite end of the field, where a reporter is interviewing his son, Michael.

"You know what? Perspective is everything," he says. "Of course we'll enjoy it. But there will be another one next year." A man walks up, shakes Fitz's hand and says, "Thank God your son has none of your athletic ability." Fitz laughs heartily at the truth in that statement.

"He's a pretty good player, isn't he?" he says.

Michael played a great game, intercepting a pass and making a key tackle on a fake punt late in the fourth quarter. As Fitz's gaze stays fixed on his son, his mood remains reflective. "I always stayed outside during the championship seasons, the big ones when the guys were being interviewed, while Coach Bitto was talking to the press. I'd wait for them," Fitz says, his voice slowing to a lyrical pace. His glance never wavers from Michael, some 50 yards away. "But I never thought I'd ever stand out here when my son was being interviewed."

"He kicked the crap out of some people tonight!" says another fan running by.

"I never thought I'd be standing out here for my kid. Good stuff. Pretty good stuff," Fitz says.

As Fitz waxes on, not wanting the rapturous moment to end, players and students wander over to the north end zone. A circle forms, extending out to the 10-yard line. The celebratory cackling hushes. Fans leaving the stands stop and lean against the railing. On the field, all within the circle clasp hands, then take a knee. In the middle of the circle stand four players— Michael Fitzgibbons, Jake Larson, Michael Cohen and Paul Madison. Still in uniform, they survey the scene unfolding in front of them. They face the crowd. Fitzgibbons stands furthest to the left. He extends out his left hand. Larson grabs it with his right. Madison clasps his right hand with Larson's left, Fitzgibbons the same with Madison. They wait for a few lingering students to join the circle. All heads bow.

The stadium lights still glow, canopied below a clear September sky. The scoreboard shines. It reads:

HOME 31, GUEST 28

It's absurdly silent, as if all humanity were taking a deep breath. The Greeks have a phrase for an occasion such as this.

The supreme moment.

∾

Larson breaks the silence.

"Our Father!"

Then, in unison, all begin to pray.

"Who art in heaven. Hallowed be thy name. Thy kingdom come. Thy will be done, on earth as it is in heaven. Give us this day our daily bread. And forgive us our trespasses, as we forgive those who trespass against us. And lead us not into temptation, but deliver us from evil!"

After the last word is spoken, helmets are raised high, and celebratory screams propel into the late evening air.

Carmel won an important football game tonight. But as the clock reaches 10:30 p.m. and its people scatter into the parking lot and back to their respective lives, it's impossible not to believe a force stronger than the outcome of a single sporting event has united them.

CHAPTER NINE

A WALK
IN THE WOODS

In 1886, a young man named Richard Warren Sears bought $50 worth of watches at a train station in Redwood Falls, Minnesota. He sold them for $500. Sears converted this one transaction into a watch-selling business that eventually evolved into retail giant Sears & Roebuck.

By the end of the 19th century, Sears & Roebuck had established headquarters in Chicago. It was common at the time for businessmen and their families to spend the warm summer months at the lakes north of Chicago. This is what Sears did, purchasing a summer home in the town of Wildwood.

"This started out as a summer home kind of place with cottages where people came out," Andy Bitto says.

He was born and raised in Wildwood. And on a cool early fall morning in this small town six miles north of Carmel, Andy takes a drive through his boyhood home. He motors along the road that skirts Gages Lake, Wildwood's landmark body of water. Where there were once summer lake homes now rest rusty shacks on neglected lots. "I don't think there's been too much remodeling lately."

Andy's father, Louis, grew up in Chicago and in the 1930s came up to Gages Lake to swim. "He always wanted to get his family out of the city and into the suburbs, which is why I think he moved us up here. He had so much fun. He wanted his kids to have fun," Andy says.

He pulls off Gages Lake Road onto Mill Road, where his childhood home still stands. To the right is another small body of water. Two parks flank the lake to the north and south.

"There was no park district when I was growing up," Andy recalls. "We had to go mow the grass ourselves. There was a horse farm nearby, Beno's. We use to shovel crap for a quarter an hour. This is where we played most of our games." He's out of the car and pointing to an open area just to the west of the lake. "When I was in fourth grade, I got to play with the eighth-grade players. It bothered my older brother Matt that I jumped him."

Matt Bitto still lives in the modest two-story home where 10 boys and two girls once crammed inside. Andy walks in and there's Matt, sitting on the couch finishing breakfast while watching the *Today* show. "You look like a toad," Andy says.

"It's nice to see you, too, Big A," Matt says.

It's the type of playful banter you'd expect from brothers close in age.

"We used to have one long table, and if you didn't make it home by dinner time you didn't eat. Right Matt?" Andy says.

"That old table that went right around the corner," Matt says, pointing toward the kitchen.

Andy wanders upstairs into a room the size of a large attic. "All 10 boys slept upstairs," he says. "No bunk beds. We had our own beds. We used to have sock fights. It was pretty much a mess all the time. My brother Alex and I used to play baseball up here. Cops and robbers. Lots of broken windows. As everyone moved out, younger guys spread out.

"There was one toilet downstairs. If you had to go, you went there or pissed on the rock in the back yard. You never wanted to go out there."

He points toward a window through where the mighty slab is viewable.

Who knew it possible to feel empathy for a rock?

"It was like a fraternity. My oldest brothers, Tony and Ron, were good role models. They helped us in determining athletically what you have to do to get it done. We learned how to do it, how not to do it."

Tony played college football at Carroll College in Wisconsin and became a teacher and coach. Ron went to Harvard. Tony was the first to expose Andy to football. "I distinctly remember wanting to be like my older brother Tony," Andy says.

He heads back downstairs. On a wall in the family room is a picture of Andy's parents, taken on their 50th wedding anniversary in 1999. Louis died in 2002 while Mary passed away in 2008.

"My dad gave me my first coaching job. He was never about winning or losing," Andy says. "He organized the dinky kids summer baseball league and assigned me to coach. Everyone asked, 'Why are you having a 14-year-old coaching?' I loved it, teaching kids fundamentals. When I was in Pony League, the manager and I did all the lineup cards and organized all the practices of my peers. I don't know why I did it, I just did it.

"My dad loved kids. He had his priorities about having kids, having a happy life. He wasn't a disciplinarian. He didn't yell at us; he instilled work ethic. He always had second jobs.

"Mom was the day-to-day, nuts and bolts, get your homework done. Mom would challenge you mentally. Hey, *did you read this?* I'd come home from college and she'd hand out books. She was from Hannibal, Missouri, the home of Mark Twain, which is appropriate because she was a writer. Very liberal. She liked to debate with me, hear my perspective, which is the opposite point of view. She liked Jimmy Carter. That should tell you something.

"But she went to Providence Catholic, which is why I think we all went to Catholic schools. My mother made a conscious decision to send us all to St. Gilbert Middle School in Grayslake. She was very religious and into social justice before they called it social justice. She had 12 kids of her own but would take my brother's friends in who had gotten in fights with their parents and gotten thrown out. We'd have 15, 20 people living at our house."

He says goodbye to Matt, hops back in the car and drives down Mill Road, turning onto Greentree. The names of these roads, avenues and boulevards read like those of most anyone's childhood: Valley, Thornapple, Eastview, Fairfield. We pull up to the entrance of a vacant park.

A breeze rushes through, rustling the leaves high above. For decades, below these trees, plastic spikes on mud and childhood vitality generated the life energy that flowed from this pasturage's green straw. It appears unchanged from the 1960s and '70s, when for the Bittos and hundreds of other boys, this mangy meadow was home to their first tackle, first touchdown, first scraped knee.

Through an open passage beyond the trees, on the other side of the lake, a few football field lengths away, you can see the Bitto home. The home's proximity made it easy for Andy and his brothers to get exposed to football. They would swap out school clothes for football gear, walk out the front door, and head for the practice field.

"My mom didn't drive, so we could just walk over," Andy says. "I don't think too many things happen by accident."

His thoughts turn philosophical.

"Football's barbaric. So, you beat another team. What does that mean? I don't want to get preachy or anything, but to do it just to do it, that's stupid. It's not just to beat another team. I don't want people to put emphasis on the wins. It's more the sacrifices for other people. What I want to add to the kids' experience is that football can add value spiritually, too.

"That belief initially came from home. My mom and dad were good people and had perspective on things. My mother raised 14 children and had to have been miserable most of the time. But as she got older she felt validated, felt valued because she sacrificed for her kids. She was a much happier person at 65 until she died than she was her whole life because it was the end-of-her-life, validation that, hey, I accomplished a lot of stuff. When you are in the midst of it a lot of times you are like, this sucks, this is hard. Why can't I just win the lottery and get the hell out of here? Those kind of thoughts happen to everybody. Why do I have to work so hard? Why did I have so many damn kids? It's that stick-to-it-iveness."

There is one sign of a modern amenity at the park. What appears to be a woodshed rests on the opposite end of where Andy is, closer to the lake.

"That's the original woodshed of the Gagewood Packers," Andy says. He's referring to the football team of his youth. "We were the first grade school field to have our own lights. We had to line the field ourselves. Motorbikes used to run through the middle of it. We had a coach named Warren Tank who used to drive onto the field with his Toyota and Japanese flag and say, 'Japan's taking over the world! Get used to it! Learn the language!' Now people would say the Chinese. But he cared about the kids, and for many of us was our first coach. He's a guy I'll never forget.

"People would come from all over. Can you believe guys would drive to this piece of crap to play?"

They did. And just as ghosts whispered to Ray Kinsella, giving the unassuming Iowa farmer permission to convert acres of cornfield into his celestial field of dreams, Warren Tank listened to the sublime force within his soul. He built it. And they came.

CHAPTER TEN

PACKER FOR LIFE

IT'S OCTOBER. Not exactly the coldest month of the year in northern Wisconsin, but Warren Tank is ready to move. He wants to get a jump on the Midwestern snowbirds. You know, the ones who wait too long before boarding up and heading south. He never had much patience for lollygaggers, the Sunday-drive types. That's OK in the country, but Warren was born a city kid. And not just any city. He's a product of Chicago's Northwest side. Portage Park. Hermosa. Whiskey breakfasts.

Warren admits the rush is more his wife Pat's doing than his. She has no patience for the cold. Warren likes the fall. "It's supposed to be chilly in October," he tells Pat. When the hard rains come and the fields get muddy around his home in Bailey's Harbor, he thinks about football, about cleats, helmets, and shoulder pads. Sunday afternoons. About how glorious a life it was.

Still trim at 75 years old, Warren's managed to hold onto his hairline along with his waist. Still sporting a '50s-style buzz cut, his piercing blue eyes and sand-dollar cheekbones make him look like the singer Tony Bennett. And every year he leaves his heart in Door County, when he winterizes the house and prepares for the move south. Outside, the temperature can reach 70 degrees on those early fall days. "How can a man supposed to do that in shorts?" Warren says about the forced winterizing. "Sort of like sunbathing in a ski outfit. It's ass-backwards." But he loads up the van, and soon he and Pat will begin the journey down the labyrinth of highways toward Florida.

∼

First there is one other space Warren must tidy up. He calls it the "Bunker." It's what most people would call a garage. But instead of lawn mowers, weed-wackers or bicycles, Warren's Bunker is populated with trophies, equipment, plaques and mementos that haven't seen the light of day in years. The keepsakes are dusty, dim, lusterless, yet Warren introduces them with the delight of a museum curator, his eyes twinkling over the illuminating story he's about to tell.

"This was our uniform," he says.

He shows a visitor his antique accouterment. Still in fine condition, the jersey barely shows any sign of age despite it first being worn 50 years ago. Its number, 50, is blue with chalky white borders. For any visitor holding the jersey, or looking at the other memorabilia in the room, it's impossible to not feel the pangs of nostalgia, a time in our lives filled with barbeques and ballgames, of fathers and sons, and great adventures.

"I was born in Chicago," he says. "That's where it all starts."

∼

Steinmetz High School is in the Belmont Cragin neighborhood on Chicago's Northwest Side. Warren attended Steinmetz, one of a hundred schools in the massive Chicago public system, from 1949-53. A shy, skinny kid named Hugh Marston Hefner graduated a few years earlier, well before he became a men's magazine mogul. Warren's time at Steinmetz did cross with Victor Spilotro, one of the infamous Spilotro brothers from a family with well-known ties to organized crime.

Warren played football with his buddies, guys like Joe Sambucci and Cookie Rizzo. They would talk on the way to school or over lunch about the athletes they'd read about in the newspapers. One time, Warren remembers the conversation steering around to the occupational function of their respective old men. Warren's dad was a blue-collar, white-knuckle guy, his expertise fixing broken water pumps. "Then one guy started talking about all the cash that was around," Warren says. "He was the son of one of the wise guys. It was a helluva long time ago."

So long ago, Warren doesn't remember if it was Spilotro talking about the cash. It didn't matter. There were plenty of kids from Melrose Park who went to Steinmetz, and in those days, if you ventured outside for a lunchtime smoke, there was a strong chance you were sharing a drag with a relative of a Chicago Don.

A 5-10, 160-pound running back for the Steinmetz Streaks, Warren was a bulldozer with a crew cut. Football was three yards and a cloud of dust in the early 1950s, and if you were tough, cranky, and knew how to lower your shoulder and take a hit, you got the football. While Warren was no track star, he was able to separate from defenders if given the slightest hole to run through. "I was going through a bunch of boxes and I found the school newsletter," Warren says. "And it said, 'Most yards per carry, 9.5 yards, Warren Tank. The next guy was 4.0. Clique. The next guy is in the twos. Clique."

Warren's Chicago roots accentuate the timbre of his voice. The city's working-class ancestry speaks through him. He could be any cop, fireman or electrician. But with this flashback, his voice changes. The emphasis on the word "clique" modulates with agitation, as if he's just unraveled a painful memory from the recesses of his 75-year-old mind.

"I would get the ball down to maybe the five-yard line and the clique would take over," he says. "I was a workhorse. I'd get it down there. It was proved at 9.5 yards per carry. Then this guy, this guy, this guy would get the ball. Three yards to the goal line and they'd get it and score a touchdown. These hot shots. I always felt afterwards, *"Hey, what was going on?"*

After games, it was that same clique that would go to Frank's Pizzeria on West Belmont. They'd talk about that three-yard touchdown run, or the one-yard plunge across the goal line all set up by Warren's gallops.

"Every organization has got a clique. A certain group of guys who hang around together. I didn't hang around. Practice was over, the game was over,

I walked home. I didn't hang around with them. There was drinking at the time. I went home. I wanted to back off from that situation."

Even then, Warren knew what he had to do. He couldn't fix things at Steinmetz. The cliques were running amuck, having their way. Smoking in the boys' room, indignantly flicking their cigarette butts at everyone's feet. Before he graduated, he remembers talking to his buddies, Joe and Cookie, who stayed as far away from the clique as Warren.

"I figured I don't want that to happen to anyone else. I know when I have a team it won't be run that way.

"So I told them, 'Let's get a team, our own team.'"

~

After graduating, Warren played a little sandlot football for the semi-pro Chicago Hornets. He tried junior college for a semester. His father wanted him to be a college boy, to study engineering at Purdue. His father had been working for the Chicago Pump Company since the end of World War I. There were a lot of buildings in Chicago that needed running water, and Warren started tagging along to get the hang of it.

He soon decided he wasn't cut out for college life, so he went to work at the pump company. He wanted to be a husband and father, and having a steady job would help him attract a wife. It worked, and he was soon married. Kids followed. All that was left was a football team. His team.

Warren wanted land. He wanted a yard. He wanted to feel grass on his feet. So, like a true homesteader, he traded the asphalt of the city for the soil of Grayslake, 40 miles northwest of Chicago, it was rapidly growing, like so many communities in Lake County at that time. Home from Europe or the Pacific, World War II veterans wanted to raise families in more wide-open spaces than the population-dense city provided. Manufacturers built plants where there was land to be had, and a burgeoning, opportunistic work force followed. Companies such as Rust-Oleum, Abbott Laboratories, and Baxter provided jobs, and populations swelled. Grayslake was a prime example. In 1946 the town built a high school, and a football team soon followed in 1949.

To birth its field, students laid the sod, donated by the Doolittles, who owned acres of farmland in the area. It was the perfect place for Warren to start his team.

He wanted to smell the clean air of the country. He wanted to educate his young children in newer schools. His brother-in-law lived on the North Side and came down with a similar case of cabin fever. So they bought some land off Route 120, near Wildwood.

"We purchased a three-acre lot. The deal was the first one to build got the front section of the lot," Warren says. "They weren't organized to start so we built the house there, facing the road."

Just a short ways down Route 45 was a pizza parlor called Florio's Kitchen. Lou Florio, a former truck driver, opened the restaurant in 1954, and by the time Warren took his family there for the first time, it had grown into a popular hangout.

While kids ate chocolate malts under the attentive eyes of their mothers, fathers sat on chrome-pedestaled diner stools and talked about the stuff men talk about—jobs, politics, and sports. Sometimes they left their "old lady" at home with the kids and drove up alone, playing poker games with their buddies on the counter tops, smoking Newports or Kents, hoping the next hand would be a royal flush. One early Saturday night, Warren was chatting up a friend on the stool next to him when Lou Florio walked up to the counter.

"I asked 'Are you interested in having a team here?'" Warren said. Lou had three young boys of his own and said, yes, it sounded like a good idea. Other fathers overheard Warren and Lou talking, asking if it was true. "Yes," Warren told them. "We need boys to play." Word about a football team spread quickly through Florio's that Saturday night. And before Warren left for home that night, he had commitments from 25 fathers that their boys would play.

~

Before he consumed his first Italian pie at Florio's, Warren was sowing the seeds for the fledgling pigskin league.

For months, while on work calls, he'd tell people about his plan. He needed equipment—uniforms, shoulder pads, helmets, shoes—and what he discovered was that the more he told, the more everyone wanted to contribute. "I was a worker in their building. I didn't come in with a white shirt, tie and briefcase. I came across as a working-class guy," Warren says.

One day he was tagging along on a call with his dad at a manufacturing shop on West 21st Street. He saw a pile of jerseys on the floor. They were light colored, with the numbers sewn on, not printed. He knew when he got a team, that was the kind of jersey he wanted. Armed with 25 commitments from fathers of boys who wanted to suit up and play, he walked back into the same manufacturing shop and said, "Hey, I was in here three years ago working on your pumps." That day the shop became the team's jersey makers.

He next walked into Riddell Manufacturing, which had an office between North Avenue and Division Street. John T. Riddell was a former high school football coach in Evanston who developed the first plastic-shell helmet. They were so good, the U.S. military had used them in World War II. Warren asked to see the owner, and after a short wait, two men appeared. "I told them I was starting a football team, and they said, 'What do you need?'" Warren says. Riddell was already supplying high schools with helmets. Warren wanted the same for his boys. He got his head gear.

One day after a job he dropped in on Alco Manufacturing. They made springs for the railroads, the big freight cars. They also made shoulder pads and thigh pads for Wilson Sporting Goods. "We were in the basement. One of the guys said, 'OK, here's the fiber for the shell, its already molded. We'll give you the foam rubber for the hip and rib pads, you just cut it out and glue it into the fiber. We'll add the padding," Warren says. "I mean, these guys are making this stuff for Wilson and they are dealing with us?"

That summer of 1959, Warren took his family camping in Wisconsin. While his wife watched the kids swim in the lake, he stayed at the campsite, gluing sheets of foam rubber into the pads' fiber skeleton. By golly, his boys couldn't play football without shoulder pads.

~

Word of Warren's mission began to spread faster than an Elvis Presley song lyric through a high school sock hop. While fixing a pump at Oak Park High School, he saw some blocking dummies the school was throwing out. He asked if he could have them. They were his. He started to go in on jobs, and he'd walk out with extra cash. "I'd be there for a couple of hours then come back with parts. I'd get paid easily $50. They would give me $60-$65 and say, 'Don't worry about it,'" Warren says. "They knew where the money was going, right to helmets and equipment."

One day late that summer, he was on a job at Luciana's, a funeral parlor on Harlem and North Avenues in Melrose Park. "The guy was very jovial. I told him, 'Yeah, I can come in on Saturday or Sunday.' Then I get a call from another parlor. The guy had recommended me," Warren says. "We go in there on the weekend and we're in the basement and the guys are playing pool. You needed a flashlight to see the place. There was one light just above the table, hanging from the ceiling. You could barely see your hand in front of your face. It was a one of those safe house places where the Mafia was hiding out. We gave them a price and the money was right there. Someone turned the lights on so I could do the work." Warren would have to go back a few more times to finish the job. "Usually you only dealt with the underlings. One day, a guy comes down to the basement to say hello. He looked just like Tony Accardo," he says.

During Warren's first line of equity funding, he may have wrestled a few extra bucks from a real-life Chicago mobster

"They knew where the money was going. All I thought about were all the extra helmets and jerseys."

All that was left to scrounge up before the boys could take the field were shoes. And a field. As always, Warren had a plan.

On West Washington Street in Grayslake was a fire insurance company. Warren had gotten a call about boxes full of shoes sitting in a room. "They had insured a sporting goods store that burned down. It was like walking into a Wal-Mart or something. There were shoes. Oh man, were there shoes." He asked the owner if he could buy all of the boxes. "I don't remember what we paid but it was well below what we would pay retail," Warren says. He had plenty of shoes for the boys—the kind where the high top came up just below the ankle—to whom he lent for $5 a pair. He went back to Riddell for the cleats.

Just up the road from Florio's was farmland owned by the Mellender family. They lent a small piece of terrain to Warren, and it became the home field of the 1959 Gagewood Packers. Most of the boys would arrive dressed for practice, as they lived nearby and could walk down the main drag, Center Street, then go north on Route 45, wearing their shiny new football uniforms. Others had to be dropped off and change on-site. Warren had that covered. "You know what our first locker was? A chicken coop. We were beggars at the time. Nobody looked down on it. Whatever we could use."

The Packers took their hits that first season. In the opening game against the Highland Park Mighty Midgets, they were down 67-0—in the first quarter—when the refs stopped the game. Warren had them run a "T" formation, which in hindsight may have been a bit ambitious for this group of football novices. "The kids did not have finesse blocking," Warren says. "By the time the quarterback got the ball, the line was folding." The Packers eventually scored a touchdown that season but didn't win a game.

After the season, the Mellenders wanted their land back, so Warren had to find a new field for the Packers. One of the fathers mentioned a vacant lot in the town of Wildwood. It was barren, harder than a goat's knee and filled with rocks. It sounded perfect.

So, in the spring of 1960, Warren went to work.

While on a job site—he was still commuting to the city every weekday—Warren talked to a plumber who had a cousin who could get a couple of bulldozers. "One Saturday, they came out and flattened the field," he says. "There was no grass, just dirt."

Warren took a chunk of the extra cash he was getting on his city jobs and bought lawn seed to supplement the malnourished grass. He needed to clean up the rocks and line the field, so he recruited some of the young Packers to be on the league grounds-keeping crew. The team would start at one end of the field, pick up as many stones and weeds as they could, and throw them out.

"How's that for a training camp?" Warren says.

Oh, and the lights. On fall afternoons, after daylight savings time, it would get dark early. The boys couldn't play in the dark!

"My father-in-law was a uniform salesman and was working up at one of the high schools, Antioch," Warren says. "They had just gotten some new lights and they had extras so he worked out a deal. It was like, 'You take these uniforms for the maintenance guys and we'll take this.' So we got these huge lighting fixtures, 1,500-watters but with big glass in front."

One of the fathers worked for ComEd, and one day four poles showed up on the field. Warren scrounged up some wiring and circuit breakers and—viola!—they had lights. "Out of all the hanky-danky teams in the league, we were the only ones who had the lights. All of these other big-time towns, they used to drool. 'Can we come over and play under your lights?'"

Another father owned a lumberyard in Round Lake. He showed up one day and built a press box—nicknamed "The Crow's Nest"—near the 50-yard line. "We wired it for sound and had a [public address] system. The coaches would go up there and tape the games," Warren says. "We kept increasing our stuff."

He had to, as what originally started as one team grew into the Northern Illinois Youth Football League. Teams from Round Lake, Fox Lake and McHenry joined, then Winnetka, Antioch and North Chicago. Soon the league had enough teams to create two divisions, with Warren as president. Because so many kids wanted to play, the Packers were now six individual teams at three different weight levels—heavyweight, lightweight, and pee-wee. This escalating growth necessitated Warren find a home base, someplace where the players and coaches could gather to prepare for games and talk football. A locker room. A clubhouse. Or something else.

"I was working at around 87th and Halsted in the basement of a guy who was the head of the Chicago motorman union," Warren says. "I saw some photos of football players on his wall. We were talking and I'm like, 'I started this team.' He said, 'You need a bus?' I go, 'A bus?' He says, 'Yeah, a bus.'"

He directed Warren to a huge depot where they stored busses in need of repair. "He said, 'Just pick one out and then go see this guy at the Merchandise Mart in the Loop,'" Warren says. He found a smaller-model bus at the storage yard, then with his brother-in-law riding shotgun, drove to the Loop in their car to complete the transaction. They double-parked in front of the Merchandise Mart and Warren bolted.

Warren soon found the guy. "He says, 'So and so said what? You are starting a team?'" The bus wasn't Warren's just yet. There was a bidding process. More skullduggery. "He said, 'I can't tell you what to bid as it's illegal. But if you bid $700 you'll get it.' So I gave him $700."

But there was a catch. There had to be a catch, right? The Packers' dilapidated starship had no front wheels. And no one knew how to drive a bus with no front wheels.

∾

They had to get the bus to Wildwood. So, Warren did as always—he called on his network of merry associates. "My old neighbor across the alley in Chicago worked for a towing company," Warren says. "So I called him and he towed it all the way from 79th Street to our field."

Since Warren had no plans to fix or drive the bus, they removed the vehicle's back tires so it would sit up straight. Before long, they brought in phone lines and electricity. A movie projector and screen came next. After much wheeling and dealing, the Gagewood Packers had their base of operations.

"It was beautiful," Warren says. "A kid would go in there like he was going to school. I don't know how good it was, but we were trying to be like the pros."

As far as Warren was concerned, his Packers would have the best money could buy. And if there was no money, they'd beg, borrow and steal to have the best. Warren saw to that. Anything for his boys. And over time, his horse-trading began to have an impact on the field.

∾

By the early 1960s, the Gagewood Packers heavyweight team—over 110 pounds—had won a league championship, the first for all levels. This created a butterfly effect: All the other teams, from the peewees on up, started to have success, too. As the older boys left, little brothers filled up the roster. No family represented this bloodline right of passage more than the Bittos.

Louis and Mary Bitto lived in a modest two-level home on Mill Road, a short walk around Twin Lakes to the Packers' field in Wildwood. Lou was a printer, and Mary stayed home to care for the brood like most women of that era. Ten boys in all Mary raised. Tony was the oldest, followed by Ron, Tom, Steve, Mike and Mark. By the early 1970s, Matt, Andy, Mitch and Alex came along, becoming Packers just as their older brothers had.

Maybe they were favorites of Warren's because there were so many of them. Or maybe it was for other reasons.

"They were a block away," Warren says. "Anytime something had to be done, they were there, always volunteering to help. They did a lot of the dirty work, picking up stones, holding up the sidelines makers. So many of them loved the game. They hung around helping the little kids.

"Never any back talk. A credit to their family."

～

Warren's seat-of-his-pants management style and enthusiastic improvisational coaching techniques trickled down to the other Packers coaches. Guys like Art Rasmussen, a World War II veteran who made the kids do leg-lifts and run around Twin Lakes to stay in shape. He coached his son, Larry, who played for the lightweight team. Art would grab your facemask if you were lollygagging and tell you to run harder. But he'd also be the first to rub dirt on a scraped knee. And there were a lot of scraped knees.

There was the time when Chris Mellender—whose family's farm was the Packers' first home—couldn't make weight. You had to be at least 60 pounds to play. What did Art do? He put his foot on the scale so Chris could get the extra five pounds and play.

And there was the time during a game when Art instructed Ronny Herzog to not field a punt if he couldn't catch it in the air. When the ball bounced and rolled to where Ronny was standing, Art yelled from the sidelines, "Leave it alone! Don't touch it!" As the other team circled the ball, out of nowhere Ronny swooped in, grabbed it, and ran for a touchdown. Those who watched the game say they can't remember a coach jumping as high as Art did, watching Ronny stomping over the stone-littered field to the end zone.

Sometime during the 1960s, the Packers truly arrived on the social map of Lake County. The sidelines at games were decorated with lawn chairs, blankets, and picnic baskets. Spectators were moms, dads, uncles, brothers, sisters, aunts, cousins and grandparents. Between the months of September and November, watching Gagewood Packers football became a Sunday afternoon tradition, a tradition that began to include cheerleaders. Art's daughters, Leigh and Leslie, were in the first group. They would dress in plaid skirts and blue-and-white sweaters, cheering on the boys—their boys. The girls thought the cutest ones played football, and many first crushes sprouted on that field, like Michelle Kuhn's on Mike Wilcox, No. 72. Michelle was adventurous around the boys. There was the time she put whipping cream in the helmet of John Gentry. When John put his crown on and discovered this bit of tomfoolery, he was not amused (he had a game to play!). John chased after Michelle, tackling her in full pads. She got up, cleaned herself off, and when the game started, she cheered for John. He was a Packer after all.

With kids ages 8-14, the Packers playbook was based on ice cream treats, with "banana split with extra nuts" meaning to go long, and "hot fudge sundae with a cherry on top" meaning a post pattern. Warren would call the plays wearing a Moosehead hat bought at an Army surplus store, looking like a World War II dive bomber pilot. Above all else, Warren wanted the boys to have fun. And he wanted to teach them sportsmanship, about responsibility, about being young men.

Warren was firm, never combative. He wanted the boys to look orderly, neat, and sharp. Like a team should look. "We treated kids like they were our own. You worry about them, you looked after them, calmed them down," Warren says. "You taught them compassion, otherwise they wouldn't be successful."

He remembers when his son, Gus, a peewee for the Packers, had his lunch money stolen on the school bus. Later that day, a group of older boys found out who'd taken the money "and showed that guy the truth. I'm proud of the fact those kids looked after the small one. Every guy counts. You are all one. There were no bullies." Those memories, even decades later, touch him most deeply.

The ones about his boys looking out for each other.

~

It's been several hours, and Warren is still inside his "Bunker." He holds a trophy—gold colored, its shape the molded body of a Gil Thorp-looking football player in full gallop. The plaque on the front says "Gagewood Packers, 1962." And in Warren's eyes, everyone who played for him deserved one.

"One guy was hollering at me one time. 'Why are you giving the second-string a trophy?' I would say, 'Because they earned it. Just because they showed up and got pushed around and knocked down.' Those types of people can't think farther than their nose."

By the late '70s, Warren's kids were grown and it was time to hand the reigns over. He estimates he spent more than $20,000 of his own money over the years. He also lost his first wife, who one day wrote a Dear John letter and left, tired of a husband who was never home for dinner. He moved to Wisconsin, remarried, and can't imagine his life without Pat. And on this day, she's anxious to hit the road. They have to finishing locking up the house in Bailey's Harbor and push off for Florida.

But those years, those precious years, are to be celebrated for all Warren gave and all that was given by so many.

"There was a lot of cooperation from the parents," he says. "People pitched in. They saw something happening and wanted to be a part of it. Kids in those days loved the game. This was an opportunity for them to be treated equally. Football. You had to get your shoelaces tied, your hip pads on. No pushing or shoving. Everyone was accepted. I just want them to remember the fun they had."

And most of all, remember how there were no cliques.

"In many ways it was just right for some idiot like me to come around."

CHAPTER ELEVEN

SOUTHSIDE HITMEN

HEAD COACH ANDY BITTO gave the team the weekend off after beating Joliet Catholic. It's a game that will be remembered for a long time, but by Wednesday, the look on Coach Bitto's face says he's already forgotten it. Or at least put the memory on ice.

Leaning back in his office chair, he's back to staring at the small television monitor propped up on a table behind his desk. He's watching game film for Friday night's opponent, Marist, and it scares him.

This is a week Coach Bitto and the coaches have dreaded since they saw Joliet Catholic on the schedule. Marist is what football coaches call a "trap game." This means your team is playing...

1. The following week after an emotional win over a rival team

2. On the road with a longer-than-usual bus ride

3. Immediately after an emotional win over not just a rival but your biggest rival

Mother Nature is contributing to the anxiety. Tuesday's practice is called off early due to a lightning storm in the area, and the team hasn't had a full workday since the Wednesday before the Joliet Catholic game. There are a lot of distractions.

"I don't like the distractions," says Coach Bitto, who also has a nagging cough. "It makes it difficult with a week like this. Maybe they'll go out and play like gangbusters, but I'm nervous."

The school bell buzzes. It's 3 p.m. Seconds after the end-of-the-day prayer is read through the loudspeaker (*"and as always, Mother of Mt. Carmel, pray for us"*), the door opens. In walks an ailing Corsair.

"Coach, I won't be able to practice today."

A tall, skinny junior named Austin Zupec speaks these words. His news is like pouring chili powder on a simmering boil.

"Do you ever watch the History Channel?" Coach Bitto asks.

"Ah, no..." Zupec replies.

"Well, I was watching this show on the Amazon jungle. Did you know that large reptiles think they're dead when their eyes are closed?"

"Oh, no, I didn't know that," Zupec says, not sure whether to laugh or fidget over his coach's trivia. "Well, the doctor said I might be out the whole season."

Zupec has missed most of the season after suffering a head injury during camp in July.

"So, this is not really a concussion, this is something weird," Coach Bitto says.

"I didn't know I had a concussion. My head hurt and I was trying to play through it. I didn't know that's what it was until it got extremely bad one day. That's when I went to the doctor. I just have to do what the doctor tells me."

"I know that. I've just never heard of a concussion lasting eight weeks. There must be something else wrong. Do you have migraines?"

"No," Zupec says.

"Well, they can't send you back if you aren't healthy. I understand. I know you are trying hard to get back. Keep trying."

"OK, I will."

With that, he leaves the room.

Zupec was expected to be a contributor on special teams. After starting the season with 60 players —a low number, compared with previous seasons —Carmel is now suiting up a few players shy of 50. Every able body is needed in order for the team to run full practices.

The attrition of the roster is concerning, but there is another reason for Bitto's sour mood. Running back Michael Panico injured his shoulder against

Joliet Catholic. It's doubtful he'll play Friday. And Jordan Kos, the team's best offensive player, missed school after calling in sick. Then he arrived on campus to practice, only to be told by Coach Bitto he couldn't.

"He's puking this morning. His dad told me. Jordan should have gotten his butt out of bed and moved around," Coach Bitto says, now standing up and cleaning off his desk. His voice is more gravely than usual. "You know what? I know he wants to practice. He just wants to miss school. You can't do that here. Rules are you can't miss one period."

This is a school rule, not a state rule. The public schools are governed by the Illinois High School Athletic Association, which says a student can practice as long as they attend one period in a school day. Carmel is private. It makes up its own rules in regards to school attendance and extracurricular participation. This is one of those times when the school's academics-first culture amplifies the boneheaded decisions of teenage boys.

Earlier in the summer, Kos missed two days of the team's July camp. Coach Bitto was so worried that he called Kos' father, Ed, to schedule a meeting.

"It's 10 evaluation days. What to leave in, what to leave out. It's a big deal," Coach Bitto said earlier of the camp. "Jordan had missed a few of the practices. Kids told me they had seen him out the night before, and I wanted to nip that in the bud and tie his dad into it and let him know three things. One, I will push him harder as I think he's that good and that I'm going to ride him because he needs to be ridden. Two, he's doing stuff he should not be doing. Three, make sure we were all on the same page. He was dating a girl from Libertyville and his priorities were being divided. We told him he had bigger fish to fry. I think the dad appreciated it as he was in the same quandary with the kid in terms of being a teenager. They all experiment. They get a girlfriend. You know about that stuff."

He leaves his office and heads down the hallway toward the athletics concessions. Coach Bitto reaches in the refrigerator and snatches a Diet Pepsi.

"Jordan's a baby. That's what he is. The coaches, we were just saying how good he's been, how he hasn't missed a practice since summertime. We jinxed it. We have a couple of scout team guys out of practice today. Now Jordan can't practice. I'll bet Logan won't be in pads today."

Coach Bitto is referring to Logan Lester, the senior offensive lineman who dislocated a finger in practice yesterday before the lightning bolts and thunderclaps forced everyone inside.

"He dislocated it. Big deal. He should have it taped and wrapped and ready to go. He needs the reps," Coach Bitto says as he approaches the field. "But I'll bet you a pitcher of beer if he's outside and not in pads."

His coughs again, sounding like he's the one who could use a day off. Instead, he says, "I could really use some throat lozenges.

"You know what? I'm going to be a jag today. This whole idea that, 'I'll be ready to play on Friday if I don't practice' has to stop. From my experience, if you are not ready on Wednesday, you will not be ready on Friday."

～

Someone owes Coach Bitto a pitcher of beer. Kos, Lester and a few more of the boys are in street clothes on the sidelines when warm ups begin at 3:20 p.m.

It's a dozen minutes later when Zupec walks across the track onto the field. Coach Bitto spots him immediately.

"Hey, practice starts at 3:20, not when you feel like getting your ass out here!"

Zupec says he's been with the team trainer.

"I don't care! Go back to Dan and get a note saying you were with him. Go! Go! Forty-eight friggin' guys not in practice today and it's friggin' Wednesday!"

With that, Coach Bitto pulls his right arm back and thrusts it forward with the force of an Olympian hammer thrower inside the Colosseum in Rome. The bottle of Diet Pepsi is now a moving, airborne object. It flies past Kos, skips off the track and caroms off the fence just in front of the bleachers, exploding like a liquid piñata.

Coach Bitto focuses his gaze at his puke-happy fullback.

"Yes, it was directed at you!" he says.

Kos is expressionless, his hands in his pockets, knowing silence is the better part of survival when his coach rants.

"We're trying to win an ESCC championship and guys are taking off!" Coach Bitto says, blowing his whistle as the team does pre-practice calisthenics. "Apparently practice is optional! School is optional!

"Oh, I have a runny nose, I don't feel so good. I had a 96.8 fever so I have to go home! The worst thing we did was get a damn trainer. The second worst thing we did was get a nurse! Toughen up! My God, if I was puking in my book bag I'd still be out here! Do you know how lucky you are to be in this position? Huh, do you? It's the wussification of America!

"And I threw my pop. That's the worst part of it!"

Zupec returns to the field. He's carrying the note from trainer Dan Henrichs. He tentatively walks over to Coach Bitto, who snatches the note, crumples it up, and puts it in his mouth. He begins to chew on his low-calorie snack while gathering the boys around him. Silent grins appear behind their facemasks. They just witnessed their coach eat a piece of paper.

"Let's go! This isn't a friggin' walk in the park," Coach Bitto tells them, his right cheek bulging. "Let's play like animals today!"

They scatter off to different parts of the field to prepare for the practice's first drill, always special teams. Coach will continue to be frosty throughout the afternoon. A lingering reason is Kos, who watches practice from the sidelines.

"Friggin sick! It's the middle of the season. You don't get sick!" Coach Bitto says aloud during a drill. "Kos wanted a day off! Why don't you just tell me the truth?"

Kos attempts to mumble an answer from the sidelines.

"I didn't ask you for an answer!"

Practice eventually shifts to the grass just west of the main stadium. Marist is the only opposing stadium Carmel will play on this season with a grass field. The hope is that simulating the conditions in practice will help them adjust faster to what will be a slower field than normal on Friday night.

When the boys move to the new location, Kos follows. Standing behind his teammates during individual drills, he processes his coach's temper tantrum.

"He wants us to be out there. I don't blame him. He's upset. He just really wants us to win this game after what happened last time."

Two years ago, Marist defeated the Corsairs 21-8 one week after Carmel had beaten local rival Libertyville 21-14 on a last-second touchdown pass. This year's seniors who were on the varsity that season said the team was too casual on the bus ride down for the game and were basically not ready to play.

"I understand where he's coming from," Kos says. "I'd feel the same way in his situation."

Against Joliet Catholic the previous Friday, Kos had what may have been the best game of his varsity career. He rushed for 141 yards on 24 carries, with one touchdown. In practices leading up to that game, he ran every carry with high energy. After one drill, he turned to the coaches and, with a huge grin on his face yelled, "I just can't wait to play this game!"

Today couldn't be more different. His shoulder pads are in his locker, his cleats replaced by gym shoes. The unshakable, confident smile is gone.

"I don't like missing school and having to catch up, but I'm sick," Kos says. "If I could have been here I would have been here. I haven't missed a day of practice all year. He doesn't want me to head down that path."

The path he speaks of goes back to the previous summer.

"I was going to morning workouts and I was lifting, but there was a time where I got a little bit lazy. He called me in and talked to me and told me I needed to be a leader, and kids were going to look up to me after being all-conference as a sophomore. I needed to set the example and be the example. He doesn't want me to cut corners. It's not just football, he's teaching life lessons, too: Not to cut corners; do things the way they are supposed to be done."

As the offense goes through its regular group of plays, Coach Bitto goes over to talk to Kos. "You can only go into battle with who's alive," he says. Then he walks over and administers a pop quiz on blocking assignments.

"Who do you block on 24?"

"Linebacker," Kos says.

"Which linebacker?"

"Inside linebacker."

"It's play-side inside linebacker," Coach Bitto says. "OK, one more Tim!"

It's Tim Serio. The sophomore backup to Kos and Brian Serio's younger brother. He's taking the bulk of the practice reps. "Let's suck it up. We'd have a break for you but someone decided to take a break today. Whatever his name is."

As his coach blows his whistle, signaling the end of the drill, Kos looks to the ground and sighs deeply.

∼

At the end of practice, Coach Bitto gathers the team on the stadium field. He has toned down the rhetoric from earlier in the afternoon, but his message is no less stern in its intent. In 48 hours, the Corsairs will play a football game, and they had better be prepared.

"Think about school or at work or TV shows," he says. "You don't have to be at the right time or the right place to do it. Teachers will let you make up a test. Your boss may give you a break and let you come in late one day. With TiVo, you know if you miss it, you can watch the Bears game later. When you are playing football it isn't that way. You have to be ready to play at 7:30 p.m., no matter what. I don't care if the band is out there naked. I don't care if the bus is in a traffic jam. I don't care if you are sick on a Wednesday. You have to be ready to play. Does everybody got that?"

Coach Bitto pauses at the end of each sentence. The first player to shout "yes, coach!" each time is Kos.

"Wish nothing. I can't caution you enough. Don't take for granted we had big victories the first four weeks, especially against Joliet Catholic. That doesn't mean squat now! All we have is one chance. There are no second chances in sports. None."

∼

The distance from Carmel's campus to Marist High School in Chicago is 57 miles. At 2:30 p.m., the Corsairs board the bus for their first trip to the city's South Side this season.

Marist is one of two schools in the East Suburban Catholic Conference to which one word does not pertain: suburban. Currency exchanges, gyro joints, and auto repair shops make up its surroundings. Its grass fields stand out against a backdrop of pavement and concrete. This is the final season on the natural lawn for the RedHawks, who are installing a turf field. The Chicago Archdiocese runs Marist. The school was founded in 1963 by the Marist brothers, a religious order started by St. Marcellin Champagnat of France in the early 19th century.

Carmel arrives almost three hours before kickoff—traffic on a Friday moves shockingly well—and the mood on the bus is as the coaches and team captains hope it would be: stern. Conversation is minimal. Any scuttlebutt is reserved for school—and football-related topics. Minutes after arrival, the Corsairs are inside the visiting locker room for pre-game meetings and ankle-taping.

Marist is a school that shares much with Carmel—Catholic designation, high academic standards—but there are distinct differences. Tom Inzinga is Marist's director of development and in charge of many things at the school, none more important than ensuring that new students keep coming through the school's doors. In such a densely populated area of Chicago, there are plenty of prospects to wear the red and white. But Marist has challengers in all directions.

"There is a lot of competition in this geo area," Inzinga says. "We have 10 high schools—Brother Rice down the street, St. Rita, Mount Carmel, Mother McAuley, Queen of Peace, St. Lawrence—so the competition for kids in the area can be enormous, where if you live in Mundelein, you're going to Carmel. You have to be aggressive with what you have in terms of selling, what you have in terms of facilities and academics."

The aggressive approach Inzinga refers to consists of outreach—he often speaks at Catholic grade schools within their recruitment radius to make the pitch.

"We are academics first, and if you are looking at a place with great facilities and good athletics, that's what we push. We feel if we can get a kid on campus and see our facilities, they will sell themselves. We have a college bookstore, it's gorgeous. A cafetorium with a big-screen TV. We just finished the other phase with our renovated chapel, another gymnasium."

He stops in front of a door that leads to the weight room, which is filled with Olympic-size racks and more dumbbells than a Gold's Gym. "We'd put this up against anyone," Inzinga says.

It's quite a display of goods and utilities. And that's the order of his emphasis—swag before services. Having the former makes it easier to sell the latter.

It's hard to argue against the marketing model. Schools such as Marist are like any business in the private sector. Every day, it is in competition for customers. Those customers won't buy unless they are convinced their money is being invested in the best product. At Marist, and Carmel, that product is education.

"Public schools don't charge tuition and have the advantage of bringing in kids from their district," said Taylor Bell, a former high school sports columnist for the *Chicago Sun-Times* daily newspaper. For decades, Bell's primary beat was the Chicago Catholic League. If there's anyone who knows how the machination of ecclesiastical football works, it's Bell. "Catholic schools recruit. They can't deny it, they don't deny it, and it doesn't make sense to deny it. They have to recruit by their very nature."

The word "recruit" is a powder keg in the culture of interscholastic football. Public-school coaches often dismiss private-school on-field success by saying, "Oh, well they recruit players." They imply that schools pay for players through scholarships, cash, or other benefits. Private-school coaches scoff at this notion, insisting the need to resort to shady recruiting tactics is unnecessary. They say the well-rounded college preparatory education, coupled with a culture that promotes spiritual values, is enough grilled red meat to convince a mother and father to enroll their son or daughter.

The debate over this issue—recruit or not recruit—has raged in scholastic circles since private schools first planted their flag alongside their public school peers in the early 20th century.

"They used to do it in the old Chicago Catholic League," Bell said. "I go back to the days when schools like St. Lawrence and other schools in the city handed out leadership scholarships or other scholarships. I remember Gary Korhonen at Richards [an Illinois public school]. Until recently he was the winningest coach in state high school history. He's in Oak Lawn. He's got Marist, Brother Rice, St. Rita, De La Salle and Mount Carmel all within a few miles of Richards.

"Korhonen used to joke that De La Salle would turn their bus around in his parking lot when they would go out and recruit kids. He would have to go out to elementary schools and persuade kids or he would lose them to any half-dozen Catholic schools. They have Providence and Joliet Catholic recruiting his kids. They have to fight that kind of thing."

He continues: "The problem with the word *recruit* is you assume you are giving them something. It's illegal to come to a school like Carmel by enticing them with a scholarship to play football. So Bitto and their admissions people have to go out to parishes and persuade them to come and get a good Catholic education and tell them 'We are going to play a good brand of football but you are going to have to pay for it.' In this day and age that's a lot to ask. Even in the Catholic League, the old alums are not sending their kids back to their schools. They are sending them to public schools in the suburbs in their district because they can't afford to send them to the Catholic schools in the city.

"You have to have alumni and parental support more so in private schools than you do in the public schools just to survive."

Let's be clear—having a good football team is anything but a hindrance to private school prosperity. After the 2003 state championship, Carmel, through donations, replaced its grass field with artificial turf. Coach Bitto immediately began to loan out the field at no cost to local youth football teams for league games. For much of the afternoon on Sundays during football season, middle school players trample the field at Baker Stadium. Once these boys graduate from middle school, they will enter high school. And having them imagine themselves as high-schoolers playing on the same field someday in front of thousands of screaming fans and adoring cheerleaders, well that's just smart—and shrewd—business.

"I'm not dumb. I know kids come here for football," Coach Bitto said earlier in the season. "For years, they see headlines in the paper about how good the football team is. They read about us winning conference championships, state championships. They are thinking, *I want to be a part of that*."

Between early September and mid-November, on most Sunday afternoons, Coach Bitto attends youth games at Carmel. It's impossible not to spot him—he's the one wearing more brown than a UPS delivery man. A frequent scenario is when a parent walks up, shakes Coach Bitto's hand and strikes up a conversation, whether about football or details on the school. According to the Illinois High School Association, this is all perfectly legal.

"As long as they approach me, everything is fine," Coach Bitto said. "I can answer as many questions as they want."

These exchanges are often one-on-one. Sometimes, while Coach Bitto is talking to one parent, others will overhear and matriculate over, and a private discussion morphs into a group conference.

This circumstance happened recently. It started when the father of a middle school boy dropped a highlight tape off at Coach Bitto's office in the middle of the week. The young man is a running back for a team in the Tri-County Youth Football League. The father of the boy invited Coach Bitto and running backs coach Tom Young, who was in the room, to his son's game that Saturday morning at Lewis Field in Waukegan, 13 miles northeast.

"So we went over," Young said. "The guy who is the superintendent of their league saw us and knew who Andy was. We told him why we were there. He knew the dad had talked to us but he was surprised we showed up."

Coach Bitto and Young took their seats. "We were going to just go over to that side and sit down and hoped that the dad would come over and talk to us," Young said. "The president of the Waukegan youth football program came over and said, 'Wait here and I'll go get him.' He went over and brought the dad over to us."

For the better part of three quarters, Coach Bitto and Young sat with the parent, watching his son play. After the game, the dad brought over his son, accompanied by a few of his teammates, their parents and coaches. "The coaches vouched for the kids and said they put the time in that was needed.

There were three other kids standing next to the fence who were on the team and listened very intently to what was being said," Young said.

Coach Bitto talked about the admissions process and the importance of getting on campus to see the school. "He must have reiterated two or three times about the open house, about the shadow day where kids can come in and we'll put him with a freshman and he can sit in the classroom and do the whole thing," Young said. "They were quite impressed with that."

Young said Coach Bitto then brought up money to the group, talking about the cost of tuition at Carmel ($8,760 for the 2010-11 school year) and if one or more spouses had a job.

"The guy was shocked at the tuition number," Young said. "But Andy said there is a system to get aid to people who need it. There is a certain amount of paperwork that is involved, and you can get as much as 50 percent off your tuition."

This tuition reduction has nothing to do with football. It has everything to do with need.

When a student applies to Carmel, they can fill out a form asking for financial help. The document is the private high school version of the FAF-SA, or Free Application for Federal Student Aid. College applicants desirous for federal grants or loans are required to submit the FAFSA to determine eligibility for such monies to help subsidize the cost of tuition. Applicants provide financial information, similar to what an accountant asks for on a tax return. This process is similar at Carmel. A third-party firm (located in Iowa) reviews the data, then determines if a family qualifies for funds.

There are 230 students at Carmel receiving aid for the 2010-11 school year. The total tuition reduction (some might call it "scholarship") totals $800,000. That comes to an average of $3,478 per student, or just under 40 percent. And just as it is with college grants, money is distributed on a first-come, first-served basis. "The sooner you apply, the better chance you will get more," Stithe said. "There are many that apply and don't qualify as 99 percent of aid is need-based, the other one percent is academic scholarship."

As admissions director, Stithe pitches prospective moms and dads at middle school-sponsored events, via brochures or letters. And while he may have to sell certain aspects of the school, one is not football. "The program has seen success for 10 years now and I think it recruits itself, which helps because we get headlines in the paper," Stithe said. "My theory is the better your sports programs are doing, it's free publicity."

The scene Tom Young described with Coach Bitto at Lewis Field in Waukegan plays out on thousands of youth football fields on fall weekends all over the country. Is it recruiting or just astute marketing?

"Again, recruiting has a negative stigma. It really is about going to the grade schools and selling the program," Bell said. "Carmel is a Carmelite school. The other two [Mount Carmel and Joliet Catholic] have won more state championships, so they are the step-sister, the young whippersnapper."

After Coach Bitto finished his talk with the interested parties at Lewis Field, "they gave us a soda and a pork chop sandwich," Young said.

At least they didn't go home hungry.

~

The sophomore game is running long, meaning the varsity kickoff will be delayed. Marist's tiny visiting locker room is one area of the school that is not being remodeled. Most of the Corsairs are clustered just outside, all in uniform, killing time before they can take the field.

Among them is defensive end Michael Cohen, his face painted in black shapes that a Sahelian tribesman would admire. Luke Venegoni sits against a wall, his headphones strapped to his ears. He listens to Cat Stevens and songs from the Texas post-rock band Explosions in the Sky. Jake Larson, who plays on the other side of the line from Cohen, also leans against a wall, headphones affixed. On the bus ride to Marist, Larson was not listening to music but reading a book titled *A Long Way Gone,* a memoir on the life of a child soldier written by Ishmael Beah.

"Teams are going to wonder, 'So how can we win state?' Read *A Long Way Gone* on your way to away games. That's how you do it," Larson said with complete assuredness.

Standing in a corner is senior Chris Georgan, the team's long snapper on punts. He is rumored to have gotten a perfect 36 on his ACT.

"Yes," Georgan says. "The first time I took it, I got a 33. But I took it again and got 36."

Georgan applied for what is known as "early action" at Yale. "You get your decision back early. I'll know by Christmas. It's not early decision so I don't have to go there. It's not binding," he says. "I'm also looking at Princeton, Harvard, Stanford, MIT and Cal Tech. Oh, and Illinois, Illinois Wesleyan and Boston College. Those are my safety schools."

He plans to major in physics, then go to medical school or pursue a doctorate in physics. "I haven't decided yet. I would love to do nuclear fusion."

Jeff Schroeder, a senior special teams player, wanders over. He injects an affectionately sarcastic view of Georgian's academic ambitions, jokingly encouraging a future in the science of blood doping. "He'd make the chemicals that are undetectable and won't hurt your body," he says.

Georgan laughs. The ability to not take oneself too seriously is most likely counterintuitive for Georgan, yet he can. It reveals a level of emotional fitness not always unilateral among the highly gifted. Such moments of unpretentious self-awareness are what endear visitors to these young men.

A St. Mary's middle school graduate, Georgan could have enrolled in one of the most prestigious math and engineering curriculum-specific high schools in the Chicago area. But he chose Carmel.

"I could have gone to Illinois Math and Science Academy, but I feel like you don't grow up at places like that. It's a place people want to go to, but it's not really a high school. I wouldn't get to do stuff like play football. School always came easy to me, so it's good to do something like this where you always have to work on it, you are always being pushed. You learn to take criticism, you learn even on days you don't want to practice—you know you have to. It's great for work ethic and time management. It's three hours I can't do homework. It forces me to get it done in a shorter amount of time."

Georgan's well-roundedness is not that uncommon among students at Carmel. Being a jock has always been cool. But in this environment, nerdiness is not only encouraged. It is embraced.

"One of my best friends is Ryan Ruddell," Georgan says. "He'll be valedictorian and will probably go downstate in the 4x400 in track next spring.

One of my friends is a judo black belt. I'm good friends with a bunch of guys on the soccer team. We're all around it and are really focused on our academics. Carmel mixes the two very well and creates an environment where you are comfortable being both. It's not that rare here."

While Chris is talking, senior linebacker Michael Fitzgibbons enters the foyer where many of the Corsairs wait. He sports two white wristbands, both with the letters "S.G." written on them. They are the initials of his girlfriend, Sarah Guinn. He wrote the same initials the previous week.

"It's going to be every week," Fitzgibbons says with conviction while stretching both bands away from his wrist. "With girls, you have to win them over and over again."

Logan Lester is messing around with his left hand. After his finger dislocation, he bought a glove he found on a website to protect the bone. It looks like a mitt of metal stolen from the set of an *X-Men* movie.

"It fits really well," Lester says. "A lot of linemen use it."

As Lester admires his hand-ware, Gus the Kicking Mule—otherwise known as sophomore kicker Steven O'Block—walks by. A player asks O'Block what his kicking range is tonight. He hesitates, not sure what to say. Lester speaks for him. "Sixty yards. Sixty yards!" he says, softly pressing his left hand against the wall, testing the elasticity of the glove.

"OK, 60 yards," O'Block says softly.

Larson overhears this exchange. He has an offer for the placekicker. "Here's a deal for you. If you make a 60-yard field goal, you can date my sister!"

O'Block is again speechless. The boys break out in laughter and head back to the locker room.

When professional athletes retire, they are always asked what they will miss most about whatever sport they are walking away from. They often say it's not the practices, the meetings, or even the games. Rather, what they say they will miss most is the excuse to act like a grown boy.

After witnessing this pre-game exchange, it's easy to understand why athletes give such clichéd answers. Because it's true. Being *with* the guys, *one* of the guys. Comfort. Acceptance.

It's all right here.

~

The coaches were right. It was to be a classic letdown game, and it's playing out in that direction. After an hour and a half bus ride, then another two and a half hour wait for kick off, Carmel's football team lays an egg all over Marist's grass field.

All game, the Corsairs—wearing white jerseys and brown pants—look flat, especially on offense. Late in the first half, junior "Z" back Matt Maher injuries his left knee. Already missing Michael Panico, who is on the sidelines in street clothes with an injured shoulder, Carmel is shorthanded at one of its most critical positions. Junior safety Brian Brennan replaces Panico to start the game and is now at "Z" back, replacing Maher. Ryan Cappis is now at "A" back, where Brennan had been in Panico's spot.

So, who's on third?

Carmel's rapidly maturing defense has kept them in the game, though, and with eight minutes remaining in the fourth quarter, the Corsairs trail 16-13. Marist is punting from its own 48-yard line. Kos is standing on the Carmel 20-yard line to receive the kick. The punt is a knuckle ball, appearing to surprise Kos by the rapidity of its descent. In an attempt to make the catch, he doesn't fully extend his arms. The ball is waist high when it bounces off his hands and rolls toward the Carmel end zone. With two Marist players trailing him by five and ten yards, Kos sprints towards the ball in hopes of grabbing it before any RedHawks can beat him to it. He wins the race, but the Corsairs have to start on their own half-yard line.

With the circumstance facing the Corsairs, the title of Jake Larson's book, *A Long Way Gone*, is an appropriate metaphor. The Corsairs may not be soldiers fighting for survival in a war-torn country, but 99-and-a-half yards are as long as a team must travel in the sport of football in an attempt to snatch victory from the jaws of defeat.

Two plays into the drive, Kos takes a hand-off from Serio and breaks off a 10-yard run. Another set of downs for the Corsairs. On second and 10, Kos gets the ball, starts right, then scampers to his left, finally getting tackled on the 23. Another first down.

After an incomplete pass and three-yard run, it's third and 7. A passing down for most teams. But Carmel is an option team. Serio keeps the ball. After a block by Cappis, in motion before the play, Serio springs free to the left side for a 12-yard gain. The Corsairs have first and 10 on their own 38, with 5:50 left in the game. On the next play, Serio fakes a hand-off to Kos, then is corralled by a Marist defender. After a three-yard loss, it's second and 13 from the Carmel 35.

Coach Berg calls for Kos to get the ball again. He snatches the hand-off from Serio and plows ahead into the right side of the line for eight yards. Third down and 5 yards to go for a first down.

On the next play, Kos gets the ball again, running this time off left tackle. He gets wrapped up just a few yards past the line of scrimmage, lunging for an extra yard before falling to the ground. It's fourth and 2 from the Carmel 46.

Perched at the top of the press box next to assistant Tim Schrank, Berg doesn't call the fourth down play right away.

"Maybe we should punt," he says into his headset.

"No way!" Coach Bitto says. "We're going for it right now!"

"OK. Then it's 31 pitch."

This is the Corsairs' bread and butter play, their bedrock, their *fortitudo et virtus.*

The first-down marker is between the 48 and 49 of Carmel. This gives the Corsairs an extra half-yard to canvass in order to keep the drive alive. Serio takes the snap and steps to his right. He fakes a hand-off to Kos. Marist's left defensive end reads the play perfectly, not falling for the fake. He crashes down on the quarterback. Just before he can grab him, Serio pitches the ball to Brennan, who gathers it on the Corsairs' 42-yard line with plenty of open field. He's tackled at the 45-yard line of Marist for a 9-yard gain. Another set of downs for the Corsairs.

The clock has only stopped on Carmel's one incompletion and three first- down runs. Otherwise, it counts down like sand through an hourglass. Four minutes, 10 seconds are left. Two plays yield eight yards and Carmel faces another third down, this time from the Marist 37.

~

From the visiting bleachers, Kos's father, Ed, is watching the action unfold. He's watching his son run with purpose. He's watching the other team make adjustments to stop Jordan and still not be able to. It's been like that since he was 10 years old, when Dan Stredler coached him in the Warren Township Youth League.

Stredler played football at Army. He went on to coach football in Texas. His son, Grant, played at Carmel. He was the first to recognize Jordan's ferocity on the football field. In those early seasons with the WTYL, Jordan had been an offensive lineman. Something about him being bigger boned than the other kids. But Stredler recognized a running back when he saw one. Jordan relished contact. He could knock kids over. He could also run around them, possessing a natural burst of speed unlike most kids his age. Rather than have him block for an inferior runner, Dan thought Jordan should be the one blocked for. And as soon as Jordan received that first hand-off as a running back, he found his rightful place on the football field, the perfect position matching his talent and temperament.

All through his son's youth football years, Ed had been his coach. He had the voice to prove it, deep and booming, just what is needed when controlling a herd of adolescent boys. Now, amid the orchestra of ambient noise inside Marist's stadium, he knows Jordan is getting the ball. For so many years, when he was coaching, he'd seen his son in the same situation run through would-be tacklers. This is what he's seeing tonight. No juking, just straight-ahead power running. The fan in Ed is mesmerized by the sequence of events taking place. But the father in him makes him stand up from his bleacher seat and yell out to his son:

"Let's go Jordan! Dig deep! Hold onto the football!"

Like a quivering echo reverberating through a cave, Jordan recognizes the cackle from where his father sits. He turns his facemask in the direction of his father's motivational aphorisms. He nods.

Serio takes the snap, then rams the football into Kos's gut. Running left, Kos breaks a tackle at the line of scrimmage, then, spinning away from another defender, his jersey is almost torn off, his body folding up like a contortionist, before straightening up and falling on his back at the Marist 31. Another Carmel first down.

On the next play, Kos runs up the middle for seven yards. Then off left tackle for two. It's third and 1, the Corsairs' fourth third down on the drive. Serio keeps it, following the pile to the Marist 20. This buys Carmel at least another four downs. They are within O'Block's range, but the grass has caused fits for the kicking game all night. O'Block had an extra point blocked and missed a short field goal. Berg is calling plays as if a touchdown would be the only satisfactory result of this drive.

"Just one chance! One play!" Lester screams to his teammates as the chains move, repeating the weeklong rallying cry of his coach. The clock reads 1:37. The ball is placed at the middle of the field at the Marist 20. Serio runs over to the sidelines to get the play. In the huddle, Brennan can't contain his impulse. As fiery as Serio is cerebral, he screams, "This is it! We do it now or we are not going to do it!" Serio returns, the play is called, and the boys line up. Everyone thinks Kos is going to get the ball. On this drive, he's carried it nine times.

As Serio ducks under center, Brennan is to his right, both hands on his knees, just a few yards behind right tackle Sean Wolf-Lewis. To Serio's left is Cappis, in the same stance as Brennan, directly behind left tackle Jack Butler. Kos is in a three-point stance behind his quarterback.

Cappis goes in motion, but stops before he reaches Serio. Center Shane Toub feeds Serio the ball. Serio takes a step to his left and appears to hand the ball off to Kos, crashing down off left guard. Kos gets hit right away, tries to break free and while attempting to regain his uprightness, gets hammered by a linebacker. Kos is pushed to the ground for what appears to be no gain.

Only he doesn't have the ball.

Holy Houdini.

By the time Marist defenders realize the Carmel fullback is a decoy, Brennan has received a perfect pitch from Serio on the left side. With the ball tucked away on his left hip, he heads straight for the pylon. Only one man lies in Brennan's way—Marist's left cornerback, Cody Bohanek. Wideout Pat

Doherty runs him off to the 10-yard line, as Brennan, running behind him, moves past the 20. Doherty flattens the defender as he tries to move up and make a play. Football players like to call these "pancake" blocks, and they are rare, especially for wide receivers. But this block is an International House of Pancakes tall stack, drenched in maple syrup and slathered in butter. If legendary football broadcaster Keith Jackson were calling the game, he would have turned to partner Frank Broyles and said, "That's a johnnycake!"

As Doherty lies on top of his victim, there is nothing but open grass for Brennan. He runs through the Marist end zone. If the band hadn't been in the way, Brennan could have hopped the fence and kept running all the way back to Mundelein. The touchdown scamper makes the score 19-16, Corsairs. The clock reads 1:22 left in the fourth quarter. Before Brennan gets to the sidelines, a trailing Toub hoists him into the air. On his way down, Doherty and Cappis join the celebration. The rest of the linemen, along with Serio, wait for Brennan on the Carmel sideline. They are so exhausted they can barely stand.

Carmel's drive is that of mythology—99.5 yards, 14 plays, 8:34 elapsed. The five third-down conversions and two fourth downs were keys in the 26 minutes of real-time drama.

One member of the chain gang asks to no one in particular, "Is it Saturday yet?" He glances to the east to see if the sun is rising. It's not, but if anyone asks about Carmel's state championship aspirations, they are ascending quite rapidly.

O'Block converts the extra point to make it 20-16. The Corsairs kick the ball back to Marist. With 1:15 left, there is time left for one last drive. The RedHawks run four plays before safety Sean Brennan, Brian's sophomore brother, intercepts a pass to seal the win.

As the final seconds count down, Coach Michael Fitzgibbons shakes hands with everybody on the sidelines, congratulating them on the thrilling victory.

"Can you believe we did it?" Fitz says.

Tom Kelly, one of the defensive coaches, walks onto the field, his daughter, Lizzie, a sophomore at Carmel, alongside him. This is a Kelly family tradition after every game, father and daughter, walking out together. There's Matt Maher, on crutches, his injured right knee heavily bandaged. He's smiling, the exuberance of victory masking whatever pain he feels.

The boys gather in the end zone for the post-game prayer. Coach Bitto is standing a few yards away, his arm around son Jack on one side, son Peter on the other. He is in tears, overwhelmed by what he just witnessed. The previous Friday, during the team's weekly chapel service, he said this to the team:

The next few minutes, I want you to take the time solely to reflect on all the awesome things in your life. How grateful you should be for where you are— from the family you come from, the teammates you have. You guys are lucky people. You can express your love for each other through the game of football. To represent yourself, your family, your friends and the school with pride and dignity. That is a gift.

The emotion shown on this night stems from more than the outcome of a football game. For Bitto and the other coaches, football is a vehicle for teaching young men how much they can truly achieve. To them, that thrill ride of a final drive is emblematic of what the sport can reveal about humanity, imbued by prioritized principles spoken of each and every day.

God. Family. Carmel. Football.

When these foundational belief structures are put into action, they yield moments beyond short-term gratification. They are intensely spiritual. It's why these men coach. In the summer before the season, Bitto verbalized this sentiment:

Football is by itself a pretty barbaric game. If we don't create an environment where our players believe they can do great things by themselves or with other people, then were aren't teaching them a damn thing. Why even play football?

Several minutes later, in the hallway outside the locker room, Dan Potempa greets the boys as they come out. After allowing a touchdown to open up the second half—received with an appropriate sideline verbal ass-kicking from Potempa—the defense pitched a shutout. For the first time all season, the Corsairs' demanding, hard-to-please coordinator gushes about his unit.

"When things aren't going well, they seem to play their best. They are all good buddies. They are friends, so they are cheering for each other and not just for themselves. That's huge. And Jordan. I have a different opinion of him than I did before. I didn't know he could run like that. I've seen him make long runs before but never like, killing guys."

"I was crying after the game, I was so inspired by Jordan and Brian Brennan, by how hard they played," Coach Bitto says. "They are just winners. How can you not be grateful for that?"

He turns to Jim Rejc. "I was saying Jordan's and particularly Brian's performance have to be in the top five in my book. In terms of his impact on the game against a really good team."

Rejc has witnessed more Carmel games as a coach than anyone, nods approvingly.

Someone asks about Maher. The early diagnosis is a torn medial collateral ligament. His recovery time will most likely be six weeks. For a moment, the game's after glow turns jaundiced.

"We have too many injuries. Especially at the running back position," Coach Bitto says. "I feel bad for Matt. He's been awesome for us. But we'll figure it out. We'll figure it out."

And for the first time all year, he says what is obvious to any observer.

"This is a good team."

~

Out of the locker room emerges Jordan Kos. He's wearing a Dave Matthews Band T-shirt from a concert he and a few teammates saw at Wrigley Field the previous weekend.

His right leg is a bit banged up, the reason for his limp. As he chats with Berg, he grins the broad grin of a young man who knows he was the best player on the field that night.

"That was the most tired I've ever been. When Brian scored that touchdown, I was like, 'Thank God.'"

It's been a remarkable turnaround for the Carmel fullback. In 48 hours, he's gone from missing practice, being in his coach's doghouse, to playing the best game of his career. Kos carried the ball 22 carries for 208 yards, 45 of them on the final drive.

"I wasn't feeling bad for myself," Kos says. "I was like 'I'm the only starter left in the backfield. I can't let these guys down.' I said to myself, 'You have to lead this backfield now. You can't quit.'"

There are athletes in need of consistent, positive affirmation. Their self-esteem demands it. Denunciation, public or private, can backfire. Whatever emotions an athlete goes through when absorbing a coach's disapproval—anger, resentment, confusion—that emotion often manifests on the playing field. There are plenty of athletes, though, who can't muster up enough reasons to apply that anger or resentment constructively if, conversely, their strengths are not affirmed on a regular basis. Not Kos. It's clear why Coach Bitto is so hard on his star fullback. He can take constructive, often blunt, criticism. Players like Kos don't need regular avouchment. They are motivated by the nature of sport, its raw competitiveness and non-negotiable climax—the result. Losing sucks. Winning is better. And when victory is achieved with your brothers, the guys you sweat with every day? The emotion is tantalizing, captivating and endlessly addictive.

Can you believe we pulled it off? Damn right we did!

But as alluring as these sensations are, they can be equally dangerous. The Greeks have a word for this.

Hubris.

Coach Bitto understands this hazard with star players like Kos. And he will make sure the euphoric ecstasy of winning does not entirely erase the mistakes.

"On the muffed punt, Jordan made a crappy play," Coach Bitto says with a long, hard cough. "He probably should have let the ball go into the end zone. It would have been a touchback. He has practiced it. He did it against Viator. He's too good of an athlete to make a play like that. You cannot give up on Wednesday reps and expect to come out and be sharp."

Unless you're Jordan Kos.

"He's a stud. A bull," Coach Bitto says.

~

Tom Biere exits onto the I-294 expressway to head home. There's still 65 miles to go before they get to Fox Lake. His father, Jim, sits in the passenger seat.

Jim turns to Tom. "Can you believe they called pass interference on LaRon on that last drive?"

"He was just going for the ball, it looked like," Tom says.

"It's a good thing it didn't cost them. I really thought the referees missed it. They should get their eyes checked or something."

"I thought he played really well. He seems to like defense."

"Oh, yeah. He's found his position. They could use him at running back now, you know, with all the guys getting hurt."

"I know. Do you think he might switch him back?"

"I don't know. As well as he's playing on defense, they may want to keep him there."

Jim and Tom go silent. The road home is all that lies in front of them.

CHAPTER TWELVE

PUBLIC HEATH PIONEER

B<small>Y THE</small> 1970s, Jim and Marion Biere had settled in Fox Lake, a farming community 50 miles northwest of Chicago. When television weathermen referred to temperatures in the "boonies," they were talking about places like Fox Lake. When officials divided the town into two zip codes, one half was called Ingleside, the other Fox Lake. Jim and Marion's house sat on the Ingleside section. In the summertime, the city's population swelled by three or four times its normal size as wealthier families rented cottages along Fox Lake, transforming the "boonies" into a resort destination. But for nine months out of the year, it was as you would expect a Midwestern rural community to be—filled with blue-collar workers, mostly white.

Jim became a painter. He always enjoyed being outside, not chained to a desk. Much of the work was on big, expansive homes closer to Lake Michigan along Chicago's North Shore. Marion worked at St. Therese's for a while after they got married, but stayed home once the babies started coming. And there were six, all enrolling in Catholic grade school St. Bede's grade school in Ingleside. Not one to sit at home all day and wait on the children to stir from their naps, Marion involved herself with school affairs at St. Bede's. At the time, a newly ordained priest, Father Tom Franzmann, had become head chaplain.

Knowing St. Bede's to be his first parish, Marion befriended Father Franzmann. She frequently invited the young priest over to the house for meals. The kids got excited when he arrived in his red Jeep. A brilliant mechanic, he restored the vehicle himself from parts he'd recovered from a junkyard. In the winter, when the snows would pile up, he'd attach a plow to the Jeep and clear away Marion and Jim's driveway, along with others in the neighborhood. Father Franzmann's passion outside of church was cars and trucks. Every summer, during the city's annual parade, he let students from St. Bede's ride with him in the fire truck as he drove through town. This was always a special day.

On Christmas Day, he'd arrive at the Bieres' and stay for hours talking, laughing, visiting. This was of vital importance to Marion, to have men like Father Franzmann not just as Sunday speakers but as a consistent presence in her children's lives, to ground them in Catholicism, to have a face embody the faith she so strongly carried and integrated into their home, a home filled with physical replicas of the spirit she carried so deeply inside of her. Throughout their house were small plastic figurines of Jesus and his apostles. On white shelves that separated the kitchen and living room were statues of the Virgin Mary and Abraham Lincoln. Marion idolized Lincoln, speaking often of how she admired his conviction in the face of crisis.

And like the man of history she so revered, Marion was vocal in defending her ideology. She participated in as many activities as possible at St. Bede's. She made suggestions to Father Franzmann, such as recommending a roller-skating party for the teen youth group. He often took her advice, respecting her maternal worldview but also her timbre. If she challenged an idea, the tone of her retort was never domineering, didactic or impolite. Those in charge at St. Bede's always knew Marion had their backs, but if she believed them to be unenlightened, she wasn't shy about letting them know.

One time a nun came to speak at St. Bede's about the problem of world hunger. The sister went on about the urgency of the issue, the necessity the church felt to assist in the global crisis. She lectured to the women in the audience how they should consider not expanding their own families, be-lieving this would leave more food for the malnourished of the world. Mar-ion approached the nun after her talk. The sister asked Marion how many children she had.

"Six," Marion said.

"Oh, Mrs. Biere, you've done your share, you've had enough children," the sister said.

Directing her gaze directly at the nun, Marion responded sharply, "I've done my share and I've done your share too, sister."

No one who knew Marion was surprised.

~

As much as Marion enjoyed being head of the St. Bede's mom's club or the church guitar group, she longed for a return to public health. She would visit her old classmates from St. Therese's and hear how much they enjoyed working, all while raising families of their own. After her youngest, Tom, entered grade school in the early 1970's, she found her entry point. The Lake County Health Department needed a nurse to go around to area grade schools and give hearing and vision tests. This lasted a few years. But the work was easy, Marion grew restless. In 1976, the LCDH earned a grant of $30,000, and it needed workers to implement a groundbreaking program. Marion was in the right place at the right time.

At the tail end of World War II, the Allies cut off the Germans' supply of opium, used to make morphine. In need of another drug to help treat injured soldiers, German scientists invented a synthetic drug they called adolphine. By 1947, the drug had made its way to the United States and was renamed methadone. In the 1960s, a Chicago-born doctor, Vincent Dole, and his wife, Marie Nyswander, started research using methadone to treat heroin addicts. Their methods became the standard in public health. Marion was hired to implement this treatment by the LCHD, which used the grant to hatch the county's first clinic for heroin addicts. Marion was back in her element, working with sick patients, just as she was when she started her nursing career at St. Therese's two decades prior.

People would enter the clinic in a messy state—battered, broken, in the throes of addiction, both arms looking hideous from heroin needles. The last place they wanted to be was in a clinic, admitting to a group of strangers they needed help.

Marion was the clinic's first point of contact. Her job was to first give them a physical examination, to see if they needed a doctor's health care. This was not infrequent. After a psychiatric evaluation, if the patient was approved for the drug, it was Marion who administered the methadone, in pill form, mixing it in with Tang or Kool-Aid, and watching them drink it down. This was challenging, as they were in withdrawal from heroin, which was making them physically sick. Emotionally, they were abused, sad or depressed. Spiritually, they were devoid of hope.

But Marion didn't see what most saw. She didn't see the penniless veteran struggling to regain a piece of his lost humanity. She didn't see a woman disheveled, lost, attempting to break off from her castigating pimp. No, she saw promise, the part of them still untouched, where human potential had not vanished. She saw assets, not deficiencies. Strengths, not weaknesses. And when the suffering looked into Marion's steely blue eyes, what they saw was compassion, tenderness, and love. They often said those eyes, that merciful face, made it impossible for them to tell a lie. That hard street persona would melt away, revealing their authentic soul. A soul desirous for a chance to make something from their broken lives.

∾

You couldn't see that much human suffering if you didn't have hope. So even when you were witnessing this, if you didn't have hope for these people and hope in your own ability and faith to achieve that result, then you didn't last long in that clinic.

- *Ed Ravine, clinic director*

∾

Brian's talking now. At the lectern. About how he and Ryan didn't really get along that much until sophomore year.

But after the Marian Catholic football game he slept over at Ryan's house. They talked, got to know each other. Now they are inseparable.

It got LaRon thinking.

Why do friendships happen?

Why do others make the decisions they do?

Someone said you could experience God's love through your relationships.

Coach May is talking now. LaRon always felt when Coach May coached him in football, he was a little hard on him. If he missed an assignment, he'd yell at him more than the other coaches. He never understood why.

Coach May is telling a story, about how when, as a kid, he entered a punt, pass and kick competition. He was so successful, earning a trip to Atlanta, where he went up against kids in his age group from all over the country. He finished in second place, so close to winning the entire thing. Coach May said how after he came home, his parents wrote a letter about the experience. They said how nice it was to be led around by an 8-year-old boy for a few days in Atlanta. How proud they were of their son, in his element, completely in control. Coach May never knew about the letter until he was 18 years old. Then he read it. Then he understood how they felt. Why it meant so much to them.

LaRon listens. It stirs so many questions about his own life.

"Why was my mom so protective?"

"Why did we fight so much at the end?"

"Why did she take me in and not leave me at that hospital?"

It's hard, thinking about the whys. At times, he's desperate for answers. Other times, he wants to run away from the past. But here, in this isolated environment, he's starting to feel safe. Everyone is so honest, sharing so much of themselves. The leery disbelieving is fading, transforming into willful trust.

He wants to heal. He's starting to feel he deserves love from others.

After all, God doesn't make junk.

CHAPTER THIRTEEN

BROWN ON BROWN

Carmel is now 6-0 after hammering Benet Academy 42-0. Coach Bitto is spending more money on ice cream than he has in years.

"It's weird. Winning doesn't matter. They want ice cream, that's the biggest thing," he says. "I really think it's kind of funny, what little things motivate them. You could give them Goldfish crackers and they'd be happy."

The youth football team that Bitto coaches, the Lake County Stallions, is also winning at a rapid clip. Gomez, Reimer, Bitto and Bitto (not a law firm but members of a football team) are keeping up with the Carmel Corsairs, win for win. The peanut gang won its fifth game Sunday and has all but sealed a postseason spot.

Three days a week Coach Bitto pulls a double coaching shift. Today is Wednesday and he has sent the Corsairs home for the night. Now, under the lights, he watches the Stallions practice. Or something like that.

"Stop it! This ain't a friggin' wrestling match! Run it again!" Coach Bitto says after a particularly untidy drill.

As the Stallions get organized, there is a visitor on the field.

～

Kate Bitto sticks around to roam the sidelines after dropping off Peter, their 12-year-old son and his 11-year-old brother Jack. She works at Abbott

Laboratories, a massive pharmaceuticals company in North Chicago. She's not much of a football fan. She doesn't attend all of her husband's home games, preferring to spend her Friday nights at home on the family's deck, drinking a glass of wine and catching up with friends on the phone. It's not as if she can't see or hear the game. The Bittos live a frisbee throw away from the school. She can see the stadium lights from the deck.

"We got married when we were 25. We were just kids," Kate says. "We had a lot in common. He's from a big Catholic family. So was I. We had the same thoughts on things. We evolved in the same direction. A lot of people don't. You have your ups and downs. We were lucky. We sweated in the same direction."

She's watching her sons be coached by their father. There was a time she believed that might never happen. In season, the life of a coach's wife can be lonesome. Tolerance is mandatory for survival.

"We've had moments. When the babies were little—Peter 20 months, Jack six months, both were in diapers—I was about to kick him out during football season. Forget about fall vacations," Kate says with a laugh. "But the spouses are generally very supportive. Support and respect for what they are doing is important. Ang [as Kate refers to her husband] is impacting far more people in a positive way than I do in my job."

That time, when the boys were toddlers, was revelatory for Kate in regards to the dogma of a coach's personality, which is often that of unrelenting sanguineness even in times of stress.

"Ang handles adversity different than a normal person," she says. "He's so optimistic. But sometimes I need him in the trenches with me. I'd say, 'Leave your coaching crap behind.'

"He's lucky to have me. If I didn't have the job I have, it would be a lot tougher for him to have the job he has as Catholic-school guys don't make a lot of money. We're pretty spiritual in that if you follow your mission, it will work out."

Her husband's gravely voice is heard in the background.

"You need a wider base, Anthony. Our splits are too tight."

Kate stops and stares at her boys.

"I talked him into this, about coaching this year. He's proud of himself. This team won one game last year. He doesn't have the time to do it but look how it's working out. Jack would not be able to participate."

Through his face mask, Jack yells out, "Hi, mom!"

"Hey, baby!" she yells back.

Kate continues. "Jack has special needs, so it's very challenging for him. Social interaction is tough for him. And this is his first year with any team sport. Jack's teammates have had to experience tolerance. He's not the best player but he's a good kid and he's having so much fun."

To any observer, Jack Bitto often looks and acts like any normal 11-year-old in shoulder pads. But there are small differences. He yells out goofy things (like when Andy gathers the boys to tell a story after practice, Jack will yell out, "he's telling a story now!"). There are times during Carmel football games he will sit on the bench, alone, talking to himself.

"He's much better than he used to be, but he's not age-appropriate socially developed," Kate says. "We're optimistic that he'll keep getting better, but it takes a lot of work. Andy does all the homework with Jack and he's awesome at it."

Kate can't stay. She's gotten her football fix for the day, and it's now time to leave the boys on the playground. First, she shares one more thought on her husband.

"Fortunately, he doesn't have great expectations on life. He doesn't need a big house, fancy car. He's just happy being who he is."

~

The boys are eating quite well this season—the Venegoni-hosted potlatch was followed by the Serios' Italian meatball-palooza, then the Lesters' steak-and ribs-fest. This Thursday's feast, the pregame meal for Friday's contest with Marian Catholic, moves to the home of the Scott and Terese Greene. Their son, Connor, is the Corsairs' senior scout team quarterback, and he may have the strongest arm on the team.

In the kitchen are the Greenes and two other couples—Scott and Beth Carr and Bruce and Diane Cappis. They are chatting and theorizing about the Corsairs' uniform colors.

"Wearing a brown jersey in Illinois high school rules is illegal. The reason is it conceals the ball," Scott Greene says. "So, Illinois grandfathered the Catholic schools in the 1950s so they can wear brown jerseys. That's why Catholic schools run the triple option, because it's all about deception and you can't see where the ball is."

"They had a powerful lobby," Scott Carr says. "It might be an urban legend."

"I don't know if that's right, the brown jerseys," says Beth Carr, whose son, Matt, is a senior on the team.

"It makes all the sense in the world," Scott Carr says.

"I don't understand the whole grandfather thing. So, if there was a new Catholic school they couldn't pick brown because they are not grandfathered in?" Beth says.

"No, they can't pick brown. You cannot have a brown jersey under Illinois rules," Scott Greene says. "It hides the ball."

"It's the ugliest color of all mankind," Terese Greene says.

"I happen to like it!" Scott Carr says.

"You think the brown on yellow looks good?" Terese asks.

"I've grown to love it," Scott Carr says.

"I love brown on brown. I really do," Scott Greene says.

"Matt doesn't even own yellow pants," Beth says.

"Yes he does. He just hasn't pulled them out," Terese says.

"No, he doesn't. Unless they're in his car. They are not in the house!" Beth says.

"They have to be," Diane Cappis says. "Ryan said they vote every week what color pants."

"I don't know. I've never seen them. I don't have yellow pants in the house," Beth says.

"Yes, you do!" Terese says.

"No, I don't. I'm telling you!" Beth says.

"You just don't know you do," Diane says.

"Because they don't wear them," Terese says with the certitude of a trial lawyer.

"They might be in the car," Beth says.

"Or they are in the bottom of his closet," Diane says.

The controversy surrounding Matt's missing gold pants is nothing more than one of life's household mysteries. But there is nothing mysterious about the Corsairs' gameday garb. Friday night is a road game. For each of the team's four home games, Carmel has worn brown jerseys with brown pants. For road games, it has worn white jerseys with brown pants, and this will be the combination Friday at Marian Catholic, located on the South Side of Chicago.

"They won't change pants color until they lose, and that won't be until next year," Bruce Cappis says.

That's the type of brave comment spoken not just in a parent kitchen, but on the practice field. For the first time this week, the coaches are talking about an undefeated season and competing for a state title. The boys are listening, and the bold, take-charge narrative is trickling down to dads and moms.

The Greenes, Cappises and Carrs are like many families at Carmel. Their sons went to grade school together—St. Mary's in Buffalo Grove—played football, and their banter is reflective of this familiarity, of common values breeding shared experiences. They easily glide back and forth between topics on family, school, college and, well, um, gold pants.

All conversation threads lead back to their favorite topic—the school their children attend.

"Since freshman year, they say football players are going to make a difference in the school," Bruce Cappis says. "[Freshman coach] Kevin Nylen said you are going to make a difference. It's not what you do on the field, it's what you do in the hallways. No one's going to get picked on. You will have influence within the school. Every kid should have that. It goes back to treating everyone the way you want to be treated. I don't think they ever lost that ideal."

Terese Greene interjects. "Aren't the kids just nicer? I had two kids go to the public school close by. The teachers there say they can peg the St. Mary's kids. They all say it. They know."

A few Carmel players walk into the kitchen. They thank Scott and Terese for the food and leave for home.

"It's funny. They kind of politely eat, they always say thanks, and leave at a decent time. Kind of cool," Scott Carr says.

"It's just different. I don't know what it is," Terese says.

Having an older son attend Stevenson High School, one of the public schools in the area, she has a unique perspective. The Greenes live in Long Grove, a city where two Catholic and five public high schools are within 10 miles. This cluster gives families an abundance of scholastic options for their children.

Terese moves to the basement where the family photos are on the wall. One is of her oldest son, Brian, wearing a Stevenson Patriots uniform.

"Brian wanted to go to Catholic school. He was the only one on his travel baseball team who was going to St. Viator. But all of his baseball teammates were going to Stevenson. He finally said, 'Can I go to Stevenson?'"

Connor Greene is seven years younger than Brian.

"Brian goes to Stevenson, and we say to Scotty, 'you don't really have a choice. You are going to Catholic school, and now Carmel is the one.' I would have loved for my two oldest to have gone to Carmel. Brian had a wonderful group of coaches at Stevenson, great friends and families. But there's a difference. I can't explain it."

As Terese talks, more boys milling about in the basement are saying their goodbyes for the evening. She wants to arrive at a more definitive place on this topic, about what's *different*.

She tells the story of how Brian and Tim Serio's dad, Paul, was late coming over to their house after a recent game because the car belonging to the girlfriend of one of the players would not start. Paul stayed and helped the girl get home safely. She recalls how Connor told her how he had to wait to be picked up after school one day. Tina Lester, Logan Lester's mom, waited with him until his ride showed up. "I felt safe," Connor told his mother later.

Terese had her answer.

"How can I help you? That's what it is. At other schools, it's more individual. My kids—how are my kids doing? Where at Carmel it's, how are your kids? More of a collective community rather than individual interests. It creates an environment where kids can carve out their own identities, be more comfortable in their own skin, more accepting of who they really are."

The house is almost cleaned out of Corsairs football players. They've all gone home, to sleep. Friday is going to be a long day. Another trip to Chicago's South Side awaits the unbeaten Corsairs.

CHAPTER FOURTEEN

BRACE GATE

THERE'S SO MUCH TO THINK ABOUT, he can't clear his head. At night. During the day. If only Luke could escape his own thoughts.

Daydreaming. Doodling when he should be taking notes. He knows he should be listening to his teacher, but what's the point? It's just more stuff. He can't think anyway. *Does anyone know what this is like?* Luke asks himself amid all the other voices. It's misery.

Football practice is in a few hours. He doesn't want to go. Luke loves his teammates. He loves having guys he can rely on, whom he can count on. But some days it's too much. Today's one of those days. He'd rather just go home and lie on the couch. Mostly he feels this way after games. But he can't. His dad, John, and older brother, Mark, want to talk about what happened. His mom will heat up some leftovers then go to bed. She knows to stay out of it. Some nights, it will be all three of them—Mark, John and Luke. Or if his older brother Mark isn't there, it's just Luke and John. They talk about specific plays, about game situations. The questions. So many questions. At times, he hears condemnation. Other times, praise.

Why were you on that side of the field?

You were really quick on that play. That was a good read.

Why can't you play that way the entire game?

That was a great hit. You wrapped up and took him down.

Luke likes the attention. He loves it when he gets a compliment. He listens to what his dad and Mark have to say, the good and the bad. Their words are motivating. That's why he plays the way he plays. He wants to be the best and he knows they want the same thing. There is no other option in his family. He was just a fifth-grader when Mark quarterbacked the Corsairs' state title team of 2003. But he read the newspapers. He knew what that team accomplished, how monumental it was. He saw how driven Mark was that season. And in 2007, he played on the varsity with David, his other older brother. Luke saw firsthand how maniacal his brother was with his training. How he could bench press 315 pounds five times. Are you kidding? For a 6-foot, 200-pound guy, that's downright Buyanesque.

Luke gets it. He knows for a Venegoni, there's only one way to be. And that's the best. But sometimes he doesn't want to be. Some nights he doesn't feel like talking, when he's bruised and banged up. Exhausted. Dad will want to talk, so he does. Mark, too. They always want to talk about football. Don't they know he can talk about other stuff? How come they never ask?

Today he just wants to relax. Not do anything. Not have to be around anybody. To try and sleep. Luke's having a hard time sleeping. He's tired, but his thoughts don't care. They have a mind of their own. Why can't it all just stop?

The medicine helps when he can't pay attention. He takes it once in the morning. It helps Luke focus on one thing, rather than on everything. The tornado stops swirling in his head. But sometimes the medicine makes him feel irritable. He gets anxious. He feels joyless. The doctor says he can prescribe more medicine. But Luke is reluctant. He's heard stories of kids so hopped up on medicine, they completely shut down. He doesn't want to shut down. He just wants a break. But he can't take a break.

~

Luke's Oldsmobile Sabre is parked out in front. Richard is running late —again!—and they don't have much time. The northern pike are hungry at Lake Canterbury today. Luke knows they are. He wants to catch one before practice. This isn't the summer. How glorious those days were, when they had all day to fish at the Salvis' private lake in Wauconda. The worry-free hours drifting by. But there's no lazy in this day. The cooler is packed with burgers and lures. All he needs is his partner.

"Come on, Richard! Let's go!" Luke yells while pressing down on the vehicle's horn. Richard emerges.

Soon they are at the lake. It's early fall, the water still not cold enough to scare off the perch and bluegill. There's plenty of bass but it's the *esox lucius* Luke wants. Richard's already bagged one. A northern pike is a fighting game fish, known to waggle and shake ferociously when caught. And are they a beautiful species! Long and multicolored with bright spots on their flanks—an electric organ with fins. To catch one marks an arrival of sorts for a fisherman. Like hunting a black-tail deer. Or a quarterback.

It's so peaceful on the lake. The serenity is seductive. It's easy to just be anonymous. Just another guy on a boat trolling for fish. From the time his feet hit the floor in the morning, Luke has to be so many other things. A student. A football player. A teammate. A son. A boyfriend. A Venegoni. That can be a lot for a 17-year-old. When he's on the lake with Richard, he can just be Luke, the Luke who likes the space of the outdoors. The Luke who, when he doesn't feel like dealing with people, will shoot shotguns for hours on an open range. Who will fish in the winter, when the lake is nothing but a reservoir of ice. Anything to escape from the other Luke. That Luke doesn't want to leave his house.

When the fish aren't biting, he and Richard talk. Sometimes their mutual friends will come out with them—Quinn, Tommy or Sam—but today it's him and Richard. That's the way Luke likes it. They have a lot in common, chatting easily about the stuff teenagers talk about—school, friends, girls, music, football. Richard goes to Libertyville High School, just a few miles down the road from Carmel. They both play football. Richard's a defensive end for Libertyville. They both share a passion for catching fish and the Dave Matthews Band. They talk about the bootleg records they like best, such as the 1998 live show at the New World Music Theater in Tinley Park. Classic Dave. They talk about who has been to more shows. Richard has. After a while, when there's no more football, friends or Dave to talk about, they'll get more serious. Today is one of those days.

He wishes it were over. Football. This season. He loves the games. Oh man does he love the games. Fridays. Wearing a shirt and tie that day in school, the admiring looks from classmates that say "I know who you are." Being in class, trying to listen to his teacher but visualizing making plays. Making that one hit behind the line of scrimmage, driving the ballcarrier to the turf. Forcing the ball loose. That's why he wanted to play defense, unlike his two older brothers. They liked to play football with the ball in their hands. Not Luke. He likes the space, seeing a play develop, recognizing his assignment, finding the ballcarrier then—pop! The sound of shoulder pads crunching running backs. He lives for that. You know what else he lives for? That feeling he gets after he turns his phone on after the last class Friday. The symphonic sound of text messages streaming in from his parents, his brothers, his cousins, his friends. The messages are short.

good luck

play hard

i luv u

play fast

Sure, he already knows he's supposed to play fast—he's Luke Venegoni!— but to read those words from the people he most cares about and who most care about him, it helps calm him, keeps him centered. He feels like he's part of something important, something greater than himself. What Coach Bitto talks about every day—God, Family, Carmel, Football. And when he puts on those brown pants, brown shirt with the number 37 on the front and back and that gold helmet with the brown "C," it affirms his commitment to those truths, of how he's playing football for a higher purpose. That's the feeling he wishes he could grab and hold onto all the time.

But he can't.

It's time to get back on dry land and leave for practice. Just a few bass today.

Maybe tomorrow those northerners will be biting.

~

It's Friday, October 8. The kickoff with Marian Catholic is at 7:30 p.m. Every able-bodied player is onsite, on the South Side of Chicago. Coaches and players are pleased with the team's preparation but the injury bug continues to bite. Carmel is losing players faster than Spinal Tap loses drummers. Tight end Pat Doherty broke his collarbone earlier in the week. At Thursday's practice, only 41 Corsairs suited up. That's an appropriate size for a jazz band, not a football team with ambitions of a state championship.

Michael Panico, the team's fastest offensive player, is playing with his injured shoulder. He sat out the Marist game, and wore a shoulder brace last Friday against Benet Academy. The plan is for him to wear the brace again tonight. Only he forgot to bring the brace.

In a hallway outside the visiting locker room, team trainer Dan Henrichs asks where the elusive brace is at the moment.

"Not here," says Panico, annoyed with himself. He is normally possesses one of the better self-deprecating senses of humor on the team, but even he can't find anything funny about this situation.

"I take everything home on Thursday and put it in my bag for Friday. I never brought my brace home, so I never put it in my bag Thursday, so I never brought it today," he says, falling on his own sword. "Thursday was when I blew it."

He asks if anyone has seen Coach Bitto.

"I think he's outside watching the sophomore game," one of the student trainers says.

From down the hall Henrichs screams, "Panico! Shouldn't you be out for specials?"

The sophomore game just ended and special teams warmups are about to start.

"I'm not going for specials."

"You can still run and catch the ball," Henrichs says.

Panico wanders off, presumably toward the football field.

Coach Bitto is nearby, talking on the phone outside the locker room. There is a developing situation in what can now be referred to as Brace Gate.

"Call Jose and ask if he can meet a guy at Door C to let a kid in to get Michael's brace," he says. "There is a kid waiting in the parking lot to get inside the locker room at Carmel to get Michael's brace."

Jose Gutierrez is the school's night shift maintenance man. Coach Bitto doesn't know the name of the emissary assigned to retrieve the brace, located inside Panico's locker. This is getting interesting.

Coach Bitto takes another call. "Hello? What is it? OK, thanks, bye."

Running backs coach Tom Young strolls over. "I did ask J.C. Pawlack if he has one. What's Jose's number?"

Pawlack is a back-up junior defensive back with an injury to his left shoulder similar to Panico's.

"Michael's about as forgetful ..." Coach Bitto says, then stops himself. "You think you'd attach that thing to your waist."

"How could he forget it?" Young asks.

"Because he's a teenager," Coach Bitto says. "His dad wants to ring his neck."

"I bet he does."

Anthony Panico has arranged to have someone pick up his absent-minded son's brace from Carmel and drive it to the game. That person is the one Jose has been instructed to let into the building and direct to the brace's location.

"For a first half, J.C. would be willing to bite the bullet," Young says.

Then his phone rings.

"Jose! Did somebody call you about letting somebody into the locker room?"

Young listens to the answer.

"They're already there? OK," Young says.

He turns to Coach Bitto. "They are already getting it."

"OK. It's a two-hour drive minimum to get here," Coach Bitto says. "Of course, Michael just wants Dan to tape the shoulder until the brace comes."

Coach Bitto's phone rings. He doesn't answer it right away. Instead, he stares at the device with a dazed expression. "Dammit! If I knew how to work a phone. I'm like mentally handicapped."

"What's Mr. Panico's number?" Young asks.

"I'll call him," Coach Bitto says. "It's like *Mission Impossible* out here."

He dials up Mr. Panico.

"Jose already let the kid in. We have another kid with a brace just like his. We'll see if he'll let him put it on him until Michael's brace gets here."

There's a pause while Mr. Panico responds.

"Tell the local police to let him go," Coach Bitto says with a laugh regarding the person charged with retrieving the brace from 1 Carmel Parkway in Mundelein and delivering it to 700 South Ashland in Chicago Heights.

He hangs up. "He said the kid will be flying to get here."

"You think he's getting paid?" Young asks.

"I don't know. Probably," Coach Bitto says with a mild chuckle. "I've said it so many times how Michael is a tough son of a gun for playing with a hurt shoulder."

"That he is."

"But I'll die trying to understand the brain of a teenage boy. How do you not remember your brace?"

~

Marian Catholic is coached by Dave Mattio. Like Coach Bitto, he doubles as athletic director at the school. Mattio is the dean of East Suburban Catholic Conference coaches, having been at Marian Catholic since 1976. After 35 years, his resume is as distinguished as any in the state—19 playoff appearances, four times to the state semifinals, one state championship in 1993. This season, the Spartans are playing well, sitting on a 5-1 record. In 2009, they qualified for the playoffs. But from 2004-08, the Spartans won only 18 games.

In his cramped, yet tidy, office, Mattio casts a figure much like that of Bob Hurley, the basketball coach at St. Anthony's High School in New Jersey that was featured in Adrian Wojnarowski's book, *Miracle of St. Anthony's*. For decades, Hurley cranked out winning teams while the school each year teetered on the brink of bankruptcy. Judging by Marian's monolithic Sr. M.

Paul McCaughey Leadership Center and expansive athletics wall of fame, the school is not on the verge of sinking into a financial abyss anytime soon. But everything that goes into maintaining the tradition established by Mattio is getting harder.

"Right now our numbers are dwindling," he says. "The demographic area is somewhat clouded because of money. There are an awful lot of people out of work, and so when people go to weigh their options between public or private, money becomes the most important factor. If you had to pay $3,000 to send a kid to a public high school versus $8,300 private, that's a big difference."

His hair is dark and straight with grayish temples. Although Mattio is in his seventh decade of life, his roundish, heart-shaped face still has traces of boyish features. "Ten or 12 years ago we had 15 or so Catholic grade schools that played some level of football. Now we are down to three. What's happening is grade schools are closing for a variety of factors. We used to have St. Jude's and Holy Ghost, and all of a sudden they close the doors or try and merge. We have St. Agnes [in Chicago Heights] and St. Ann in Lansing, which are the last vestiges of teams that play. We no longer have the large numbers like we had. We are not turning people away like we used to."

Marian is run by the Archdiocese of Chicago. Its president and principal are both nuns. So is the school's fencing coach, Dorothy Solak. Yes, a saber-carrying sister roams the Marian Catholic hallways.

Mattio blames the school's sour numbers on economic, not spiritual, conditions.

"I think religious education is still important to people in this area. But those people that used to live here have moved out west and now live in Mokena and New Lenox," Mattio says, referring to the suburbs. "We had six or eight former athletes of ours that now send their kids to Lincoln-Way East." That's a public school in Frankfort, 12 miles west of Marian Catholic.

"It's what happened to jobs in this corridor and affordability. Twenty to 30 years ago, parents were accustomed to working two jobs to make ends meet and send kids to private education. Today both parents are working to make ends meet and still want private school but it's difficult to afford. So there is an interest level in keeping numbers at a high level but you don't have the people to pick because money is so tight.

"I was accustomed to running a practice with 55 kids. Now we have 42."

When asked about his colleague, Coach Bitto's tone is more kindred than competitive. He sees Mattio as a mentor figure, someone who helped shepherd him through the rough patches when he first became an athletic director in the early 1990s. Over the years, they have become good friends. When Coach Bitto won his 100th career game in 2009, Mattio drove up for the post-game party. When Coach Fitzgibbons' father died, Mattio showed for the funeral. "He came to my parents' wakes," Coach Bitto said. When Mattio was hospitalized a few years back, Bitto and Fitz went to visit.

"The guys in our conference will cut your throat to be successful," Mattio says. "But before and after, we are in the same boat and there is a mutual respect."

That was evident earlier in the day, when the home team lent the visiting team use of its chapel for pre-game services.

There's a lot at stake tonight. Both enter the game unbeaten in the conference. The conversation switches to football.

"What I'm most impressed with this year is they have Kos, Panico, Serio. You might gear up to stop one for a while, then you have second or third options that can come in. Most teams you play have a good running back and you can focus on taking that away, I don't know if you can do that against Carmel. They may have a Panico kid who runs better than anyone we have, but we have to find a way to compete. You have to learn how to be emotionally and physically better.

"But no matter what the score is, the winner and loser are going to shake hands and you are going to leave the field."

As he finishes the last sentence, a Spartan player enters the office. He needs some time with his coach.

"Excuse me," Mattio says.

Kickoff is 90 minutes away.

~

Brace Gate is resolved before the half with the arrival of Michael Pani-co's shoulder harness. The deliverer is still a mystery, whereabouts unknown. Only Mr. Panico has the answer.

Just like two weeks ago against Marist, Carmel comes out flat on offense.

Kos fumbles on the game's first possession. Panico looks tentative run-ning the football. Blocking specialist Matt Maher, injured against Marist, is desperately missed. The Corsairs' lone-first half touchdown comes a on a 27-yard pass from Serio to running back Brian Brennan. But the good news is the defense is again dominating.

Each week, coordinator Dan Potempa has integrated themes into prac-tices, more a motivational technique than a schematic one. This week, the theme was inspired by Guns 'N Roses album, *Appetite for Destruction*. Ironi-cally, as Marian Catholic ran onto the field before the game, a song from that album, "Welcome to the Jungle," blasted through the stadium loudspeakers. That "jungle" might as well be anywhere the Carmel defense is playing.

Marian's offense is like that of almost every team the Corsairs have faced this season—a spread offense. This scheme works against bigger, slower de-fenses, but not against Carmel's. Fast linebackers Luke Venegoni, LaRon Bi-ere and Mike Fitzgibbons, along with juniors Tyler Lees and Kevin Cox, can outrun most plays, arriving to an assigned gap or spot on the field at the same time as the ball. And Carmel has a terrific inside-out pass rush with seniors Michael Cohen and Jake Larson.

The Corsairs are fast, but not big. Larson, at 6-2, 191 pounds, possesses the body type of an Olympic-level sprint swimmer. Nose tackle Sam Duprey is a stocky 5-9, 205 pounds, and Cohen is a lean 6-3, 212. Marian has a 200-pound bull of a running back, Jeruel Taylor, who could potentially gash the Corsairs with runs up the middle, directly behind the center and offen-sive guards.

Already razor-thin at running back, Carmel's worst nightmare almost occurs in the second quarter. A Spartans defender falls on Kos' left leg. Kos limps off the field. Henrichs' initial diagnosis is that nothing structural is damaged. "More likely a deep knee bruise or a contusion," he says on the sidelines. But during tests, Kos has no burst in his legs. His quadriceps is not firing. This makes the ligament vulnerable to injury, and Henrichs declares him out of action. He's replaced by Tim Serio, the quarterback's sophomore brother.

Carmel leads 7-0 at halftime. Coach Bitto is mildly agitated by the team's first-half performance, reflected in his brief talk to the boys. "We need to play with a lot more purpose and enthusiasm in the second half!" he says. He's more concerned by Kos' leg. And he's annoyed by the mercurial full-back's body language after the injury.

During several offensive series after he was removed from the game, Kos sat alone on the bench with his helmet off. Told by Henrichs to not put weight on the leg, he obeyed. But his withdrawal from the rest of the team gave off a sulking, self-indulgent vibe, feeding into his narcissistic reputation. "He likes the attention," freshman coach Kevin Nylen says.

Coach Bitto knows they will probably have to win the game without their best player. He can't control the injuries infecting the team like an airborne virus. But he has to let Kos know that kind of attitude won't be tolerated. He seizes the opportunity to send a message to the Carmel fullback as the team makes its way back to the field to begin the second half.

"Whatever you do, put your damn helmet on. I don't want to see you walking around without your helmet on!" Coach Bitto says.

Just before the second-half kickoff, on the sidelines, Coach Bitto says quietly, "He's too friggin' talented to get hurt."

Kos does as instructed. He keeps his helmet on the entire second half.

～

Dave Mattio's prediction comes true in the second half. It's next to impossible to keep the Corsairs dexterous running attack down for the entire game. With less than a minute left in the third quarter, Panico scores on a one-yard run. It gives Carmel a three-score lead, 17-0. Then, with just under five minutes left in the fourth quarter, Panico shows off his sprinter's speed with a spectacular 49-yard touchdown run. Carmel's lead is 24-0, and the fat lady may not be singing, but she sure is clearing her throat. After forcing another punt, Carmel gets the ball back for what surely will be its final offensive possession of the night with just over four minutes left in the game.

The first play is an inside handoff to Brennan. Away from the play, a Spartans defender gets knocked down and rolls up on the left leg of Carmel tackle Sean Wolf-Lewis, who drops to the ground and doesn't get up. Henrichs sprints out to the huddle of players around "Wolfy," as they affectionately call him.

Several minutes later, Wolfy is helped off the field, unable to put any weight on his left leg. Once on the sidelines, he is propped up on the trainer's table behind the Carmel bench, the injured leg wrapped with ice. Thinking the leg might be broken, Henrichs attaches a splint for the trip home. If it's a break, Wolfy's football career at Carmel is most likely over.

The development curbs the joyfulness of the 24-0 victory but not the meaning: The Corsairs have clinched a share of the conference championship.

"It's hard to win on the road in this league. It's hard to maintain that 375-percent effort," Coach Bitto says to a reporter on the field a few seconds after the final whistle sounds. Then he adds: "Oh, my God. Can we get anymore guys hurt?"

Typically at this point, players matriculate toward the end zone for the post-game prayer. But this time, they gather around the trainer's table, where their fallen buddy lies.

Wolfy's head rests on the table, both hands at his side, his legs stretched out, one encased in ice. He is motionless, staring upward into a cloudless sky.

Michael Cohen is the first to approach him. Cohen grabs Wolfy's right hand. Kos limps over and grabs his left. Wolfy moves his head from side-to-side, staring up at Cohen and Kos, their expressions a mixture of intensity and compassion. Within seconds, all of Wolfy's teammates, coaches and trainers, surround him, hands locked. Coach Ben Berg breaks the silence.

"Our Father, who art in heaven ..."

~

The prayer session ends, and the boys walk toward the locker room and prepare to head home. Wolfy remains on the training table, he now sits upright.

"There's a cart coming so we can get you to the locker room," Henrichs says.

"Is it OK if I just wait here a little bit more?" Wolfy says.

"Sure," Henrichs says.

Now alone, Wolfy can't fight the tears any longer. He looks into the clear Chicago sky and he sees nothing but darkness. But inside, deep within the recesses of his soul, he feels everything a human could possibly feel.

～

The official diagnosis on Wolfy is a broken fibula. Out for the season. Unless Carmel can make it to the state championship game Thanksgiving weekend, then there's a chance.

The next morning, Wolfy sits up on one of the tables in Carmel's training room, a splint attached to his left leg. His dad stands to his side.

"It's always the left side, everything that's happened to him," Tim Wolf-Lewis says.

His son had surgery on his left knee, broke his left thumb, separated his left shoulder. Now a broken left leg.

"There's nothing you can do about it," his son says. "I'm not going to be depressed about it. I'm doing OK."

Coach Bitto walks into the room. He puts his right hand on Wolfy's right shoulder.

"You've been a great player for us. A great model for what we are trying to do here. Get healthy. We still want you here, to be around the guys."

Wolfy directs a sheepish grin toward his coach. He has a long road of rehabilitation ahead of him.

Tim Wolf-Lewis looks at the coach and says: "You made him a man. You and the coaches. My money is well spent, as you've really turned him into a man. We're very proud of my son for what he's done and accomplished."

There's silence in the room as the words sink in.

"And there's something else. You hurt with him. I know you do."

Coach Bitto takes a breath. His eyes are red, his face weary. He gently squeezes Wolfy's right shoulder.

"I do. Yes, I do."

～

The training room late in a football season is as congested as a MASH unit after a long battle.

Knees. Ankles. Shoulders. Hips. Backs. All requiring some form of therapy, remedy, rubbing or manipulation. It's a chaotic place, a mix of pandemonium, bedlam and just plain lawless disorder. It takes a special person to be in charge of this unpredictable *mise en scène.* Someone just crazy enough to subject himself to such bedlam.

"You don't learn in school how to deal with teenagers," Dan Henrichs says. "You don't learn how to deal with different personalities."

Which makes his job one of the most important in the program.

Athletes have a unique relationship with their bodies. In order to play their sport, parts need to be working. For the first time in their neophytic lives, teenage athletes are dealing with the reality of these parts being infallible. These ailments require icing, massaging, stretching and lots and lots of taping.

And just as critical as the remedy for the body is the soothing of the soul. Young athletes need someone to talk to. Someone to reassure them that what hurts is just part of the natural order of the universe. It's nothing *they* did. At Carmel, Henrichs is just this person.

Like so many others, he left, but came back. He's where he wants to be, where he believes he is meant to be.

"That's the benefit that I get from the job," says the class of '92 alumnus. "It's rewarding to see the athlete get injured and then see them through physical therapy and back on the field. It's awesome. It's not awesome that they are getting hurt. It's good to see them when they are going back, to see the positive."

Earlier that morning, Jordan Kos was in the training room getting treatment on his bruised knee.

"He's one of those athletes who is aware of his body. He knows when something is wrong, even if it's little," Henrichs says. "When we played Marian Catholic Friday night, his knee didn't feel right and he was worried if he played, he'd only make it worse."

Coach Bitto was hard on Kos on Friday night, his demeanor an uneasy balance between impatience and pugnaciousness.

"I don't know what he's doing," Kos said about his coach's behavior. "I wish I knew, but I don't. He's always barking at me."

The trainer knows why.

"I see it every year. It's guys Andy knows are leaders, that should be leaders, and if they are not, he's going to ride them a little bit longer. Jordan comes to me at times afraid to go to practice. He'll say, 'I'm going to be yelled at.' I say, 'You have to know it's not because he hates you. He's trying to get under your skin. He likes you. If he likes you, he's going to give you shit.' That's his personality. That's one way he shows his affection toward his players. But kids don't get that, they hear the yelling."

Henrichs must be a great listener to teenage angst, the program's surrogate big brother, and an ally of whom the derision is directed. It's a daily balancing act he juggles as deftly as a seasoned politician.

"I took a sports psychology class as an undergrad, and as a graduate student, a child-development class. I thought the psychology class was one of my favorites. It made me look at athletes in a different way. Andy sees potential in Jordan. He knows he is a good player and can be a better player."

Henrichs' youthful face and easy smile—followed by a loud, cackling laugh—is an asset. He doesn't look that far removed from the other side of the training table, the one hurting rather than helping. He has a natural ability to put teenagers at ease, to get them to reveal what's ailing them. Once a diagnose is made, he can often, in one visit, one conversation, mend their malady. It makes him an irreplaceable cog in Carmel's athletics program. Not that the Corsairs have to worry about replacing him. Ever.

"I go online looking for other jobs. My wife tells me, 'What are you doing?' I'll say, 'I'm just looking.' She says, 'You'll never leave; why are you even doing it?' I love dealing with the kids on a daily basis. And I know I'm going to deal with coaches who care about the kids. I honestly say I love coming to work every day. I love my job. I'm not going to leave."

It's standing room only inside Dan Henrichs' house of boo-boos. He reaches for a roll of tape and goes to work on another wounded body and soul.

Andy Bitto with son Jack after a Carmel victory. Bitto leads the Corsairs football program with a balance of intensity and humility.

Carmel players and coaches pray during a pre-game chapel service. Defensive coach Michael Fitzgibbons (middle) leads the service.

One last fiery speech is heard before the Carmel Corsairs take the field to play Notre Dame in 2010.

Quarterback Brian Serio makes a call at the line of scrimmage during a playoff win against Rockton Hononegah.

Fullback Jordan Kos is Carmel's best offensive player. His powerful legs are an important reason why the Corsairs are state title contenders in 2010.

Linebacker Luke Venegoni is one of the Corsairs' defensive leaders. He eyeballs the St. Viator quarterback during Carmel's 39-0 victory.

Safety Michael Fitzgibbons is an important member of the Corsairs' stout defensive unit. He shows a relaxed game face before Carmel takes the field.

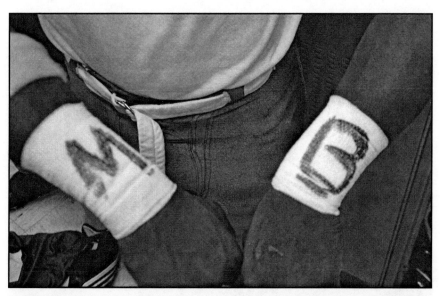

Before each game, Carmel players write the initials of a family member or friend for whom they are playing. Linebacker LaRon Biere dedicates this game to his adopted mother, Marion Biere.

Biere (left) and offensive lineman Logan Lester (right) smile broadly after the Corsairs pound Elgin 55-7 in the first round of the playoffs.

Carmel fans storm the field after the Corsairs shut out win over St. Viator. The relationship between fans and the team is one of the school's many virtues.

Serio races past a Joliet Catholic Academy defender during Carmel's 31-28 win over the Hilltoppers.

Carmel coaches wait outside the team's locker room after the team's dramatic win over Joliet Catholic Academy. In a few minutes, they would recite the Lord's Prayer.

CHAPTER FIFTEEN

MARION'S THIRD ACT

As Marion Biere got more involved at the Lake County Health Department, her home life adjusted accordingly. Often she would work second shifts—nighttime was when more patient care was needed—and would be leaving for work when her husband Jim or the kids would come home. And while it was impossible not to be aware of Marion's absence at the dinner table—she would lead discussions on school topics and current events—she otherwise structured things so a seamless family environment was in place.

In the morning, she'd prepare that evening's meal. There were a lot of casseroles served in the Biere household in those days, warmed up in the stove or microwave. Shepherd's Pie was a family favorite. Jim would come home and help finish what Marion had started that morning before she left for work.

Because she had fostered relationships with the neighbors, they were happy to pitch in. Tom, her youngest, would come home from school and stay with a neighbor across the street until Jim got off his shift. This was an era in America when families thought of helping their neighbors as not a burden, but a responsibility. And how could they refuse Marion? She was always inviting people into her home, offering friendship, kinship, and opportunities to build affinity.

Every summer, while working at the health department, Marion threw a picnic for her colleagues. Tom looked forward to the picnic every year, as it was a chance to meet his mother's co-workers. People of various ethnicities would come, and this was important to Marion, to expose her children to the melting pot of nationalities she saw every day at work. The Bieres did not live in the most racially diverse area. In Tom's four years at Grant High School, he remembered having one African-American classmate. There was an insistence from Marion that her children view the world as a bigger place than through the narrow prism where they resided.

By the 1980s, there was an emerging demographic entering the clinic: people with HIV or the AIDS virus. Within this alarming trend was a sub-demographic: pregnant women infected with the virus. Or, if they were not HIV-positive, they had become addicted to heroin, increasing their chances of becoming infected.

It was along the front lines of this public health crisis where Marion entrenched herself. She reached out to her old hospital, St. Therese's. The women she was diagnosing at the Lake County Health Department clinic were in need of prenatal care. With drug-using patients, there was a higher probability of fetal distress, potentially resulting in a spontaneous abortion. Mother and child were at significant risk. Methadone had to be administered to wean the mother off heroin and help avoid birth defects. A program was born to provide nurses and doctors training. It was Marion who personally educated the nurses on how to handle the troubled women.

"They may look a bit worse for wear, but treat them like any other patient," she would tell them. "They are working on making a better life for themselves and their baby."

A baby birthed by a drug-addicted mother is likely to take its first breath dependent on whatever poison its mother has been ingesting. In this program, before a woman gave birth at St. Therese's, Marion or the nurses she trained would monitor the child. If the mother was on a methadone regimen long enough before birth, the child was born less damaged. A preferred scenario was for a life to begin not addicted to but withdrawing from heroin. Even with this circumstance, however, the newborns were not out of the woods. Babies in withdrawal are fussier than healthy newborns. Their cries are more high-pitched, their bodies tremulous. This makes swaddling exceptionally difficult. And if a mother was HIV-positive, there was risk of transmission to the child. Bottom line: They needed more attention, requiring specialized treatment.

There were times when this reality, coupled with a drug relapse, would cause the mother to abandon her child, leaving the sick newborn in the hospital's care. But in most cases, the women kept their children. This scenario spawned a new set of questions that needed answers: Once released from the hospital, where were they to go? How could these single mothers support a family?

To Marion, what could not happen was a circumstance where mothers wanted to care for their children but, because of a lack of education and skills, were unable to. This was unconscionable. But these women faced a hard reality. They never learned to take care of themselves, let alone a household. Basic, fundamental domestic skills like cooking, cleaning or driving a car were foreign tasks to them. Marion was desperate to help integrate these young mothers into society and make them self-sufficient. But she needed unilateral support for her mission. Fortunately, she had President Reagan on her side.

Just before he left office in 1988, Congress passed the Omnibus Drug Act. At the heart of the legislation were laws containing more heavy-handed penalties for drug traffickers. But buried in the bill was the framework for states on how to receive grants for the treatment and rehabilitation of drug users.

Ed Ravine, the clinic's director, monitored this legislation. He and Marion worked very closely every day, often discussing boundaries in regards to patients. To them, there was a fine line between ardent submersion and compassionate detachment. Walking that tight rope was a daily battle. Ravine, along with Lou Collier, a Vietnam veteran who worked at the clinic, would take young men out to dinner on Friday nights, or play pick-up basketball games at the VA in Waukegan. On Thanksgiving, they'd get donations and put meals together. On the Wednesday before the holiday, Marion would hold a cooking class, teaching the women and men how to prepare a stuffed turkey and other holiday side dishes. All of this time and money—often Ravine, Collier and Marion would pay for meals out of their own pocket—was impactful in the short term, but there was a limit to its effectiveness over the long haul. There were just too many people coming into the clinic. They needed government money.

Ravine wrote a grant proposal with designs on receiving funds for a women's treatment facility. This was Marion's long view public health vision—transitional housing for young mothers to receive ongoing medical care but conjoined with elementary parental training. The family structure had to be built from the ground up. Many of the women in the clinic had other children, and these children would be allowed to live with their siblings at the facility. At the time, the late 1980s, the idea of a women's residential service program was innovative. Empowerment was not as much of a buzzword as it is today. But that is just what Ravine sold Nancy Reagan in Washington. And it worked. The money became available when the president signed the proposed legislation in November of 1988. Soon after, a facility was built in Libertyville, then Vernon Hills. Women, mothers and their children finally got the care they needed. There were many to thank— Ravine, Collier, the Lake County Health Department, the state of Illinois, the Reagans—but Marion was the driver, the advocate, and in the end, the missioner doing what she believed to be God's work.

And she was by no means finished.

∼

Marion Biere needed a third act. She had been a mother and nurse, followed by a champion for women in public health. What next? Retired from the clinic, she knew this about herself: She was not going to stay at home and watch soap operas all day. She tried joining the Garden Society. She and the other senior citizens took a bus trip, touring large gardens in the Midwest. Marion had fun and enjoyed the company, but that was part of the problem. It was too leisurely, too recreational. She told her sister, Joanne, "That just isn't me!" She had to find an outlet for her benevolent self.

She learned of a foster-care program run by Catholic Charities in Waukegan. Marion was still tortured by memories from the clinic, of young mothers having their children taken away. Where did they go? What became of them? Foster care allowed her to develop a deeper relationship, to connect on an emotional level with another human being. When Marion would pray, she often asked, "How can I be of service?" She believed being a foster parent would bring her closer to God.

So she began to let children into her home. Some were newborns, others teenagers—always with problems, just as she saw at the clinic. It was hard not to get attached. One was a white teenager who had been sexually abused. Marion had many long chats with her, helping her work through her emotional issues. But then she was gone, adopted by a wealthy couple in a neighboring suburb. That's when Marion got frustrated with foster care. The recycling. The rotation of the children. They'd stay for a few weeks, even a few months. Just enough time for Marion to learn their story. Just enough time for her maternal instincts to kick in. Then one morning, they'd be gone.

"This isn't working," she told Jim. "There has to be a better way."

Then one day, she got the call about a sick child that needed help.

~

Having raised six children, she decided on the eve of her seventh decade that she wanted another. Marion needed a purposeful project, and baby LaRon needed a home. So he would stay.

Just as she had every time she brought a new baby home, Marion had a room prepared in the house. Normalcy, routine, consistency in daily life— that's good for a child. Even a newborn needs stability. But surrounding LaRon with the ordinary could not wash away the poisons he was saddled with at birth. His mother's addictions—heroin, cocaine—meant LaRon was born with the same dependencies. There was also a chance he would be HIV-positive, as was his mother. It would be months, if not a year, before doctors would know for sure. What they did know was that if LaRon's diagnosis revealed him to be HIV-positive, he could die. Marion knew the risks. She had spent a portion of her nursing career taking care of mentally ill children. Only this time, the sick child was hers.

LaRon suffered immensely through those first months. Yet Marion never left his side. She utilized all of the nurse's training she had acquired over the years. She wrapped him tightly in a blanket to keep him soothed when he fussed, which was often. Because LaRon was so aware of sound and motion, swaddling was difficult. Cooing could set him off, his body instantly tremulous. His nerves were desensitized. Marion had to rub his skin to recalibrate the nerves to respond. Feeding was laborious. And his cries were unlike the attention-grabbing cries of other babies. When he opened his mouth, out came a shrill yell, much like that from a burning teapot. When Marion could get him to eat food, he would often vomit it right back out. And he was so small when he first came home, weighing less than six pounds. To see a human life in such a state of disrepair would break the heart of any witness, but Marion had no time to mourn her child's current state. She had to ensure his future health.

∾

Marion mothered LaRon through his drug-induced pain and suffering. By the time he was two years old, doctors at Children's Memorial Hospital in Chicago confirmed the HIV antibodies were out of his system. This meant he would not acquire the AIDS virus. He was putting on weight, smiling, laughing, acting like a normal toddler, a joy to be around. The bond between mother and son was now irreversible. And this time, no one called to take him away.

Not everyone was wildly enthusiastic of the adoption at first. Tom, their youngest child, was often his mother's confidant. He understood his mother's decision, what was driving it. He had witnessed the transient public health environment where Marion worked for so long. How a patient would get treatment and counseling, only to relapse, succumbing to addiction's unrelenting temptations. This would at times leave Marion feeling helpless, questioning if she was being Pollyannaish about her impact. But by adopting, the end result would be different. She could seize control of the outcome. Tom would explain this to his older siblings, many of whom now had families of their own. They would call and ask, "What is mom doing? What the heck is she thinking?"

"You have to let her make the decision. It's her choice," he would say calmly. "She is the one that has to put the work and the effort in."

Soon after she decided to adopt LaRon, Marion decided to attend a St. Therese's nurse's reunion. While there, she told her friends and former colleagues of her decision. Reaction was a mix of shock and idolization. Joan Zupec had known other couples that had adopted, and whom had taken in black babies. But not when they were 60 years old. Marion's ex-roommate, Nadine Sedar, wondered the same as Joan.

"It was pretty much disbelief when we all heard about it. Not that she adopted a black boy but because I know a number of people that have done that. But at their age. That was the thing. To me that is about the most selfless act that I have ever been aware of. She acted in a way that we idealize in the church, which is giving sacrificial service. She lived that out," Joan Zupec said.

"Now? At her age? Does she have the energy?" Sedar asked.

Marion believed she did. And as LaRon blossomed into a highly active young man, she would also call on her reservoir of spiritual vitality in dealing with the inevitable issues of raising a black child in a mostly white community.

~

Marion and Jim had a cottage at Rock River Leisure Estates in Wisconsin. That's when I got to know her as an adult. We could visit. Just her and I. That's when I saw the depth of the faith she didn't talk about all that much. It wasn't something she wore on her sleeve. It was always there and that it was what she felt when she looked at this little baby. "God is asking me to take this child." That's the way she put it to me. "God is asking that of me."

- Sister Joanne Wegener, Marion's sister

CHAPTER SIXTEEN

BRUISED FULLBACK

It's homecoming week at Carmel. The team is 7-0, reaching its highest peak to date in the polls—No. 5 in the *Chicago Tribune*, No. 4 in *Chicago Sun-Times*. Tim Halloran, the prep information guru who goes by Edgy Tim online, has Carmel at No. 3. Comcast SportsNet, a popular cable channel out of Chicago, is on campus this week to do a story. The suburban newspaper *Daily Herald* is featuring Carmel as part of its weekly web series. If there were ever a time to be puffy-chested, now would be it. Yet Monday at practice, accolades and rankings are not on the boy's minds.

"I think I'm going to stuff her car with balloons," Austin Zupec says. "I don't know what else to do."

Zupec is referring to a girl he plans to ask out to Saturday's dance.

"I thought about putting a piece of paper in the car with 'homecoming' on it."

It's been a few weeks since Zupec has presented a note to someone. The last piece of paper was devoured, chomped, chewed, gnawed and ultimately gulped. But this does not faze Zupec. He understands that simply asking a girl to the homecoming dance is not an option. Presentation and intent are equally consequential.

"I could just ask her, but it would be boring," Zupec says. "I think girls like it when you do something rather than just ask them."

Tyler Lees strolls by. The linebacker has a girlfriend but has yet to officially ask her to the dance.

"I have a plan," Lees says with a mischievous grin.

For this generation of high school boys, having a plan is a matter of social etiquette, of what the French call *de rigueur*. Showmanship over simplicity.

Lees and Zupec better not disappoint.

~

"We need everyone at practice. We don't have a lot of guys left, so get to practice on time, OK?"

Head coach Andy Bitto addresses the team in the weight room before the thinning-by-the-day roster heads out to the field for Monday's light practice. Carmel will be lucky to dress 40 players.

"This is our championship week," he tells them. "We can win the championship outright Friday night."

The boys hoot and holler back at the straightforwardness of their coach's message. Win Friday against Notre Dame, and they are conference champs.

Minutes later, Coach Bitto is in his office. He's listening to a voice mail.

"Hey, Andy, it's Bill calling. I wanted to make sure you got my message. I think for 10, 12 and 15 you want to make it as simple as possible in terms of multiple fronts."

Bill is Bill Mack, the Corsairs' offense consigliore. Earlier that morning, Bitto and Mack met for their weekly schematic chitchat at a Wauconda diner. Often, Mack will call Coach Bitto a few hours later with additional ideas.

"This is like the second message," Coach Bitto says.

He continues to play the voice mail, Mack's voice providing an unceasing background soundtrack as running backs coach Tom Young walks in.

Coach Bitto asks him if he's spotted Jordan Kos in the training room.

"He was walking around with a little bit of a limp," Young says.

"He didn't even get hit. That's not even how he got hurt," Coach Bitto says about Kos's injury from Friday. "He fell and hit his knee on the ground."

"What a dork," Young says.

"Here's the dork right now," Coach Bitto says as Kos strolls in.

"Hi Jordan!" Young says.

There's silence from Kos. All that can be heard is Mack's unbroken voice through the phone speaker. "You want the fullback to have the option to cut both ways ... to run the backside A gap consistently ..."

"What?" Coach Bitto says impatiently to his gimpy fullback.

Both of Kos's hands are in his pockets. He's wearing a white T-shirt and sweat pants. "Dan sent me in here to ask you when would be a good time today to get treatment."

Coach Bitto doesn't respond to Kos's question right away. Mack is still talking endlessly through the phone speaker—"I was wondering when Kos got hurt ... he ran into the pile a bunch of times ... I was wondering what his situation is ..."

"Coach Mack is ripping you," Coach Bitto says. He turns to the voice recorder as if speaking to Mack directly. "I don't know, maybe he has a girl-friend who dumped him?"

Kos stands in front of Coach Bitto's desk, hands still in pockets, expressionless.

Coach Bitto finally stops Mack's stream of consciousness. Temporarily. There's another message.

"Hi, Andy, Bill calling ... give me a call ... I think we can put together a simple game plan that's pretty effective and gives them some significant problems ..."

"This is like the fifth time he's called me today. It's all the same message," Coach Bitto says. "I love Bill."

He turns his attention to Kos. "What were you saying again?" he asks.

"Dan wanted to know when the best time would be for me to see him, during running or after practice?"

"Why do you want to be with your teammates? Let's go now. Why hang out with your teammates? Do the prima donna thing—stand around and do nothing. Go inside, come out, whatever."

"That's not really an answer," Kos says.

"No, it is an answer. You need to think of the perception of how people are thinking of you," Coach Bitto says. He walks toward the storage room to grab something for practice. "Jordan, I was a running back. I know how people perceive running backs. So, you make your decision."

"If I'm out there with the team, then when would the best time be to come down to get treatment? After practice?" Kos says. "I'm asking you for advice because I really don't know what to do."

Coach Bitto looks up at his bruised, and now vulnerable, fullback. He lowers his voice. "Go outside now, watch them run so at least they know you're alive. Then come inside, and when they go to the weight room, get treatment. Make sense?"

"It does," Kos says. "All right."

He walks out.

This is one of the more honest two-sided exchanges between coach and star player all season. Kos asking for advice is better than the alternative, but Coach Bitto was hoping he'd go further, to figure out for himself what his coach just instructed him to do.

"There's a prima-donna factor he has to get over. He doesn't know any better; he's been treated that way his whole life," Coach Bitto says. "So, my goal is to get him to think that he needs to be more part of the team, especially when he's hurt."

What has Coach Bitto further exasperated is how Kos injured his knee. Running backs get hurt all the time in football, but Kos's affliction was self-induced, and worse, self-motivated.

"OK, so he cut his knee pads in half, then he got a knee contusion. I'm upset because it's 'I'm going to do it my way' and he gets hurt. Instead of, 'We were going to win this game anyway, get your 100 yards and get out, let's go.' It's not that he got hurt, it's the fact he modified his equipment that got him hurt. It's more Jordan doing Jordan's thing rather than doing what he's supposed to be doing.

"You lose more games with guys who do things their own way."

~

As the healthy boys run on the track, the wounded rest their aching bodies on treatment tables. The Carmel training room is a crowded space on this day.

Running back Matt Carr lies on one of the tables. Carr broke his left foot against St. Viator on September 10. Sean Wolf-Lewis, fresh from weekend surgery on his broken leg, wanders in and hops on to the table next to Carr. Carr looks away from his phone to ask Wolfy a question.

"Sean, can I see your foot?" Carr says.

Wolfy yanks off his boot and pulls back the bandage to expose the surgical scar. He then pulls up an image on his phone of the X-ray, showing the break.

"Shit, yours is way worse than mine!" Carr says.

"Yeah, you just cracked yours."

"Mine was lower, and the bone didn't separate."

The mutilation show over, they both lean back down on their respective tables and get back to quietly playing with their phones.

Just another afternoon in the Carmel sick ward.

~

After the boys run, Coach Bitto holds open tryouts for punt returner. Two muffed punts last game has him miffed.

"Catch it! We can't drop punts anymore! Catching punts is like catching a baseball. You have to look the ball into your glove," Coach Bitto says while standing next to a ball-launch machine. "Second, you can't run and catch at the same time. You have to almost freeze-frame when you catch. Just catch the darn thing. I don't care if you gain a yard. Two phases: Catch it, then return it."

As Tom Young loads another ball into the machine, Ryan Cappis and LaRon Biere arrive from the parking lot. Today is a half day at school, and most of the players went home before practice. Cappis and Biere are late, their nap having lasted longer than planned.

"How late did you stay up?" receivers coach Tim Schrank asks Carr, who has hobbled out onto the field after foot therapy. Carr is best friends with

Cappis and Biere, both of whom frequently spend the night at his house. Last night was one of those nights.

"I was in bed by 10. I didn't know they had stayed over until I saw their cars in my driveway when I woke up," Carr says. "It's kind if weird. My house is different. It's kind of a …"

"Youth hostel?" Schrank interrupts.

"For my friends, yeah," Carr says with a laugh. "I'll be home at random times and they'll be staying there. LaRon's car will be there and he'll be sleeping in my basement."

On the field, Biere lines up in a punt-return position. He has the wrong helmet, the color white verses the normal gold. Cappis is wearing a T-shirt he grabbed from Carr's closet.

"What's wrong with your helmet?" Coach Bitto barks at Biere. "Eyes on the ball when you come down with it!"

Young loads a ball into the machine, which shoots it into the air. Beire catches it perfectly with both hands.

"Get over here Frick and Frack," Coach Bitto says, calling Biere and Cappis over. "Do you want someone to call you tomorrow? Just to get you out of bed? It's like you guys need a concierge service."

"That would be great," Cappis said with a half smile, fully aware of his coach's mood—agitated over their tardiness but not hysterical.

"OK, gassers. Now before you run, remember, being on time is very important in life. Do you know what happens if you are late for work? You get your ass fired."

They respond in unison. "OK, Coach Bitto. We're sorry."

"Ready … go!" he barks, blowing his whistle.

And then they run.

～

Carmel's defense continues to be its most consistent unit, on a pace to be one of the best in school history. Marion Catholic managed a paltry 98 yards of total offense on 43 plays.

One player who stood out against the Spartans was Biere, who had four total tackles, one for a loss of seven yards.

"He's been a pleasant surprise," defensive backs coach Tom Kelly says. "We're playing him in limited schemes but what he does, he does well."

What Biere does well is run in open space. His first three seasons, he played running back. But when the decision was made in the summer to have Kos and Panico to get most of the carries, the coaches moved Beire to defense.

It took August practice and the first week of the season for Biere to adjust to his new position as an edge linebacker. But 18 combined tackles against Libertyville and St. Viator showed how far he's come. His confidence grew after six more tackles and a sack against Joliet Catholic. In the Marian Catholic game, he was in the right spot on the field almost every time.

"I pretty much always knew that I understood plays and formations," Biere says. "It's making reads, it's the progression where I'm better. I can see more plays, see where the running backs are going to end up and see where it's going to work out. We're doing a lot more changes as we get better reading offenses."

Biere says one of the reasons the defense is playing so well is because of how well they get along.

"Last year, if someone on the defense didn't like you as a running back, you got nailed. If I talked about starting over someone else, I would get my ass whipped by the other seniors. This year, it's less about trying to hurt you and more like, 'let's hit, make solid tackles and go onto the next play.' This year, we are all friends, juniors and seniors.

"We have the best chemistry."

In charge of coaching defensive backs is Tom Kelly. In his 16th season, he's held just about every positional coaching job within the program. When Carmel won its only state championship in 2003, Kelly called the plays as the Corsairs' offensive coordinator. He played quarterback at Bishop Mc-Namara, a Catholic high school in southern Illinois, before moving on to St. John's University in Minnesota, where he spent one season as a Johnnie under coach John Gagliardi, the octogenarian who holds the all-time record for victories by a college coach.

"He wrote me a thank-you note after I left the program," Kelly says. "I'll never forget that. Hand-written."

Kelly is pleased overall with the defense. It's hard not to be, with back-to-back shutouts against Benet Academy and Marian Catholic. Against the latter, the Corsairs moved Michael Fitzgibbons from cornerback to a hybrid linebacker/safety position to replace Brian Brennan, who started the season on defense but is now a permanent running back. It worked, as Fitzgibbons' height (6-5), speed and natural football instincts gave Marian Catholic fits. Luke Venegoni is playing as well as any linebacker in the conference. Ricky Acosta might be the league's best cover corner.

While Kelly can be as loud and shrill as any coach during practice, his style mirrors that of coordinator Dan Potempa—cerebrally intense.

"You see a lot of defensive coordinators who are so testosterone-oriented. They think the best way to motivate kids is to get in their faces and scream at them. Our kids are intellectual kids. It's not the way they've been taught to solve problems. We've had games where we've started slow and teams have had us on our heels, like Joliet Catholic. But we keep our composure under duress. A lot of that comes from Dan. He'll say, 'Let's make an adjustment here, our scheme is good. Let's not panic.'"

A distinguished science teacher at Stevenson High School in nearby Lincolnshire, Kelly chooses to make the nine-mile drive to Carmel every day when it's a short walk from his classroom to the Patriots practice field.

"Carmel is a tremendous place to coach. Collaboration is the nature of the coaching staff. It's not one person dictating. It's what can we do as a group."

All coaches receive stipends. Private schools typically pay their coaches much less than their public counterparts. Carmel pays between $2,700 and $4,500 per season. "It's half of what I'd make at Stevenson," Kelly says. "I get asked a lot by some of my closest friends at Stevenson, 'When are you coming back? Why aren't you coaching here?' There's pressure on me, so I have to think this through. But it's really clear."

He pauses.

"The emphasis that is placed on Carmel football is how we teach kids to be good people and try and teach these kids to become young men and leaders of the world. That culture is so good that it transcends to the coaching staff. I'm a better person because I'm around men teaching that every day. It's good for me spiritually; it's good for me emotionally. I'll get to pray three times on a Friday night. When the students run onto the field after games and we say the Lord's Prayer together, those moments are some of the highlights of my life.

"I mean, on the morning of our state championship game in 2003, we had chapel. You know who served me communion? Jack Simmons. I'm receiving the body and blood of Christ from one of the players I coached. It's the best thing that happened to me all season. Little moments like that keep me attached to Carmel."

～

The day ends with a film session. Kos and Serio, along with Serio's sophomore brother, Tim, cram into Coach Bitto's office to review plays from the Marian Catholic game. Kos's fumble from the opening drive is on the screen.

"How could you lose the ball when a guy grabs you from behind backwards? You want to know why? Because the ball is away from your body. Keep the ball high and tight," Coach Bitto says to Kos, sitting to his right. "You can't be fumbling when we are in the red zone or almost in the red zone."

Coach Bitto fast-forwards to the next play, a designed quarterback run. Serio scampers for a six-yard gain. Kos blocks one of the Spartan linebackers but, from Coach Bitto's vantage point, he doesn't do it well enough.

"I don't know why you are not more physical in your blocking. This is a minus-1," he says, referring to the grade on the play he gave Kos for his postgame evaluation. "So even before you decide to cut your knee pads off and hurt yourself, you are not playing at an all-conference level yet."

Coach Bitto hits the stop button on the remote control and turns to Kos, who stares blankly at the screen.

"I don't know what you are thinking. Did your girlfriend break up with you again?"

"No," Kos says, a grin creeping up his mouth, acknowledging his coach's playful tone.

"Maybe she should. Get rid of her. That would be good."

∿

It's 6:10 p.m. Brian and Tim have left the room to head home. What awaits them is a hot meal, school homework and more football film study. Coach Bitto asks Kos to stick around. The television monitor is off.

"Jordan, you realize you are our best player, right?"

"Yes."

"You have a bit of an image problem where you think you can miss practice. We need you to practice as hard as you can because the team is going to respond to how you behave. I'm going to be hard on you because the rest of the team has to know you are on task.

"Now, that's not fair. But that's the way it is. Guys look to you. When it's fourth and one, they want you to have the ball. I want you to have the ball. I only push you because you are so talented. You dig?"

"I do."

"OK. We're done. Get your rest and we'll see you tomorrow."

Kos walks out. The office door closes behind him.

"It's important he understands I don't hate him. I like Jordan. He's an awesome kid and so gifted," Coach Bitto says. "I'm trying to teach him that when he's at his best, we are at our best."

∿

Outside, darkness has enveloped the fall sky. Shadows of light hover above the tops of the stadium grandstands. On the field, the Stallions youth football team congregates in the end zone. Tonight is the final practice before their weekend game. There is much to prepare for, as there is much at stake—one more regular season game before the playoffs. But the Stallions' coach is running late. He has yet to punch out from his day job. Something about a film session with his starting fullback.

One of the Stallions tires of the wait. In full gear—black pants, black jersey with red trim—12-year-old quarterback Peter Bitto directs his mini-mite teammates in a warm-up drill.

"Ready … go!" he screams out, his voice crackling with the tone of a pre-pubescent soprano. "Coming back … go!"

His teammates take the instruction as if it's the natural order of things. They run in two lines on either side of where Peter stands in the end zone.

"I wish I had a whistle," he says under his breath.

He resumes his clamorous instruction.

"100s … last one! Go!"

And with that, Peter's father is spotted walking through the entrance gate, a Diet Pepsi in his right hand. He will soon affix whistle to mouth and continue what his quarterback has begun.

With each patter of cleats landing on turf, the sun's natural light fades more out of sight. Another diurnal arc in a football season rapidly evolving into something truly extraordinary.

CHAPTER SEVENTEEN

HOMECOMING

It's Thursday. Coach Bitto addresses the team after its final practice before the homecoming game versus Notre Dame.

"Tomorrow is Brown and Gold day at school. We are wearing our ties, no jerseys," he says. "Ties tomorrow. Routine."

He stops for a moment.

"Seniors! You want brown pants or gold?"

"BROWN!" they all yell back.

∿

Just a few yards away, sophomore coach Larry Whittier huddles with his boys.

"Tomorrow is tie day. Button-down shirt, Carmel school pants. We're going to be on the same schedule, 3 p.m. in the cafeteria. We need to get there right away so we can get taping done and get on the field for specials. Friday routine stays the same.

"Our uniform is brown jersey on gold pants."

The boys give a collective groan.

"Gentleman, gentleman. We are not the varsity. When you guys get to be on the varsity, you can go brown on brown. We're not brown on brown. Not yet."

Whittier pauses. His right hand, now a fist, rests on his right hip. Clumps of grey hair jet out from the edges of his cap. His eyes are squinty, his gaze focused downward on the eager faces staring back.

"We are going to be Carmel. We are going to play Carmel football. Does that make sense?"

"Yes, coach!" they all say back.

~

It's just over 48 hours before Carmel's homecoming dance. And Tyler Lees finally acts on his inspiration.

Inside Salvi Gymnasium, a girls volleyball game is being played. Lees's girlfriend, Megan Brennan, is one of the players. On one side of the gym, Michael Panico and Mike Schostok each hold up handmade signs. One sign reads: "H."

The other: "C."

Another sign, held by Brian Brennan, has a question mark written on it. Lees holds a bouquet of flowers while his teammates do the grunt work.

As the boys work through their on-the-fly, jumbled system—do we hold the signs up at once? Should we yell her name first? Does volleyball have a halftime?—it's obvious they believe strongly in the adage that it's better to beg for forgiveness than ask for permission. They yell out the name "Megan!" several times before she finally looks up from the gymnasium floor in their direction. In unison, the pigskin barbershop quartet all scream:

"Homecoming!"

During a timeout, Lees walks down to the Carmel bench and hands Megan the flowers, which she accepts. She wears a conflicted look—half bewilderment, half thankful. It's as if she's saying, 'Nice effort, but…"

"I had a different picture in my mind of how it was going to go," Lees said later with a big grin. "It didn't go that well."

But he got his yes. He has a date to the homecoming dance. And no matter what road Megan Brennan takes in her life, she'll always remember the night her high school boyfriend interrupted a volleyball game to ask her to homecoming.

And gave her flowers.

~

When Coach Bitto talks to the team after every practice, he's not averse to using pop-culture metaphors to make a point. He's fused the Pope, Erik Estrada ("You look like the guy from that cop show. The guys on the motorcycles. With the big hair. Chippendales.") and wrestling singlets all in the same conversation.

By Friday, he's all business, though.

It's less than an hour before kickoff. Meetings are over. Everyone's eaten. Chapel held, Communion received.

There's a gymnasium just around the corner from Coach Bitto's office. It used to be the gym before Salvi Gym was built. Now it's referred to as the "old gym." This is where Coach Bitto gives one final oration before game time. Inside, the boys all take a knee and clasp hands, awaiting the arrival of their coach.

He walks through the door and enters the gym.

"Homecoming conjures up a lot of cool stuff," Coach Bitto says. "I don't know if it does at other places, but I know it does at Carmel. Carmel is a place where if you play football, part of you stays with the next team and the next team and the next team. So, therefore, anyone who has ever played Carmel football is with us this year. You're taking the next extension of that idea. I shook hands with so many guys that played in the 1960s all the way through last year. They are reliving their Carmel experience. I'm not talking about football. I'm talking about Carmel! What does it mean to be at Carmel? That's what makes homecoming different. What does it mean? It means to do whatever it takes to make this community the best in the country. You guys are here because you want to be better people and better players. Most of all, Carmel homecoming is great because you guys are going to fight for each other and fight for all those players before you, because tonight you are representing the greatest high school in the country, Carmel Catholic High School!"

The boys let out a roar and head out for warm ups. Their coach's speech is the perfect crescendo as the clock inches closer to the game's momentous kickoff. The excitement is palpable.

Over the years, the assistant coaches have heard hundreds of Coach Bitto's speeches. After so many listens, they are in the habit of offering reviews.

"A good effort tonight. Good effort," Tom Kelly says.

"I thought he climaxed a bit early," Tim Schrank says. "But an A-plus."

"Not bad. An A," Joe May says.

"He took the crescendo to another level. Just when you thought it couldn't be more dramatic, he crossed the mountain," Schrank says.

"The content is always the same," Kelly says. "It's about Carmel."

~

Carmel is doing what it's supposed to do during a homecoming game —kicking the crap out of its opponent.

It's midway through the third quarter, and the Corsairs are moving the ball at will. Deep in Notre Dame territory, the Corsairs are driving for a touchdown that would give them a 17-7 advantage. Jordan Kos carries the ball to the one-yard line. On his way up after being tackled, he shoves a Dons player in full view of the officials. A flag is thrown, moving Carmel back 15 yards. A few plays later, the Corsairs finish the drive with a touchdown, and Coach Bitto is waiting for his fullback as he comes off the field.

"When did you think you can play without poise! You are going to get hit a thousand times! Everybody is going to play dirty, hit you, twist you, punch you. If you are going to be a champion, you have to get back in the huddle and score touchdowns against them!" Coach Bitto walks with his agitated fullback toward the bench. "You don't tell them that, you just play like that!"

The coach walks away, having said his piece. Kos is still clearly upset over the penalty.

"They fucked with the wrong dude!" offensive guard Logan Lester screams while taking a seat on the bench.

"Watch your language!" Coach May barks back at the bench.

On the bench with the other offensive linemen, someone asks what got Kos so upset.

"They twisted his ankle," Lester says. "They were trying to twist it, trying to break it."

Notre Dame is an all-boys school run by the Archdiocese of Chicago in Niles, 25 miles south of Carmel's campus. Unlike Joliet Catholic or Marist, where recent history has produced competitive games, the Corsairs have beaten the Dons 12 consecutive times.

Kos had fumbled on the opening drive—which was a far greater cause for concern than the personal foul—leading to the Dons' only score of the game. After the third-quarter ankle twist, Kos runs for a 42-yard touchdown, and for the game, he finishes with 109 yards on 15 carries. In the fourth quarter, backup Tim Serio replaces Kos and runs for a 47-yard touchdown. Carmel scores 30 second-half points and pounds Notre Dame 40-7, sewing up the fourth conference crown in school history.

The rushing disparity in the game is startling—314 yards for Carmel (on 51 carries) versus 1 for the Dons (on 20 carries, about a half-inch per rush). Notre Dame manages 121 yards of total offense, with most of the yards accumulated in the fourth quarter after the starters were pulled. Carmel's linebackers—Kevin Cox, Tyler Lees, LaRon Biere and Luke Venegoni—are credited with 32 tackles and a sack. In six conference games, the defense allows 51 points. Statistically, it's one the best defenses in the 36-year history of the program.

"They are playing unbelievably," Coach Bitto says. "I don't have to worry too much about them."

The victory has Carmel sitting on an 8-0 record. It's only happened three other times in school history. The last time, 2003, Carmel won the state championship.

Under the lights, the field is a mass of jubilation. Players celebrate with their classmates, coaches with each other and their families. Moms, dads, brothers, sisters, uncles, aunts, cousins, English and science teachers. All a unified mass. It's what makes fall Friday nights so extraordinary, so *esse singulari*.

Coach Bitto is holding court with reporters in the middle of the field.

"Wow, 8-0...who would have thought that?" asks Bill Pemstein, a reporter with the weekly *Pioneer Press*.

"I like it. I get to keep my job," Coach Bitto says.

"Is the AD going to fire you?" Pemstein asks.

"I'd have to fire myself," Coach Bitto says with a chuckle. His son, Jack, is standing to his left.

"Dad, I accidentally hit my brother below his belt," Jack says.

"Well, don't hit your brother in the privates anymore," Coach Bitto says without moving his head.

"How do you get ready for a team you haven't seen?" asks Kevin Reiterman, sports editor of the *Pioneer Press*.

He's referring to Carmel's final regular season opponent, Elder Catholic, which plays in Ohio.

"It's hard to match-up unless you see them live, although we don't see a lot of teams live anymore, as everyone plays on Friday nights. It's hard to get team speed and size on tape," Coach Bitto says.

"Is this the first time you've gone out of state?"

"It's the first time my team has."

~

Amidst the chaos on the field stands breathless linebacker LaRon Biere. Coach Potempa gave him more first-team reps in Tuesday's practice, and Biere responded by having one of his best games of the season. He finished with three tackles and played with poise and discipline. At times this season, he's drifted in practice, not always given consistent reps. This has translated to the games when Biere runs too far up the field or doesn't fill the right gap. Carmel's defense is based on players executing specific assignments on each play. Often, that assignment isn't designed for a player to make a tackle. It's about creating open space to allow a teammate to make the tackle.

Tonight, Biere's stellar play was more about sacrifice than statistics.

"You know, I may not go somewhere and play at a great place in college. I may not do much, but this is great for my first senior start, to win the conference, and just an amazing feeling and I know all the seniors are with me on that. It is just amazing, just being a part of this. So much drive. It's all the inspiration I need for anything," Biere says before being swallowed up by the frenzied crowd.

Linebacker Luke Venegoni hit plenty of Dons on this night. His 10 tackles mean that for the sixth time in eight games, he recorded double-digits. He was a beast. Venegoni is still on the field, being interviewed by a reporter. His head is wrapped in a black scarf. This is his signature game-day look, the cloth extending from the top of his head to just above his eyebrows.

Before the game, in a ceremony on the field, the school admitted his brother Mark—the quarterback on that 2003 team—into the Hall of Fame.

"That was awesome," Luke says. "He worked really hard back then. His high school career made him successful. I'm happy for him. He's my leader."

Mark and John Venegoni, the boys' father, were in their Baker Stadium seats that night. They could occasionally be heard over the normal rhythmic cadence of crowd noise.

"You have to pick it up, 37!" Mark could be heard shouting at one point during the game. "Let's go! Hit somebody!"

The game has been over for 10 minutes. Fresh sweat beads still leak down the linebacker's dark forehead and cheeks. His piercing pupils appear like caramel-colored sand dunes. He's about to be pulled into the swarm.

Luke turns his head behind, and then back again.

"I always have to live up to their expectations, to please them, to do better than them," Luke says. "It feels better to do better than them."

And then he's lost in the crowd.

CHAPTER EIGHTEEN

RAISING LARON

Kids say the darndest things. Whatever pops in their head, out it comes. No filter. We laugh at their naiveté, cry at their sweetness. Often scold their boldness.

"Ma, when am I going to change to white like you?"

This was the question second-grader LaRon Biere posed one afternoon in the family kitchen. Earlier that day at school, there was a discussion on parents. Who are your parents? Where do they come from? What do they look like? LaRon asked his teacher, "My mother and father are white. Why am I black?"

Now he was asking Marion when he was going to look like her.

"It's not going to happen," Marion said. "You are black and it's a beautiful color."

Being a child, he accepted his adopted mother's honest answer.

At that point, he was officially LaRon Biere. It took three years, but the adoption had gone through. Marion was relieved, as she feared that at any time he'd be taken away. During the adoption process, the natural mother, the father or another family member often will emerge and claim a child. There also can be innocuous, bureaucratic reasons hopeful adoptive parents never officially become moms and dads. In Jim and Marion's case, every six weeks Catholic Charities would send someone out to inspect the house, checking the furnace or the light bulbs, looking for something, anything that might indicate they were unfit to adopt.

"Why does this matter? Can't they see this is the best home for him?" Marion would say to Jim.

"They just have to do what they have to do," Jim would say.

With LaRon, no one stepped forward. He had tested negative for HIV. He was free to develop into a normal boy. He soon took up judo and became a rising star. Marion and Jim would take him to tournaments all over the Midwest and Florida. He discovered a talent for writing poetry, and a few of his poems were published in the school's literary magazine. And he was becoming a Catholic, baptized at St. Bede's Church. This was dearest to Marion's heart, a turning point for the family. The entire family came to witness this sacrament before God. Marion's face beamed that day. My how far her sick little baby had come.

LaRon was their son, Marion and Jim's. No relative or adoption official would knock on the door in the middle of the night and whisk him away. But the everyday reality—a black boy being raised by white parents in an insular, homogenized community—was challenging.

There were small moments. Like the trip to the car dealership. They had an appointment for first thing in the morning, but when the clock struck 11 a.m., the car still had not been serviced. Marion grabbed LaRon and left. At restaurants or at the grocery store, there were occasional long stares. At his kindergarten graduation, all of his classmates got a hug from the principal. All except LaRon. She was furious.

In grade school, there were taunts on the playground. In second grade a group of kids bullied LaRon, saying he couldn't play with them because he looked different. One of his friends called him a bad name and LaRon pushed him to the ground. A fight ensued. It was the early 2000s and the school was dealing with racial integration for the first time. LaRon was the only black child attending.

When Marion heard of these abuses, her response was ferociously protective. She would jump in the car and drive to the school.

"This behavior is unacceptable," she would tell exasperated officials. "How are you letting this happen?"

She and Tom would talk to LaRon about the incidents. He was quiet and shy in grade school. They believed this was a defense mechanism, a way of coping with the anger simmering inside. It was important he not internalize his feelings, but resorting to violence was not the right way to express them, either. Finding middle ground was difficult.

"Even though they are mean to you, try and get to know your classmates. Approach them and be comfortable being yourself," Tom would say to LaRon. "If they can look beyond the color of your skin, they will see how great you are."

~

Marion was a realistic person. She had gone to the classes offered by Catholic Charities. She listened when they said how interracial adoptions could be formidable, laborious. They told stories of American couples adopting Vietnamese children. Isolated from their culture, many children grew up to become angry adults. Marion took all of this to heart.

Things got better at school. Marion loved the religious education LaRon was receiving. He was learning about Jesus, developing a foundation of spirituality, a consciousness about his place in the universe. Nothing was more important.

But the accumulation of incidents had a lingering effect. It forced Marion to question if it was best to stay in a predominately white area. Her and Jim talked of moving. They would include Tom in these conversations.

"Is this the right situation for him? Should we find an area more integrated?" Marion asked of Jim and Tom while seated in the living room of the family home after dinner.

"What about his education? Will that be affected if we move?" Jim said.

The decision had to be made with high school in mind, which LaRon would soon be starting.

They needed to find an environment where LaRon could expand his spiritual footprint, where not only he would be embraced, but where the family would be accepted for who *they* were.

Marion knew of such a place. In her heart, she believed it to be where her son belonged.

~

LaRon is good at analyzing people. He likes to shape them up, figure out their angle, get inside their head. Where are they coming from? Can I trust them? He likes to talk to new people, but he's not completely giving of himself at first. Will this person slow me down? LaRon can't be slowed down. He's got places to go, things to do. People to see.

Within these hallways, sound is sparse. Candle wax drips audibly.

It's Matt's turn to talk. LaRon writes down something Matt says in his notebook.

"Sometimes I'm afraid to be who I am because you might not like who I am."

He's talking about wearing masks. How we all do.

There was this time at a school dance. LaRon was talking to a girl. Another guy didn't like that he was talking to this girl. So he called LaRon a nigger. Not to his face, but to a group of other kids. LaRon's friend, Tyler, overheard. He walked over to LaRon and said, "this dude, he called you a nigger." It was the first time he remembers hearing that word, but knew it was bad.

LaRon went over to confront the kid.

"Were you talking about me?"

"Yeah," the kid said.

LaRon punched him in the chest.

Marion had always taught him to do the right thing, to look out for others. That's what he felt he was doing. This kid was a bully. Someone had to stand up to him. If LaRon had just cried about it, said nothing, what's to stop this kid from saying that word to somebody else?

If you are not going to stand up for yourself, then call me, dammit! I sure as hell will. Somebody's got to make a move. The school, my classmates, they all deserve better. That's what my mom would want. To live my life for other people.

That's why she wasn't all that mad about what happened. She knew his heart was in the right place. On drives to and from school, Marion talked to LaRon about how people would look down on him.

"If someone is injured, you have to help them," Marion said. "You have to be strong, stronger than them."

Those are times LaRon misses most. When Marion would talk to him about everything. School, teachers, his friends. His future. If something bad happened, like at the dance, she'd tell him what she thought. Straight up. Honest. But then she'd get over it. Let it go. Move on. She trusted the message was heard. And LaRon loved how Marion had so much faith in him.

She had worked all of those years at the clinic, after all. She saw people come in at the lowest point, only to leave with hope. She believed people could change. She had to. Otherwise, why would she have done what she did?

But the anger scared her. LaRon knew that. The older he got, the harder it was to control. Like at the dance. Or that time a girl discarded LaRon for someone else. Rejection from girls always hurt LaRon deeply, sending him into an emotional tailspin. It would often lead to him making poor choices. Then there was the time he and a friend were buying energy drinks online at a discount. LaRon would sell them to athletes at school for a profit. Marion found the drink cans and poured all of them out. When LaRon saw the empty cans, he flew into a rage. He tossed a chair across his bedroom. He punched the wall so hard, he broke his hand. He was screaming, crying. And while he wailed away, he realized something about himself.

He couldn't for the life of him figure out what he was so mad about.

Listening to Matt, it starts to make sense to LaRon. Sometimes, he does wear a mask.

∼

A clock ticks in the hall. Next to its swinging pendulum, on the wall, is a plaque. It reads: "This clock does more than mark the passing of time ... We touch our beginnings and face the future with confidence."

Chris stands in front of a lectern. He starts talking.

"Getting to know God is like getting to know any other person. It takes time and energy," he says. "God is the almighty bookkeeper. He keeps track of all the good I do and all the bad."

A piece of paper is passed around the room. Words from scripture are printed. It's from The Gospel of John.

God sent his messenger, a man named John, who came to tell people about the light, so that all should hear the message and believe. He himself was not the light; he came to tell about the light. This was the real light—the light that comes into the world and shines on all people.

The Word was in the world, and though God made the world through him, the world did not recognize him. He came to his own country, but his own people did not receive him. Some, however, did receive him and believed in him; so he gave them the right to become God's children. They did not become God's children by natural means, that is, by being born as the children of a human father; God himself was their Father.

The Word became a human being and, full of grace and truth, lived among us. We saw his glory, the glory of the one and only Son, who came from the Father, full of grace and truth.

After he reads the gospel, Chris asks the group to write down four questions.

How does God reveal himself?

What is he saying to me?

What is he asking me to do?

What is my response?

LaRon thinks about the questions and what Chris is saying. There were so many good times. Especially the holidays. The Christmas party at his brother Pat's house. The entire family would get together, play secret Santa. The grab bag, where everyone would pick a number, then take out their gift. What LaRon remembers is how as soon as one of his brothers or sisters or cousins would open their gift, everyone else wanted it more than the one they had. There were always shenanigans around the presents, a cousin trying to steal another cousin's toy. All playful, in good fun. He loved it whenever he got a new snowboard or video game. If anyone tried to take those away from him, LaRon might show them a few judo tricks he learned as a kid. He can still hear the laughter.

It wasn't the same this Christmas. Not without her.

~

How does God reveal Himself?

"Any experience in life that is meaningful and good can be considered an experience of communicating with God and prayer," Chris says.

LaRon never thought about if people knew about him. About where he came from. It never felt like he had to. But there were times when they acted like they knew.

Like Mrs. Lester, Logan's mom. She would always bring stuff. After practice. Her son Steve went to the Air Force Academy so she brought a sweatshirt from the school. LaRon remembers the shirt's sharp blue and silver colors. And the cookies. God, how he loved the cookies.

"Make sure your dad gets some, OK? Don't eat all of them before you get home," Mrs. Lester would say when handing another tray to him. LaRon would walk over to Matt's car before he drove home.

"I can't believe she keeps doing this," LaRon said. "She's so nice."

How did she know?

And Mrs. Venegoni. The picture frame she gave him. It contained the newspaper article where LaRon talked about his blood brothers and sisters. About how he knew they were alive somewhere.

How did she know?

Or that Saturday morning at the Carrs'. Mr. C had made breakfast. The *Daily Herald* article, the one where LaRon talked about Marion, was on the counter in the kitchen. Matt, Ryan, Ricky and Brian read it first. Then LaRon came up from the basement. He was always the last one up. He took the article and sat on the sofa. As tears slowly trickled down his cheeks, Mr. C walked over and gave him a hug. Then Matt, then Ryan.

"We love you," they all said.

How did they know?

How does God reveal Himself? What is He saying to me? What is He asking me to do?

"You can communicate with God by how the people you love show their love," Chris says.

As he listens to Chris, LaRon stares straight ahead, lost in his thoughts.

Chris stops talking. Only the pendulum clock can be heard.

CHAPTER NINETEEN

ROAD TRIP

IT'S THE MONDAY AFTER THE NOTRE DAME GAME. The last week of the regular season. Carmel head coach Andy Bitto and assistants are fastidious about routine, but today, routine is taking a holiday.

The old gym is filled with players from all levels—freshman, sophomore and varsity. They are lined up in rows. There is no space on the gym floor.

Butts on the hardwood, their eyes stare straight ahead. Senior football players sit on chairs lined up against a wall. Each is called to speak.

First up is Jake Klahs, a wide receiver and special teams player:

"You may not know this but I moved here from Columbus. That's one of the hardest things anyone should ever have to do. I spent my entire life there. My best friend, everything. I came into this situation knowing no one. I can legitimately say that. Now I can legitimately say I love all of you. That's what it's all about. That's what you are here for."

Quarterback Brian Serio:

"What I can say is don't take it for granted. The years go by pretty fast. I remember coming in my freshman year not knowing any of these guys and now they are all my best friends. Second, you get out what you put in. It's really important to work hard and do plyos [plyometrics] in the summer and it sucks, but you have to do it. You may not be starting now, but you never know what might happen."

Linebacker Luke Venegoni:

"Carmel football has been in my family for a long time. My older brother won state. My other brother went pretty far. I go to my brothers for anything and tell them what's on my mind. I always had to meet their standards and do better than them. It made an impression on me. I wouldn't have wanted it any other way because that makes it better, being able to go home and tell my brothers, 'I'm better than you. We won state and I'm going to beat your ass.'"

Defensive lineman Jake Larson:

"I was in seventh grade and I didn't know about Carmel at all. I was at a baseball tournament, so we are staying at this hotel and Coach May was there. We were in the lobby and Coach May said, 'Check this out.' It's a ring that says '2003 state champs.' I said, 'Damn.' That week I was like, 'Mom and Dad, can I go to Carmel?' I started going to the camps. And here I am today. Here's the thing—it was those guys in 2003 working their asses off to win a state championship and that's why I'm here today. It makes me think every time I go out on that field I'm not only working for myself, my teammates and my coaches, I'm also affecting the lives of somebody out there."

As Larson speaks, the mass of bodies in T-shirts and shorts stare back. What they are listening to is an annual tradition at Carmel started by former head coach Michael Fitzgibbons and continued by Coach Bitto—the senior talks. Always the Monday of the final regular season game, each senior stands up in front of the room and gives a speech. It's a chance for them to reflect on their football experience and share those ruminations with their younger classmates.

"Our seniors really drive every season we have," Coach Bitto explained earlier. "We want them to take a minute or two and talk about what Carmel football has meant to them and impart that on the lower-level kids so they would be inspired to have the same experience. It's an affirmation of what hard work and dedication can do. When you can impart that on younger people, you have done a great service."

There are 31 seniors on this season's team, and almost all give speeches. One of the last talks was that from Fitz's son, Michael.

"What I would say is take advantage of the time you have here. Carmel football has been a part of my life since I was born. I was a ball boy in the third grade and couldn't wait to be one of the cool kids on the field. Now I'm up here, standing, talking to all of you. Remember all these times. Take advantage of it because it flies by, and before you know it you will be up here."

Michael walked into his dad's office and started messing with stuff. He messed with his dad's desk. He messed with his dad's computer. Frankly, he just messed with his dad.

"That sweater is quite slimming," he said sarcastically of his father's choice of clothing that day.

"What are you so nervous about?" Fitz fired back. "Where are you going?"

Michael Fitzgibbons, the football player, took several brisk steps toward the door. Before he left, he turned around and said, "I'm going to throw up."

"What are you getting so worked up about? It's just a football game."

Later, Michael talked about his dad's less than sympathetic manner toward his game-day anxiety.

"I get real nervous before games. He'll make fun of me for being so nervous. That really helps me a lot, as he'll make fun of me for overreacting so much about something so small as a football game. He makes it seem like it isn't that big a deal, like it isn't life or death, even though I think it is."

As a kid, football didn't make Michael Fitzgibbons sick to his stomach. His family lived on McKinley Avenue, in Mundelein, 10 houses from campus. Fitz would walk to work every day. Afternoons, Michael would get off the bus from grammar school, Santa Maria Del Popolo, throw his backpack in the house, change clothes, and run as fast as he could to join his dad at practice. It was there, on those dusty fields, where the energetic child met his heroes. It was there he watched his father lead and coach them.

He envisioned a time when he would grow into a young man and be coached by his father. But his father had another son, a daughter and wife at home, and his priorities were with them. This was hard for a prepubescent to understand.

"I was so mad because I was looking forward to being able to play while he was the coach. He took time off as he wanted to spend more time with us, but I was selfish. I was like, 'We can spend more time on the football field!'"

When Michael finally enrolled at Carmel in 2007, he was hardly a football prodigy. He stood 5-6, weighing 135 pounds. No one knew where to play him. So the freshman coaches put him on the offensive line, at guard. "No one wants to play offensive line," Fitz said.

His sophomore year, he played tight end plus multiple positions on defense. But he didn't start. Fitz would walk into the coach's room that season and scurry out as fast as he could. Michael asked his father if he would talk to the coaches about why he wasn't playing.

"Nope. I'm not getting involved. That's not the parent I'm going to be. If you want answers, talk to the coaches yourself."

His junior year, 2009, a growth spurt shot Michael's height to well over 6-foot. Like his physical stature, his acumen for the game accelerated, as if the reservoir of wisdom built up from all those years shagging footballs as a wide-eyed Carmel ball boy finally burst open inside of him.

He was a good defensive player that season, playing in every snap after the first quarter of the first game. Fitz would go to the games and watch like any parent—proudly, his eyes fixated on his son's movements.

At the end of the 2009 season, Carmel's defensive coordinator unexpectedly quit. Dan Potempa, then a position coach, took over. Coach Bitto placed a call to Fitz to see if he could help out through the rest of the season. For the last regular season game, against Nazareth, there was Fitz, on the sidelines, as loud and boisterous as ever. Only now, his son was there with him. It was just the circumstance Michael Fitzgibbons, the boy, had desired. But Michael the teenager?

"It was the complete opposite of how I felt when I was five years old. I was mad," Michael said. "We had the same name but I was making my own name. I felt like him coming back he was trying to steal what I'd done."

Fitz knew his son might feel that way. He was a professional counselor, after all. He did not want his son to feel like his senior year was being hijacked by his father's presence. He talked about it with Bitto and Potempa.

"I never would have done it if he hadn't started his junior year. Wouldn't have happened," Fitz said. "But I knew he was going to play senior year and I wasn't coaching his position, so I had nothing to do with whether he played.

I didn't even want the misconception, 'Oh, you know he's playing because he's Fitz's son.'"

Although father and son talked about Fitz joining the 2010 coaching staff, it was August when the decision was sealed. Michael came home from a retreat. Two-a-day practices were starting in a few days. Fitz approached his son. He needed his blessing before he could officially say yes.

"Unlike when he came back and coached that Nazareth game, I was excited. I said, 'Hell yeah, you better take the job or I'm going to be mad at you again.' I knew how important my family was, and being able to join the family part and the football part—I mean, they were always joined because of who we are, but having him be an actual part of it, I felt luckier than I can imagine.

Now, every weekday at 3 p.m., Fitz leaves his day job as Carmel's ministry director, changes his shirt, pants and shoes, and races as fast as he can to Baker Stadium. He barks out instruction to his defensive lineman ("If you're getting double-teamed, don't just stand there! Rip inside or outside!"). His son, Michael, is just a short distance away, running through drills coached by Potempa, whom his father once coached and whom Michael idolized as a boy all those years ago.

"To watch him turn himself into such a good football player, that's one half of one percent," Fitz said. "To be with some of the best friends I'll ever have in the world and I'm watching them influence my son and I'm watching the influence occur first hand? I mean, that's a special thing. It's just a wonderful, wonderful gift."

~

About 10 years ago, Fitz became a published author. He wrote *My Senior Year*, a novel written from the perspective of a high school senior.

"The guy in the book had way more success with girls than I did," Fitz says with a laugh. "It's pure fiction. I sprinkled in pieces of my own perspective. It's a satire on how we expect so much of kids. We expect our kids to do so much, to learn so much, and be so much. They are running around acting like adults. But they are kids. That's my perspective."

If he were to write an updated version, Fitz says he'd include technological advances that have since become part of our daily lives. And that, according to him, has made our lives more enriching.

"I'd add cell phones. In the book, notes get passed in the hallway. It's weird," Fitz says. "I hear parents say, 'But we managed.' But we managed worse. This is so much better. I mean, were the good old days really good old days? Bullshit. Kids are basically the same. They adapt to their environment. I talk to my friends on the South Side and they tell me, 'Oh, I'm driving and I see the parks and they are empty. The kids are at home in the air conditioning playing video games.' I say that's because they are smart! They aren't in 103-degree weather trying to set a baseball diamond. They are online communicating with people all over the world rather than with their three buddies down the street playing baseball. I don't think better or worse is involved. It's just different."

Everyone has left the gymnasium. Fitz is standing alone. His phone beeps. It's a text message.

"Some people say texting is not a real conversation. But you know what? At least they are doing it," Fitz says. "I know that if I could have thought about what I was going to say, I would have had a lot more girlfriends."

∿

Among Chicago's many food staples—deep dish pizza, hot dogs with grilled onions and mustard, (hold the ketchup)—chili does not make the cut. And according to Carmel running backs coach Tom Young, no one can touch one Cincinnati restaurant version.

"You've got to try Skyline chili; it's the best in the world," Young has been saying after practice for a few weeks now. "It's spaghetti, chili and cheddar cheese. I don't know how they do it, but it's terrific."

There is a reason behind Young's evangelistic narrative. The Corsairs are closing out the regular season Saturday in Cincinnati against Elder Catholic. Elder is historically one of that city's best teams, having won a state title the same year Carmel won its only state championship.

This is a game hatched of necessity.

After the 2009 season, longtime East Suburban Catholic Conference member St. Joseph's left the conference. This left a hole in Carmel's 2010 schedule.

"We had no one to play the last week of the season," Coach Bitto said earlier.

His first preference was to play an in-state opponent. That option was soon off the table.

"Schedules were full or no one wanted to play us," Coach Bitto said.

Calls to schools in Wisconsin, Indiana and Michigan went nowhere. Finally, a call to Elder Catholic in Cincinnati was not only returned, but with good news—they had a schedule gap in late October.

Once Coach Bitto got school administrators to sign off on it, the game was put on the schedule.

"It took some work. But I think it will be a good experience for our kids and our community," he said.

Young has a personal interest in this game. He grew up in East Palestine, a small, conservative town resting in the northeast corner of Ohio. It only takes a few miles before a driver headed east along the main drag hits the Pennsylvania border. Its location makes it closer to Pittsburgh (50 miles) than Cincinnati (296 miles). That fact did not matter to Young when he was dodging defenders as a 5-10, 170-pound quarterback for the Bulldogs in the 1950s.

"I love Ohio and I love Ohio football," Young says over a bowl of chili (just kidney beans and ground beef—no spaghetti) at Grandma V's diner in Mundelein. "The type of game they play is very physical."

There wasn't much industry in East Palestine while Young was growing up, just ski shops and pottery stores. His dad was a laborer who worked at those stores, performing odd jobs. Young had one of his own—delivering milk. He made $15 a week making stops at doorsteps all over town.

"That was a lot of money back then. The problem was, I never saved it. We didn't have a car, so I would help buy gas for kids who did have cars."

There was a right way and a wrong way of doing things in the Young household. Grades were emphasized, and as long as Young got As and Bs, he could leave the house and spend his milk money.

"If I got a C, I wasn't going out until the next report card. It was a very strict upbringing as it was for my sisters and all my friends. I like to do things a certain way and that comes from how I grew up."

Young grew up in a community where football was the biggest game in town. In a town of 5,000, Young says they would draw as many as 3,000 on Friday nights. One contest stands out from his senior year, a moment that timestamps Young's strict sense of right and wrong. The Bulldogs were undefeated and playing rival Lewisville. The score was 13-6 just before the half.

"I was playing defensive back. I picked off a pass near the sidelines and ran it back 80 yards for a touchdown. But one of the referees called it back. We were going off the field for halftime and one of the kids went to me and said, 'Tom, your mom is on the field yelling at the ref.' I asked her after the game what she said and she wouldn't tell me. I can tell you this. She probably called him a rotten son-of-a-bitch."

Young chuckles at the memory, a smile broadening his furrowed, weather-beaten face. A gold-colored Carmel cap sits atop his head, covering an orderly combed crop of thinning gray hair.

"She was a very fiery lady, my mother. She went to every game. We ended up beating Lewisville 41-6 and made it to 10th in the state. That was my last game, as they had no playoffs back then."

All Young and his East Palestine teammates could do was imagine what it was like to play the state's big dogs.

"We compared ourselves to those schools but we never played them. And the thought of ever playing against a team like Cincinnati Moeller? It was like, 'Shucks, that will never happen.'"

But Saturday he will get his chance. More than 50 years after he left his hometown, Young is finally getting the game he never got to play.

"For it to finally come to fruition, I'm going to be emotional. I think I'll be OK on the way down there but..." his voice trails off. "Both my sisters still live there. One of them will be at the game, I told them it will be on iHigh [an online streaming service]. Listen, to get my older sister to watch it on a computer? That is pretty significant."

During his chats with the boys this week, Coach Bitto has sprinkled in "Coach Young is from Ohio" a few times.

"I think they know how important it is to me to play a team in Ohio," Young says. "I would never say, 'You have to win this game for me.' That's egotistical. We're 8-0. They are playing for themselves and each other first. But man. I'm hot to get there and hot to play."

As hot as a steaming bowl of Skyline Chili.

"It will be the best you've ever had," Young promises.

~

"A 15-year-old Amish boy and his father were in a large shopping mall. They were amazed by everything they saw, as it was the first time they had been inside any mall. Two shiny, silver walls that would move apart and then slide back together again especially struck them.

"The boy asked, 'What is it father?'

"The father, having never seen an elevator, responded, 'So, I have never seen anything like this in my life. I don't know what it is.'

"While the boy and his father were watching with amazement, a rather elderly, overweight woman moved up to the moving walls and pressed a button. The walls opened, and the lady walked between the doors into the small room. The walls closed. The boy and his father watched the small numbers above the walls light up sequentially.

"They continued to watch it until it reached the last number. Then the numbers began to light in reverse order. Finally, the walls opened again, and to their amazement, a gorgeous 24-year-old blond woman stepped out. The father, not taking his eyes off the young woman, grabbed his son by the arm and quietly said:

"Go get your mother."

Meet Mr. Saturday Morning, Father Pat Tonry.

Carmel is set to play Cincinnati Elder Catholic in four hours. The team is gathered in a ballroom inside a hotel eight miles from the Elder football stadium. The room serves as a makeshift chapel, with Father Tonry giving mass. His joke—while unexpected—hits the perfect note. The boys are relaxed, yet uncertain. Unfamiliarity is all around them. In the last 24 hours, many of them have taken the longest bus ride of their lives [330 miles]. They slept on a mattress that felt weird, or they had a roommate who snored or was texting his girlfriend all night. If routine is the currency of success, what they are now experiencing is the opposite. Throw in an octogenarian priest spinning a yarn about the Amish man and the elevator, and you could have emotional chaos. But instead, a peaceful opulence permeates the room.

Father Tonry may like to delve into poppycock and tomfoolery now and then but he has a day job. And that's to spiritually nourish the soul. His homily is back on point.

"In Rome there is a church called the Basilica of St. John Lateran. It's an immense church, and you look this way and it's just an immense mosaic. And a mosaic is a picture made up of tiny little pieces of stone. The mosaic itself is an immense picture of Jesus. And it has all these tiny pieces, and if one piece is missing, you notice. It's just not right. Every single little piece is necessary for the picture to be complete. And every piece is different. That's the way it is for a team. You have to have every little piece, and every little piece is important. That's what it is with a team. If a piece thinks it's not important, that piece does not connect.

"Carmel has a wonderful history and opportunity. Remember this year and continue the wonderful work you are doing. Dedicate yourselves to one another. Remember this—a team has been given a legacy of all of those who went before you. Some of your coaches here today played before you. Handle it with trust and honor and add your own special gift to that legacy so you can pass it along to others. You have no idea even now how this will influence your own lives."

Father Tonry is done with his sermon. As is tradition at chapel, Fitz asks everyone to reveal for whom they are playing the day's game:

"My brother."

"My family."

"My grandfather."

"Everyone injured on the team."

"My sister."

"My grandmother."

"Mom and dad and this team."

"My family and teammates."

"This team."

"My wife and kids."

"This experience."

When Father Tonry talked about the little pieces of stones that in unison make up Rome's Basilica of St. John Lateran, he could have been talking about the sign of peace. Only now, in this hotel ballroom on the outskirts of Cincinnati, we are witness not to a metaphoric edifice, but a living, breathing life force, its virility encapsulated by an act of brotherhood.

If Michelangelo were in the room, he would reach for his paintbrush.

"When you see high school boys do the sign of peace before a game, that is the most intense sign of peace you can ever imagine. Those are real hugs. You are building a team," Fitz said earlier in the year.

As they embrace during the sign of peace, a few of the boys say words of encouragement to one another.

"Good luck today."

"Peace be with you."

"Kick some butt."

The boys line up to take communion. The sacrament is served by three men—Father Tonry; Brandon Paluch, a Carmel graduate who lives in the area and is going through what the church calls "discernment," or thinking about becoming a priest; and Coach Jerry Rejc. One by one, they receive the Body of Christ.

A few weeks ago, defensive backs coach Tom Kelly shared a memory from before the state title game in 2003, about receiving communion from Jack Simmons, Carmel's all-state tight end.

"There is something really right about that," he said.

Mass ends. Everyone files out of the ballroom to board the bus to the stadium.

"It's time to go play a football game," Tom Young says.

~

Jim Biere could sit and watch his son all day. Whatever sport or activity, it doesn't matter. He's been doing it since LaRon was five. When he took up judo. Oh man, was he good. A natural, his coach said. No fear. That had its drawbacks, of course. Like when LaRon used to climb the evergreen trees in the family's backyard. The biggest one was 40 feet high! The little daredevil once took a Dixie cup and stuck it between two branches high up. Can you believe that? He wanted to show his mother what he could do. She was beside herself.

"What are we going to do with this child?" Marion would ask Jim. "He's a risk-taker, that one."

"I know, I know," Jim would say. "He likes to go his own way."

Who else would play drums in an adult rock band? He was in grade school. There were a bunch of local guys who liked to play together at resorts. Tony Schoenberger was the front man. He was the husband of LaRon's grade school teacher, Colleen. They played '50s and '60s rock 'n' roll. Elvis Presley, Jerry Lee Lewis, Everly Brothers. Tony encouraged LaRon to play the drums. Before you knew it, he was playing with the guys in front of crowds at bars and restaurants around Fox Lake. "Wipe Out" by the Surfaris was one of LaRon's favorites. Or the classic "Rockin' Robin." He never took lessons. LaRon could never sit long enough for that. He just had an ear for music. It was his way of talking to the universe and hearing it talk back to him.

If Marion were here, how they would share a laugh at the memory.

Jim is thinking of her as he leans forward, resting his forearm on his leg. He's in Cincinnati for the game. Sitting next to him, his daughter Ann snaps pictures. How sharp LaRon looks in his white number 25 jersey—brown pants and gold helmet sequestered from the busy fall colors that surround him. It's good to have Ann here. Grown up with a family of her own, Jim doesn't get much alone time with Ann or any of his adult children. He'd been looking forward to the windshield time for months. During the drive, they called Mary, Ann's sister, in Washington, D.C. He always called Mary after games to give the score and fill her in on how her little brother LaRon played.

This season has been so much fun. For home games, Jim would get to the stadium well before the sophomore game at 5 p.m., just to reserve a section of seats. It was needed, as often, several family members would come to each home game. Brothers, sisters, aunts and uncles, all sitting together, all watching LaRon.

Jim is so anxious about this game, his stomach dances with butterflies. On the drive down, just a few miles after they crossed the Ohio border in the car, Jim told his soft-footed daughter to step on the gas. Intolerant of out-of-town speeders, a state trooper pulled Ann over and handed her a ticket.

"How's that for father-daughter bonding?" he said to Ann with a chuckle as they started back on the road.

"Dad, we won't forget this for a long time," Ann said, masking her bemusement.

It's almost game time. If only Marion were here to see. How proud she'd be of LaRon. He was so sick when she took him home from the hospital that day, years ago. All of those sleepless nights. The adoption. The hurtful looks from strangers. Their own battles, when LaRon became a teenager. Gosh would they fight. Like cats and dogs. Some days it was awfully hard. But she never gave up. Not Marion. Not on LaRon. She fought so hard to make her son, their son, have faith in himself, to believe he could accomplish anything. To trust God. He had a plan. Open your heart and let Him in.

Knowing this about Marion, knowing the sacrifices she made, there is something Jim doesn't *understand*, one thing that still pains his heart.

Why hadn't God granted his wife just one more wish?

～

Elder's football field is nestled in the Price Hill neighborhood of Cincinnati, five miles west of the city. The high school campus shares the same streets as modest two-story, single-family homes. Peyton Manning could bounce a ball off a shingled rooftop if he threw it from the 50-yard line. The school refers to its stadium as "The Pit," calling it one of the "premier high school facilities in the country." It seats 10,000 and in 2001, *USA Today* called it one of the 10 best places to watch a high school football game. Elder's fans sit on grey slabs of concrete on the east side of the stadium, extending around the south end zone—in contrast to the conventional steel bleachers found at most high school facilities. The horseshoe shape, combined with the fact the stands are just five yards from the sidelines, means the stadium amplifies sound, creating an atmosphere equal to that of a small college.

The purple jersey and pants of the home team provide a startling contrast to Carmel's brown (pants) and white (jersey). Boosting the inverse chromaticity are the fans. They are decked out in mulberry-stained tops and bottoms (mostly shorts as it's a warmer-than-usual October day), reflecting the school colors. Fans fill out most of the rows behind the home bench. But the atmosphere is detached, complacent. More appropriate for a Yanni concert in the park than a football game. Elder is having an uncharacteristically poor season, losing five of its seven games. That could be the reason for the purple placidity. Or maybe nervousness over the unfamiliarity with these option-running boys from Illinois.

On the other side of The Pit, the visiting stands are peppered in brown and gold. Scott and Beth Carr, parents of injured senior Matt Carr, along with Bruce and Diane Cappis, parents of running back Ryan Cappis, rented an RV, drove into Cincinnati, and parked the vehicle in the stadium lot. Brian and Tim Serio's older brother Mike, a running back on the 2003 championship team, flew in from New York to watch his little brothers play. Coach Bitto's elocution about bringing Carmel's tradition to Ohio is anything but hyperbole.

In the visitors' locker room, Coach Bitto gives his weekly pre-game speech. He's standing on a bench, looking down on the boys as they kneel in front of him.

"I heard from a lot of people this week. I heard from guys I played with —guys who played before me and guys I've coached. There are thousands of people who live vicariously through you. There are thousands of people in our community who live vicariously through this team. But guess what? This journey is not theirs, it's yours. You are the guys that have earned it. And you know something else? We bring all of that tradition, our tradition, to this state of Ohio. What makes this more special is, we bring that tradition and we're 8-0. Let's show them how we do things, how our brand of football is played. You are the guys that have earned this moment!"

Minutes later on the field, Coach Young watches warm ups and shags waywardly thrown balls. He spots his sister, Mert Chamberlain, in the stands. She sits on the Carmel side. He walks over to where she is. They share a laugh. He re-enters the field.

His eyes moisten.

"I can barely talk right now. For 10 years since I was around Carmel I have wanted to do this. I just want us to play up to our capability, make them know that we can play football."

~

It's the drive of the second half and the score 14-14. An Elder player catches a pass near the Carmel sidelines at the Panthers' 40-yard marker. Sophomore safety Sean Brennan tries to bring him down, but the ball carrier dodges the tackle, spinning away toward the Carmel sidelines. Stumbling at the 45, he almost falls down at midfield. But he regains his balance and sprints into Carmel territory. Defensive back Ricky Acosta and linebacker Tyler Lees rapidly gain ground, but it is linebacker Luke Venegoni who emerges from the backside and brings down the runner out of bounds at the Carmel 40.

As the pile of purple and brown pants separates, a pair of white pants remain on the ground: those of Young. When the Elder player hit the ground, Young was standing right in front of him. He tried to move out of the way, but when the player's right shoulder nicked Young's right leg, the momentum knocked him backwards. His head hit the ground violently.

Lying supine on the ground, both hands clutch either side of his head. He says nothing, his face wearing a look of anguish and disorientation. Carmel trainer Dan Henrichs gets Young to his feet and onto a cart. Over and over, Young repeats, "I'm fine, I'm fine. How are we doing?"

The cart drives away. Carmel stops the Panthers and the score remains even at 14.

~

The Corsairs hit a big pass play for a touchdown at the end of the first half but otherwise can't get much going in the passing game. This is nothing new, as going into the Elder game, the Corsairs had completed just 19 of 38 passes all season. What's surprising is how Carmel can't move the ball on the ground. Elder is as advertised—big, strong and physical. Carmel has not been hit this hard all season. But Panthers are also an intelligent defense, accurate with almost every read and filling almost every gap. And when they tackle, it's akin to watching video of crash test dummies. Only this is in real time. It's now easy to see what Young was mythologizing about. Ohio football *is* different.

When it's their turn, Venegoni, Lees, Jake Larson, Kevin Cox, LaRon Biere and Michael Fitzgibbons and the rest of the Corsairs' defense apply their own smackology on the Panthers, East Suburban Catholic Conference-style. The unit matches Elder hit for hit. Blocks are crisp, tackles clean; pad on pad. This is football at its most basic: brutal and beautiful all at once.

With just over a minute remaining in the game, the score is the same as it's been since halftime, 14-14. Elder has the ball on the Carmel 33. Panthers quarterback Ben Gramke tries to hit a seam route up the middle of the field. Playing deep safety, Fitzgibbons reads it perfectly and picks off the pass. Carmel gets the ball back on its eight-yard line with 1:06 left in the game. Coach Bitto is content to play for overtime.

Only his fullback makes a costly mistake.

Offensive coordinator Ben Berg calls for an inside hand off to Jordan Kos. It's the kind of play a coach calls when the intention is to run out the clock. Kos takes the hand off from Brian Serio and runs through a hole up the middle. A few yards beyond the line of scrimmage, an Elder linebacker hits Kos. All he has to do is fall down with the ball safely cradled in his arms, and the clock runs closer to double zeros. But upon contact, Kos tries to fight for extra yards, and he's carrying the ball with just the left, away from his body, as opposed to a more secure two-handed grip. Before he hits the turf, his left knee knocks the ball out of his own hand and sends it rolling up the field. An Elder player falls on the loose football. It's first and 10 Elder from the Carmel 30-yard line.

The Corsairs' defense, impenetrable for most of the game, can't stop the Panthers' offense one last time. Three plays later, the Panthers score the go-ahead touchdown. It's 21-14 Elder with 28 seconds left. Carmel gets the ball back, but there are no miracles tonight. And just like that, the perfect season is over.

Postgame handshakes complete, players and coaches dejectedly gather at midfield. Each coach says a few words to the team. This is the first time they've had to do so after a loss.

Tim Schrank: "This chapter is over. A new one begins Monday. We'll be focused. I know you will be, too."

Berg: "Here's the thing: Let it hurt for a few days. We are still a good football team. We didn't execute and play with enough poise at the key moments today. We got down 14-0, and you could have rolled over but you didn't do that."

Jim Rejc: "Let's use this as a learning opportunity. We have five games left if we decide to do that. Let's be sure Coach Young is OK."

Coach Bitto: "That's why we play sports—is adversity. It didn't go the way we wanted. However, if you take adversity and don't get better, you're a turd. If you take this game and do the same damn things, you are a turd. But I think there's a lot of gumption on this team. And I know next week we'll play 10 times better, especially on offense. The key is to keep this experience going. It should hurt. I'm proud of you because you played as hard as I've asked you all year."

Bitto speaks last. Like all the coaches, he strikes the right chord between disappointment and disaster. It's appropriate to be upset. But it's just one game, not the end of the season. The Illinois state playoffs are next.

∾

After the coaches' brief speeches, players quickly head to the visiting locker room, grab their stuff and go outside to greet waiting family members. After most of the boys exit, the locker room is filled with tape, food wrappings and other random droppings. It's up to the coaches to clean up all the trash. And they do—when you stay at someone's house, you make the bed. This is all part and parcel of the coaches' deeply ingrained moral code. Duty, honor, and obligation are always top of mind, front and center. Quite simply, cleaning up your own mess is the polite thing to do.

Running back Michael Panico is one of the last players to linger.

"Some guys are trying to forget about it, but I can't," Panico says, gingerly removing the harness protecting his still-injured left shoulder. "It was brutal. We could not move the ball at all. They started blitzing the corner, and we didn't see it. Not on film, anywhere. They weren't fast. But they hit so hard. It was a painful game. I'm hurting right now."

Coach Bitto overhears him.

"Michael, I know you're hurting. Most guys wouldn't even be out there. You've been a great team player for us," he says. Coach Bitto then attempts to lighten the mood with another Justin Bieber reference. "Are your vocal chords hurting, too?"

Panico smiles wearily, too tired and frustrated to continue the familiar narrative. He reaches for his gym bag.

"Where's Coach Young?" he asks.

"He's in the hospital," Coach Bitto says.

"We've got to go get him."

∾

On the bus, Coach Bitto's been taking calls from reporters about the game.

"We just shot through the booger," he says. "I'm kind of hoping they are mad for a couple of days then we'll reassess.

"Somewhere in the third quarter, our running backs coach Tom Young got nailed and went to the hospital. He's got to get out of the way faster. I don't think he knew what day it was after it happened. I don't think he knew he was from Ohio."

Coach Bitto is still talking when Rejc's cell rings.

"Hello?" he says. There's a pause. "Coach Young! We're coming for you! We're about two miles away."

Coach Bitto is done with his interview and overhears Rejc.

"Hey, tell Tom we lost the game and it's his fault."

Rejc laughs and hangs up.

"How's he doing?" Coach Bitto asks.

"He got his head checked out but I think he's OK."

A few minutes later, the bus pulls into the hospital parking lot. Young is spotted. He's on his feet, about 50 yards away under the awning by the hospital's front entrance.

"He's not in a wheelchair," Coach Bitto says. He's the first to jump out when the bus comes to a stop. Everyone else follows, all 30 passengers. It's a much more sparse group than on the way down. Most of the players chose to ride home with their parents.

Young approaches the bus walking slower than normal.

"You all right coach?" Ryan Cappis asks.

"The doctor looked me over. I'm fine. I'm just mad we lost the darn football game."

"It's your fault. I'm blaming you. I have to blame somebody," Coach Bitto says with a smile. "So, you're OK?"

"My knee hurts but otherwise I feel fine."

"Now it's the knee. That's what got hurt? Is that the bad clot leg?" Coach Bitto says.

"No, this is the clot leg," he says, pointing to his left. "It's the other one. How the heck did we lose that football game?"

"We gave it away, Tom. We gave it away," Coach Bitto says.

Everybody files back on the bus, relieved their coach is all right.

~

It won't be long before the state of Ohio is a distant image reflecting from the bus's rear-view mirror. Soon after the vehicle pulls onto I-74, a peaceful solitude washes over. *Invincible*, the movie about a bartender who earns a roster spot with the Philadelphia Eagles, is shown on the way home.

A few hours later, Brian Serio and Cappis sit next to each other, in good spirits, talking quietly.

"We have to forget about this one but remember what it felt like for the rest of the season," Serio says. "We're still in good shape."

He's asked if any positive can be taken from a loss like that.

"Maybe. Just to know how it feels to lose and be motivated to not lose again. We can't lose again or we're done."

Just as Serio finishes, Cappis squeezes his chest with his right hand. "Oh, man. My ribs are so sore."

Serio glances at his tired buddy. "We need to stay healthy."

But they aren't. The Corsairs were beat up on the way to Cincinnati and head home looking like a traveling infirmary. The loss knocks Carmel down from a potential No. 1 playoff seed to No. 3. What that means is they will most likely face a more challenging opponent in the first round of the post-season beginning next weekend.

Coach Bitto is done with his post-game media obligations. He sits in the front row, talking with coaches Rejc and Berg. The disappointment from the loss is still in his voice, but neither he nor the coaches are dwelling on the missed opportunity.

"I know these guys," he says of the boys. "They will practice extremely hard this week. I've never had a team play poorly after a big loss."

The conversation turns to Young. He's across the aisle, attempting to fall asleep.

"You know, Tom was crying on the sidelines before the game," Coach Bitto says. He pauses and looks through his seat's window. All there is to see is the benign concrete of the Ohio Turnpike, reflected by the endless row of highway lights.

"Life goes by pretty fast, doesn't it?"

Someone asks Young if he wants to turn back, reminding the weary coach of a promised stop for Skyline Chili.

Young smiles a sheepish grin. "Next time. Next time."

∾

Young slept a good portion of the ride home. After stubbornly refusing to admit the obvious—"Don't say concussed or any derivative of that word!"—he later admitted to suffering a "mild head wound."

∾

For Christmas, Ann Biere gave her father a framed picture of the two of them sitting in the stands at The Pit in Cincinnati. The inscription read:

"Speeding ticket, $75. Hotel, $99. Spending time with dad, priceless."

CHAPTER TWENTY

FUMBLED OPPORTUNITY

IT'S MONDAY AFTERNOON, Carmel's first practice since the Elder loss. Friday night, the Corsairs host Elgin High School in the first round of the 7A Illinois High School Association playoffs.

The boys are in the weight room, having completed their Monday weight-lifting session. They sit on benches and on the floor. Everybody listens to Coach Bitto announce the Corsairs who made the all-conference team. Carmel had 10, the most of any school. The almost 20-percent monopoly of players reflects the team's superiority.

On offense: quarterback Brian Serio, fullback Jordan Kos, running back Michael Panico, offensive lineman Logan Lester and tight end Patrick Mulroy. On defense: linebackers Luke Venegoni and Tyler Lees, defensive backs Ricky Acosta and Mike Fitzgibbons and lineman Michael Cohen.

"They are voted on by the coaches. It's an individual award but it's also a team award," Coach Bitto says. "There are probably four or five guys that should be on the team but there's a maximum of 10. This is certainly not an indication of the value of the players who didn't make it. It's just a numbers-crunch thing."

He acknowledges players who could have made the team: defensive lineman Jake Larson, safety/running back Brian Brennan, offensive lineman Michael Dyer, center Shane Toub, kicker Steven O'Block and linebackers Kevin Cox and LaRon Biere. An argument could be made for the entire starting defense. The unit's 51 points allowed is the fewest by a conference team since the 1995 season.

With the exception of the conference it plays in—the Upstate 8—Friday's opponent, the Elgin Maroons, are a complete unknown. This makes film study an essential part of the week's preparation. What scheme do they run on offense and defense? How well does their offensive line block? Is the quarterback a runner or thrower? Or both? Within the familiar confines of conference play, these questions are often answered before a single second of film is viewed. But not now. The difference between advancing to the next round or going home is which team can best grasp its opponent's tendencies, quickly design a game plan, then execute that game plan. The coaches—always fastidious about film study—adopt a more persnickety tone in preparation for the "second season."

There's nothing finicky about Coach Bitto's short speech to the boys in the weight room before they split up to watch film. It is an old-fashioned verbal butt-kicking.

"There is nothing in my make-up that makes me think losing a game is an educational process. All the way home, everyone's giving us bananas and candy—we had so much food I gained 47 pounds. You can have all the fun and candy you want, but we still lost the game. And we lost the game because we didn't execute the times we needed to execute, especially on offense. Now if you're OK with that, we'll go right into the playoffs and get our asses knocked off in the first round. Because everybody is good.

"And there's always an excuse. 'Oh, we drove six hours and it was a Saturday game and they wore purple and I'm allergic to purple' …you can name a thousand reasons, but we lost! And we lost not because Elder beat us, but we lost! We let them beat us. If you think for any moment I'm happy, you're wrong! Am I proud of you? Hell yes! Do I love you? Hell yes! But it's time to crap or get off the pot! I expect more out of each and every one of you, and you should out of yourself. We have to coach better, too. I'll be the first to admit it. We put all this time in over all these months and we are not going to beat ourselves again. Let's learn from our mistakes. And the rest of the week I want guys flying all over the place to get better, not get frustrated, and beat Elgin and beat the next team and the next team and the next team. Because I'm pissed off and so should you be. Now let's go."

The boys funnel out of the weight room with shoulders square, heads high, and faces stern. Today is all business.

∼

A few minutes later, Coach Bitto is in his office. He's less concerned about the opponent than he is about his own team.

"Elgin is scrappy. Better on defense. They have a big-play offense, good special teams. They set up scores with punt or kick returns. Both lines are small. They play four or five guys both ways. We just have to figure out how not to fumble the ball to the other team."

Tom Young pointed out to him how the Corsairs have fumbled the ball on the opening drive in three consecutive games. This stat fell through the cracks the first two times, as Carmel's offense more than made up for the lost possession. But Saturday, the turnover led to an Elder touchdown. This time, it was the difference in a seven-point loss. "We haven't been mentally sharp to start games and I've been denying it," Coach Bitto says. "Not anymore."

The weekly film crew arrives—Jordan Kos, Brian Serio and Serio's younger brother, Tim. On the screen is Kos's fumble in the waning seconds of the Elder game.

"You have to be smart enough or savvy enough to know where the game is. There's a minute left. We are trying to end the game and send it into over-time, right?" Coach Bitto says to Kos, sitting just to his right.

"Yeah, well I was trying ..."

"Don't say a word. Just listen to me. We can't do anything on our six-yard line. So think about it. Anytime you make contact inside your own 20-yard line what should you do?"

Silence. After almost 10 seconds, Kos breaks the tranquility.

"Hold onto the football?"

"How do you do that?"

"I'm not sure what ..."

"Two hands, that's what I'm looking for. And not kick it out of your own hands. The ball wasn't knocked out until you kicked it out of your own arms. Part of the problem was he hit you high and you staggered and tried and fight for a few extra yards and kicked the ball. I'd rather have you stay low, keep two hands on the ball and get an eight-yard play, line up and do it again.

"You dig?"

Kos gives his best poker face. Which is appropriate, considering he has no hand with which to play.

Coach Bitto continues: "So you have to make a good play a good play and keep a good play a good play. And if you think I'm wrong, I want you to look me in the eyes. You blew it. So don't act like you didn't. It drives me crazy."

He stops for a few seconds before switching gears.

"It's not that play that you blew it. It's because you didn't practice. You have to practice. You've done a lot of great things, but when the game's on the line we need you every time. And we need you for five more weeks. I'm trying to teach you something here."

Coach Bitto believes Kos was tired at the end of the game, contributing to the calamitous events. A lack of reps during the week due to his bruised knee made his fullback a mistake-prone football player.

Brian Serio rewinds the DVD to the Corsairs' final possession of the first half. With 28 seconds left, he threw a 23-yard touchdown pass to Ryan Cappis. It made the score 14-12. Because the Corsairs missed the extra point on an earlier touchdown, they were forced to go for two to tie the game. On the conversation attempt, Serio fakes the hand-off to Kos and runs through a small hole off left guard and scores, tying the game at 14. But that's not what Coach Bitto wants to talk about.

On the play, Kos's job is a tough task for any offensive player—he must block 6-2, 220-pound Jacob Lindsey, rated as one of the best linebackers in

Ohio. He played that way against Carmel, consistently shedding blocks and making tackles. He was one of the main reasons Carmel rushed for only 207 yards in the game, well below its season average.

On the two-point conversion, Lindsey sprints through the left side "A" gap (between the center and left guard) before Kos gets there. The Elder linebacker hits Kos so hard behind the line of scrimmage the Carmel fullback almost falls into Serio, almost destroying the play.

"He's a Division I football player and you're not," Coach Bitto says. "You can be, you have the ability to be one. But you're not there yet."

"That offends me," Kos says.

"Do you want to take it from him?"

"No."

"Then get your ass down and beat it. Is he D-I?"

"Is he?"

"I'm asking you. Is he D-I?"

"Yes."

"He just proved it, didn't he? You'll get in a film room in college and they'll run this a thousand times and you'll be sweating your ass off before you leave because you'll want to get the hell out of there. He won. That's embarrassing. You're a better player than that. I know he's a great player but so what? You should take the challenge and say, 'I'm going to beat the best player.' He's one of the best in Ohio. Everyone's talking about him. I can see why. It doesn't mean you should take it from him. Beat his ass, knock him in the end zone, maybe you'll get a scholarship. So what do you think of that?

"Stop getting offended. Just get better. Offended isn't going to get you anywhere."

Coach Bitto picks up the clicker and fast-forwards to the next play. Kos stares ahead at the television screen.

CHAPTER TWENTY-ONE

DECLAN

A SOPHOMORE AT THE UNIVERSITY OF NOTRE DAME, Declan Sullivan was a videographer for the 2010 Fighting Irish football team. His routine was filming practice, and he did this while on a scissor lift, suspended high above the football field. On Wednesday, October 27, it was very windy. The Irish had practiced indoors the day before due to a tornado warning in the area. But on this day, they were back outside. And so was Sullivan.

At 4:54 p.m., he was standing on the scissor lift filming the Fighting Irish, when a sudden burst of wind knocked the lift down. Sullivan did not survive the accident.

~

Christine Hartnett was at home when she got the call.

A guidance counselor at Carmel, she had a unique relationship with students. While teachers might have a student in class for one semester or an entire year, Hartnett meets with every student twice a year. Carmel touts itself as a college prep school, and Hartnett functions as part of its nerve center. By the time students make a college choice, Hartnett has shepherded them through—advising, consulting and often making recommendations on where they should spend the next four years of their lives. Meeting with more than a thousand students a year, it's difficult for Hartnett to develop relationships that go beyond her specific job duties. But once or twice a year, she makes a deep personal connection with a student. Declan Sullivan was one of those students.

The 2006-07 school year was her first year as a counselor at Carmel. It just so happened to be Sullivan's junior year. He was bright, funny, and charming, with a wide, toothy grin, and shaggy brown hair, and quickly became one of Hartnett's favorites. When she would talk about the boring stuff—the graduation requirements, the classes he had to take—he would respond in a way that made it obvious he was listening, that he valued her input, which was not always the case with high school students.

Teenagers can be very day-to-day, an evening's homework easily pivoting from a workable task to a point of stress. When they struggle, they don't always open their eyes to the support that surrounds them. Not Sullivan. He took control of his present and future, a master at the art of self-advocacy. He didn't wait for others to define his future. Instead, he sought out mentors who could help propel him in the direction he'd mapped out. He played football his first three years at Carmel. He was a musical person, playing the guitar in the school band. He wanted to write screenplays and produce movies. Film school was his dream, either at Notre Dame or the University of Wisconsin.

"How do I get there?" he would ask Hartnett.

She loved how much he cared. She also loved how grateful he was to others who cared for him.

Sitting in Hartnett's office one time, they picked classes for his senior year. English and History were his favorite subjects. Math was not. Somehow calculus wasn't fitting into his schedule. This did not disappoint Declan. He wanted to know if he would need the class on his transcript for the colleges he was applying to. Hartnett made some calls. The answers satisfied Declan enough to where he was comfortable avoiding calculus. But when he was accepted into Notre Dame, his first choice, the school told him he would have to take the dreaded math class he'd avoided with such inventiveness. Declan's mom called Hartnett and told her about her son's startling mea culpa.

"He said, 'Arrgh ... Maybe I should have taken that calculus class after all,'" she told Hartnett with a laugh.

Hartnett still doesn't know how she let him get away with that. She wouldn't have let any other student. But it was classic Declan. Endearingly deviant.

Before graduation in the spring of 2008, Hartnett arrived at school one morning to find a bouquet of flowers outside her office on the floor in front of the door. She picked them up and set them on the table in her office. There was a handwritten note. It was from Declan. He thanked his guidance counselor for all of her help. He wouldn't have gotten into Notre Dame without her, it read. Declan also wrote he would always remember what she did for him when he became famous, which was part of his plan.

~

Notre Dame was Declan's dream school. If accepted, he would be free to spread his wings in an environment conducive to expressing his creative energy. Carmel could be suffocating at times for Declan. The rules—uniforms, schedules, do this, do that—did not always mesh with his intellectually curious view of the world. He was a questioner.

One of Declan's favorite teachers was Jim Schuster. A bit of an outlier at Carmel—Jewish, married to a Catholic—Schuster had a previous career in business before getting his teaching license. Schuster taught Declan in two classes: AP World History and European History. The AP class is a bit more freewheeling as it covers the history of mankind from the Ancient Romans to current events. Schuster pushes his students, and at times, they push back. Declan was one of those students, though never in a disobedient way. He was far too respectful. But playfully contrarian? That was Declan. At times, just to test his teacher, he would vocalize answers he knew were not well thought out. Schuster would fire back.

"Come on. Be serious here. Give me some effort. Stop seeing what you can throw out quickly and put some energy into this."

Declan would respond to his teacher's challenge by doing the work. And often, his work was exceptional.

There was the museum project. It's become legend at the school. Students taking European History are asked to write four papers over both semesters. At the end of the year, they take the content from those papers and create a presentation based on what they learned. Schuster's room becomes quite the sight by the month of May as students prepare exhibits on a variety of subjects. Declan's presentation was on medicine. And it was not to be forgotten.

Using China as his muse, he talked about the country's use of acupuncture. How did this connect to the concept of chi? How did the energy flow of chi reflect the society's religious beliefs? He went on to compare this to Native Americans, who use natural remedies found in their native soil.

"That's where their gods were. So that's where they went," Declan said, integrating visual artifacts into his presentation to show the religious aspect of the Native Americans' way of life.

It was brilliant. For years after, Schuster kept his exhibit as an example for how students should construct the project.

∾

Schuster was at home that evening. The news was on. A Carmel student had died. He heard the name and thought, "Oh, my God. Don't tell me." But there was no mistake.

∾

Sean Brennan is getting something to eat after football practice, with his older brother, Brian. They are at Jack's on Highway 83 in Mundelein. Sean's mom calls. She has terrible news. Declan Sullivan has died.

At home that night, Sean has so many questions. He grew up with Mac, Declan's younger brother. They went to middle school together, at St. Mary's in Buffalo Grove, and are now in the same grade, 10th, at Carmel. Mac plays on the sophomore football team while Sean is on the varsity. Sean knows Declan how most everyone does—as an infectious free spirit. He knows how much Mac looks up to his big brother. Now he's gone? What is Mac going to do? For all of Sean's questions, there are no answers. How do you make sense of something so senseless?

~

After Hartnett gets the call, she can't believe it. They have to be talking about somebody else. It can't be Declan. She has to confirm it is true. Hartnett calls her daughter, Allie, a freshman at Notre Dame. The previous year, when Allie was deciding on a college, she did an overnight in South Bend. Who was the young man who gave Allie a personal tour of the campus? Declan. Along with his younger sister, Wyn, they introduced Allie to their friends, going out of their way to make sure Allie was comfortable. He was working with the football program. He enjoyed his film and history classes, gleefully sharing his experiences. He loved Notre Dame and was sure Allie would thrive as much as he was. That was Declan. Hartnett had helped him, so he was going to help her. Hartnett remembers how Allie came home later that weekend after the overnight at Notre Dame and said, "Mom, this is the school for me."

~

And we know that for those who love God all things work together for good, for those who are called according to his purpose.
- Romans 8:28

~

Hartnett is talking to Allie about the accident. Allie is with Wyn, Declan's sister who is also a freshman at Notre Dame. So is Maria Skorcz, another Carmel graduate. They are there to be with Wyn until her parents arrive. Hartnett can't believe it until she talks to Allie. It's true. Declan is gone.

~

On this night, coach Michael Fitzgibbons is counselor Michael Fitzgibbons. His phone keeps ringing.

Word about Declan's death is trickling out. People have questions. "What do we do at school the next day?" "How do we remember him in prayer?" "How do we help Mac?" Fitz knows Mac is hurting, his family is hurting, his friends are hurting, his classmates are hurting. Fitz's daughter, Molly, who graduated with Declan, is hurting. They need him. But so do the people in his office. He has a private counseling practice and a full schedule of patients to see. How do you choose? This is always the hard part. The deciding. So he does. He sees his patients that night, returning calls in between. There would be a team prayer the next day, involving Mac's football teammates and friends from St. Mary's, his middle school. That would be followed by a prayer service for the entire school.

∿

Sean Brennan is sitting in his homeroom class Thursday morning when Fitzgibbons makes the announcement on the PA. He grabs his books and goes to the chapel. All his friends from St. Mary's are there. They sit together, not a word spoken. What is there to say? How are we supposed to act? Sean isn't sure.

Fitzgibbons is now in front of them. He's talking. He doesn't know much about the what. Nobody did. But the what doesn't matter. All they know is their classmate, their teammate, their buddy, had lost his brother.

"This is going to be a sad time for Mac," Fitzgibbons says. "What's important is he knows we are there for him."

Sean glances over to Matt Campbell and Connor Lynde. They all went to St. Mary's together. They are crying. He can't remember the last time he saw them cry.

∿

All the hours they spent together. Their talks about college but also about life. The laughing. The thought that he was gone was unbearable for Hartnett. She was a counselor. Her job was to help others. But how could she offer support when she was in so much pain? She needed a safe haven to grieve for her student and friend. To pray for his family.

On Thursday, the day after in the accident, she's in her office. Hartnett listens to the morning prayer. Then later, at the chapel. The service. To walk in and see so many there. Some didn't even know Declan, or even Mac. But they came. Amidst the anguish, she finds solace.

～

The son of a union electrician, Fitzgibbons grew up on Chicago's South Side. He was one of six kids from a classic blue-collar Irish Catholic family. His grade school was on "the boulevard," Garfield and 55th. The church is still there. It's a landmark. It wouldn't be otherwise. Since the 1970s, gangs have taken over the neighborhood.

He wanted to become a priest. After all, he was one of four boys. His mother told him all great Irish Catholic families produce a priest. His older brothers had already made it clear they weren't interested. He was the family's last shot.

An altar boy, he'd wear the cassock. Holding the candle. Walking down the aisle between the church pews. The May Crowning. The Holy Ghost. The mystery. It spoke to him. All of it. That's why he enrolled at Quigley South. To explore the idea of becoming a Carmelite priest. His heart was open. Or at least he thought it was.

He ended up at Carmel in 1976. Not as a Carmelite priest, but as a teacher. Then as a coach. Then as a counselor. Today he's all of those things. All of his life experiences prepare him for what he faces now. A chapel filled with people in pain. Who don't understand. Especially the kids. They hear so many things. They need something to hold onto. Something real.

He starts talking.

"Here's what we know. We lost someone we loved. And someone who is one of us is grieving. That's what we know. What we know is we need to be there for each other. The rest is commercials. You'll hear 4,000 different stories about what should have happened, and if you get lost in that, it's energy in the wrong places.

"We don't understand. A lot of you will say, 'Why would a good God take him?' You'll hear 'God wanted Declan more than we did.' God didn't take Declan. A wind blew him off scaffolding and killed him. That's not God. It's an unfortunate accident. God didn't do that. If you start blaming God for things, you'll be mad at God your whole life. The Lord we pray to and believe in holds us in the palm of his hands and tries to help us through these tough times.

"What we know is Mac needs support. We are supporting Mac. The Sullivan family needs support. That's what we know. That's what we do. We take care of each other."

∾

Sean Brennan stays in the chapel, along with Connor Lynde and Matt Campbell and several other St. Mary's classmates. They talk about everything, including the why. Fitzgibbons keeps saying, "What happened, happened. You have to be strong for Mac." There was no manual to give out, no instructional guide. Just be there for your friend. That they can do. That they knew how to do.

∾

Friday, the next day, Hartnett drives to South Bend for a prayer service. Sitting with her in the pews at the Basilica are Mark and Sherry Skorcz. Hartnett turns her head to look behind her. The pew is filled with Carmel parents and students, there to support the Sullivans, to pray for Declan, to grieve together.

As the priest begins to speak, she closes her eyes and bows her head.

∾

It's the Wednesday after the accident. Mac is due back at school. He arrives that morning, Connor and Matt greet him. They want Mac to know they are happy to see him. And although they didn't understand what he was going through—how could they—they want him to know he is not alone. This they know how to do.

Sean saw Mac at the wake. He'd texted and called him after but he hasn't seen him. Sean walks out of his first period class and spots Mac in the hallway. Sean walks up to his friend, flashes a big grin, gives him a hug and said, "It's great to see you, Mac."

"Thanks, Sean. It's great to see you too," Mac said. "Thanks for being there for my family."

And then they go to class.

∼

Put life in a little perspective. One of our very own, a former football player, band member, Declan Sullivan, was in a tragic accident. His little brother Mac is a sophomore football player. He has an older sister who goes to Notre Dame.

I've told you many, many times we are all connected, in a lot of different ways. In this case, we are connected through Carmel. His loss puts a heavy feeling on our hearts. We want to pray for him now as a team as we always would, but to understand when you are part of the family it means not just recognizing the good times but the bad. It's also important at a time like this to use the power of prayer for his family. I can't tell you the grief that they must be sharing right now is. That's not entirely true. I might be able to tell you.

When I was 21, my sister was killed in a car accident. She was 25, and it was by far the hardest thing I had to deal with as a young person. Declan was 20; his brother is only 15. It's very difficult to understand why these things happen. That's why we must use the power of prayer and God to get us through. We are praying for their family and somewhere in this tragedy hopefully we can make sense of it and find something good. So let's all grab a hand and say the Lord's Prayer.

- Head coach Andy Bitto to the Carmel football team.

CHAPTER TWENTY-TWO

PLAYOFF DRIVE

In a few short hours, Carmel will take the field to play Elgin. To the winner, the right to continue the season. To the loser, a Monday reservation with the equipment manager.

In the coaches' room, the Carmel staff is making last-minute preparations. The weight of the mission in front of them is heavy, and tension is palpable.

Finally, one of the coaches breaks the silence.

"Oops! ... Close," defensive line coach Michael Fitzgibbons says, grabbing the edges of a desk to keep the momentum of his 360-degree chair spin from propelling him through the room. He lets out a belly laugh heard round the world. He only has the one.

"Can't take you anywhere," defensive coordinator Dan Potempa says with a wry smile. He only has the one.

"When are you going to grow up?" running backs coach Tom Young asks.

"What's the rush?" Fitz says. "You know, I spilled something on myself the other night. Mary [his wife] looked at me and laughed and said, 'Thank God you're funny and make enough money, otherwise you'd have been gone a long time ago.' I make her laugh. That's important."

"Laugh *at* you?" Potempa says.

"Doesn't matter as long as she's laughing."

~

Athletes talk all the time about not thinking. About seeing first, and reacting second. About being in the moment. Jack Nicklaus once said his ability to concentrate on each golf swing was the best antidote for anxiety. He also said: "Golfers have a tendency to be very masochistic. They like to punish themselves for some reason."

You could say the same for Carmel's fullback.

On the Corsairs' first offensive series against Elgin, Jordan Kos again puts the ball on the turf. It happens on a third-down play from the Maroons' 38-yard line. Two Elgin defenders just behind the 35-yard line hit him. On his way down, the football squirts loose. It appears to hit the turf after Kos is tackled, but no whistle is heard. Maroons linebacker Adrian Martinez scoops up the loose leather and runs 65 yards for a touchdown. Just like that, it's 7-0 Maroons.

"That Christian attitude has to stop in the playoffs," linebacker Luke Venegoni says in the direction of Kos.

Coach Bitto makes good on his threat to sit Kos if he fumbles. When Carmel takes the field for its next offensive possession, Tim Serio is the fullback. Kos remains on the bench.

After Coach Bitto's wake-up-call speech Monday, the Corsairs snap out of their 48-hour post-Elder funk. They practiced hard all week. Watching film reaffirmed a season-long truth: Carmel is better than its opponent. Elgin is small on defense, and offensively, it runs a mediocre version of the spread offense. It's a team the Corsairs should manhandle.

Because Carmel knows it's a better team on this night, the reaction to Kos's latest fumble is not a crisis. There is no panic on the sidelines.

"We spotted them a touchdown. So what? If we play our game, we'll be fine," Young says to the offensive unit, waiting to get the ball back.

Even without Kos, the Corsairs' superiority comes through on their next possession, as they move easily down the field before stalling at the Elgin 17. With 3:50 left in the first quarter, Carmel settles for a 24-yard field goal by Steven O'Block.

After forcing the Maroons to punt, the Corsairs take over on their own 39-yard line. Coach Bitto puts Kos back in the lineup. He has made his point. Now it's time to win the game.

A 41-yard scamper by Michael Panico gives the Corsairs great field position. With 19 seconds left in the first quarter, quarterback Brian Serio scores a touchdown from one yard to give Carmel the lead, 10-7. Then, a few minutes later, safety Mike Fitzgibbons picks off a pass and the Corsairs' offense takes over on the Elgin 28-yard line. Kos finishes the drive with a nine-yard touchdown run.

On Elgin's next possession, the Carmel defense makes a statement. On a first-down pass play from Elgin's 40-yard line, Maroons quarterback Lee Jackson throws a swing pass to the right side of the field to running back Jordan Dean. Dean cuts it back toward the middle, a mistake. Dean is gang tacked by half the Corsairs' defense and is stripped of the football. Carmel recovers and takes over on the Elgin 46-yard line. On the first offensive play, Serio throws deep to wide receiver Ryan Cappis on a fly route, only to have the pass intercepted.

The turnover is nothing more than a distraction. Elgin punts it right back, and the Corsairs begin their next drive on the Maroons' 42-yard line. On the drive's second play, Kos breaks off a 16-yard run, punishing Maroon defenders before being dragged down. A 40-yard touchdown run by Panico is called back for holding. But the self-inflicted wound is of no mind. On second down from the Elgin 40, Serio again steps back to throw. This time, he hits Brian Brennan at the Elgin 25-yard line, and Brennan outruns a Maroons defender into the end zone. Before the half is up, the Corsairs tack on two more touchdowns to take a 38-7 lead.

"I don't wish them any ill will, but I hope we have a running clock tonight," Young says. A 40-point lead in the second half is required for the operator to ignore the off switch.

"The tide turned when you guys started belting them around. They don't like getting hit," Coach Fitzgibbons says to the defensive players huddled behind Baker Stadium. "I don't think they've ever been hit like that. Think about that the first time you go out there in the second half."

Fitzgibbons' son, Michael, intercepts a Maroons pass on the first posses-sion of the second half. His development is one of the main reasons for the defense's extraordinary play. Strictly a cover cornerback early in the season, Fitzgibbons' versatility allows Potempa to use him as a linebacker or safety. Because Fitzgibbons is so athletic and intuitive, Potempa can line him up five yards off the line of scrimmage—even up to 15 yards depending on the coverage. This confuses an offense, and in football, the more confused team usually loses.

When Kos scores a four-yard touchdown late in the third quarter, the score is 45-7. Without its starters, Carmel tacks on 10 more points [Young gets his running clock] and rolls to a 55-7 win. For the game, the Corsairs nearly rush for 500 yards. Three runners finish with more than 100 yards on the ground—Serio (12 carries, 133 yards), sophomore Josh Walinski (eight carries, 114 yards) and Kos (14 carries, 109 yards). On the flip side, Elgin manages a paltry 16 yards on 24 rushes. The defense forces six fumbles, re-covering four.

"The best thing about this victory was we won by 40 and we can still get better," assistant head coach Jim Rejc says.

Kos's fumble on Carmel's opening possession is almost forgotten until a reporter asks Coach Bitto about it after the game.

"It's the fourth week in a row we've fumbled on the first drive, so we can work on some things," he replies. "We're talented, and we try and make big plays when they should be first downs. We need to figure that out a little bit more. I wasn't too nice at some points tonight, but I'm proud of how our kids responded. When we need to make big plays, we make big plays."

Back in the locker room, Coach Bitto surprises the boys by giving them Saturday off.

"He's a prophet," wide receiver coach Tim Schrank says.

Coach Bitto shouts over the jubilant buoyancy of noise. "Dudes! Listen! I asked you guys to come together tonight, and you did that. I asked you to play for one another tonight, and you did that. There are more important things than yourself. The more you get that, the better this team is going to be.

"Winning teams are guys who are willing to put themselves aside for someone else."

∿

It's barely after 10 p.m., and the post-game party is in full swing.

The amiable hosts are Scott and Beth Carr, parents of Matt Carr. With all the injuries the Corsairs have suffered this season, Matt should be playing in the defensive secondary or seeing action at running back. But the bone he broke in his right ankle against St. Viator in Week Three has taken longer to heal than expected. The good news: Doctors are expected to clear him for practice beginning Monday.

Scott, an insurance man, is an excellent host. He mixes up rum and cokes, gin and tonics, and pours glasses of wine for parents. The topic of conversation is what it always is in the homes of football parents on late Friday nights after games: the boys, the season.

"We live for this," Scott says. "I get through the work week to get to Friday nights. It's such a special time.

"During football season, Matt goes to school, he goes to practice, comes home, eats something, does his homework and goes to bed by 9. The whole discipline football brings—I just love to see."

Beth holds a glass of red wine at the bar. "I love when they first come home from the game. They can't stop talking. That's the best. The first 10 minutes. You get it all," she says. "It's the same after the school dance. You want the kids to come to your house to change their clothes because Sunday morning they are not telling you what happened last night. It's done, it's over. But that first 10 minutes in a bubble is the whole night."

A few more sets of parents stroll in—the Greenes, the Serios, the Cappises.

"Wasn't that fun!" says Scott Greene, who then orders a scotch.

"Were we that good or were they that bad?" asks Bruce Cappis, grabbing a Budweiser handed to him by Scott.

"A little bit of both," Mary Serio says.

"We were pretty darn good," Paul Serio says.

Then the boys arrive. Conversation stops for a brief moment as everyone listens for them come in through the garage door. Beth excuses herself and heads into the kitchen to greet them.

She doesn't want to miss her 10 minutes.

~

With each successive round, the opposition gets tougher, and that looks to be true of Rockton Hononegah, whose 9-1 Indians are based 60 miles west of Carmel's campus.

They have a better offense than the punchless Maroons, averaging 34 points per game with a versatile offensive attack. Quarterback Chase Robinson is athletic, posing the type of run/pass threat that causes paranoid defensive coaches like Dan Potempa to lose hours of sleep. In their first playoff game, the Indians put up 50 points on Chicago Taft with Robinson throwing four touchdown passes. Defensively, the Indians have only given up 183 points all season (although that's significantly more than Carmel's 113 points allowed).

So, on paper, Rockton Hononegah looks to be Carmel's toughest in-state opponent since Joliet Catholic. The Corsairs expect to be in a four-quarter game Saturday night under the lights at Baker Stadium. Possessions must be valued.

That's why concern over Kos's fumbles has reached a tipping point.

"Jordan will fumble once, and that will be it. He ain't playing again," Coach Bitto says before practice Monday.

He's no longer keeping his frustrations in house. For the first time, he talks about it publicly.

"If you can't protect the football, you ain't getting it," Coach Bitto tells *Daily Herald* columnist Patricia Babcock McGraw that week. "If we want to keep advancing in the playoffs, we won't have a glimmer of hope if we keep fumbling the ball."

One of football's unwritten rules, come playoff time, is that coaches transition into a reverse-psychology mindset. Here's how it works: The week of a playoff game, the coach of the higher-seeded team (Team A) gives interviews. During interviews, coach of Team A espouses the virtues of their opponent, Team B. Coach of Team A makes comments saying how Team B is "great up front" or "sound fundamentally" or "well coached." About his own team, coach will eschew positive platitudes, instead opting for a narrative featuring self-evident clichés such as "we can't make mistakes" or "we have to protect the football" or "we will have to play our best to beat such a quality opponent." And while all of these observations about his own team are true, what the coach of Team A says about Team B are often flat-out fibs.

Privately, there is nothing about Rockton Hononegah that worries the Carmel coaches. The Indians are not particularly big on defense and they don't have much speed on offense. And the game is at home, where the Corsairs haven't lost in over a year.

Before they step on the practice field Monday, offensive coordinator Ben Berg says to Coach Bitto: "If we don't help them—and that's the only concern I have—they can't play with us."

~

Berg's right. And Tom Young gets another running clock. It's 28-0 after one quarter, 42-0 at halftime.

There is another fumble scare on the game's first play as Kos drops the hand-off from Serio. Only a fortuitous bounce saves Carmel from another early disaster, and Kos falls on the ball before an Indian can snatch it. He redeems himself later in the drive by taking an inside handoff and galloping 38 yards for a touchdown. It's the first of three touchdowns on three straight offensive plays. In fact, four of Carmel's six first-half touchdowns come on runs of 35 yards or more. The first-team defense is stout once again, not allowing Rockton Hononegah into Carmel territory the entire first half. At halftime, coaches meet not about schemes but about how soon to insert the second team.

In a season filled with outcomes decided by the second quarter, these 24 minutes of football might represent the most thorough blowout.

~

With Carmel leading by six touchdowns, the only intrigue for the second half is what scout team players will take the field. Coach Bitto decides on the first series. Freshman Nick Grandolfo will go in to replace Serio at quarterback. Sophomores Josh Walinski and Tim Serio will take snaps for all three running backs. Offensive line coach Jerry Rejc is already making post-game plans.

"I think our defense is outstanding. They play option was well as anybody. These poor guys just ran into a buzz saw," Rejc says. "I'm praying we don't give up a touchdown here so we won't lose the running clock.

"Our tradition is cheap wine and cheap pizza on Friday nights after games. I want to get home while there is still some left."

~

Hononegah punches one in on fourth and goal with four minutes left. No shutout, but the final score of 42-6 means Carmel has outscored its two playoff opponents 87-13.

"Round three baby!" defensive lineman Jake Larson shouts into the microphone of the iHigh sideline reporter.

Coach Bitto stays the course in his post-game speech. He avoids any potential bulletin-board material that might leak to Carmel's quarterfinal opponent. "It's fun to watch you guys get better," he says in the cramped, yet gleeful, Carmel locker room. "It gets tougher every week, so we have to get better every week."

Carmel will legitimately have its hands full against its next foe, St. Rita, ranked No. 2 in 7A. This time, comments made to newspaper reporters about the brilliance of the opponent will not be smoke screens. If and/or when the Corsairs punch the Mustangs in the mouth, they will punch back. Like Carmel, St. Rita is a one-loss team, albeit in the arguably tougher Chicago Catholic League, a conference that features Mount Carmel, Loyola, and Providence, all of which have won state championships in recent years.

After Coach Bitto gives his brief statement, most of the assistant coaches mirror the low-key tone of their boss in their short speeches to the players. With one exception. Coach Berg can't help but ramp up the bravado.

"This is what you are going to hear all week. You are going to hear how tough the Chicago Blue [conference] is. How tough and physical they are. You know what? We are just as tough and just as physical. And we have more weapons. It's been a long time since we played them. They talk about their great tradition, but we've played them three times and kicked their ass three times. I don't expect anything different next Saturday."

The boys' faces are still smeared with sweat, wearing the spoils of another commanding victory. Each grabs the hand of the guy next to them. They bow their heads and say the Lord's Prayer.

CHAPTER TWENTY-THREE

AFTER LIFE

IT WAS A BRIGHT, warm spring day when friends and family gathered at Jim and Marion Biere's house. There was much to celebrate at their son LaRon's 14th birthday party in May of 2007. Marion's heart was filled with much joy that day.

Earlier that year, LaRon had passed the entrance exam for Carmel. To help ease the burden of tuition, LaRon had qualified for a Daniel Murphy Scholarship. The organization specialized in working with students from unique backgrounds such as LaRon's. With that final hurdle climbed, it was official. He was going. He would enroll at Carmel for classes beginning in August. They had found a way.

Marion was by no means Pollyannish about the road ahead. She understood the next four years would not be easy. After all, she had raised six children who were teenagers before becoming adults. She was aware of the challenges. But Marion preferred to indulge her emotions not on anxious thoughts of adolescent shenanigans but rather on LaRon's education. Her adopted son had come so far. To be accepted into a private school as prestigious as Carmel was significant. Inside those school walls he would be free to evolve into the man he was meant to be. A man who would walk with God.

∽

That was a wonderful choice for them to make. He would not have had a wonderful four years at [the public school]. I think there would have been a lot of problems. At Carmel, I think LaRon blossomed there and was so well accepted. I think it was a wonderful decision on their part. I think they watch out for each other. He'll do a lot of growing up.

– Marilyn Adams

Once we added all the parts in and made it less open-ended, it was obvious he was going to Carmel. There's a lot of support—my dad, my family and the coaches, which filled that third piece which was needed. Especially from a supportive, discipline way. They saw him every day, I didn't. They saw him at school and in class. We didn't know that at the time, but this is just another plus or benefit that we saw in the program itself. I don't think he would have gotten that at a public school. Not to say they don't care about their kids, but they don't have the time to put into it, which he definitely got at Carmel.

– Tom Biere

I don't believe he came here by coincidence. Someone made his parents want to adopt him and send him to this school. He could have gone somewhere else, but they chose here. It doesn't just happen. There's a greater good happening.

– Carmel ministry director Michael Fitzgibbons

∼

Marion's third act was in full motion. Her prayers—combined with action—had LaRon started on the path to academic and spiritual success. It was to be celebrated. But as she, Jim and the rest of the family were awash in gratitude over their good fortune, they were equally conscious of another, less-exalted reality—Marion's age. She turned 76 years old in 2007. Having worked in health care for so many years, she was acutely aware of time, how life and death is a defined period, with a beginning and end. On a trip to Rock River Estates in Wisconsin when LaRon was 11, she shared these concerns with her sister, Joanne. During a long walk, her sister's deep faith came more into focus to Joanne. Marion was not unrealistic about her future. The end was near. As the Lord giveth, He taketh away.

"All I ask of God, the only thing I pray on, is to let me live long enough to get LaRon through Carmel," Marion said. "When I pray, I say 'Let me live to see him through high school.' If he's 18 years old, I've given him that time.

"I know he'll be OK."

~

This is when I knew she knew death was at the doorstep. In other words, I knew when she said that, she's accepted the fact that she will struggle on, that she has accepted the reality of her death.

– Sister Joanne Wegener

~

It's later in the day. The sun fades. Artificial light fills the room.

Mr. Rejc is talking now. About sacraments.

"Sacraments are actions, not things. They are something we do, not done to us. They are experiences that put me in contact with something greater than myself. A person, thing or event when I experience God in a new or deeper way.

"Who is a sacrament in my life? Who enables me to experience God in new and deeper way? What experiences have been sacramental?

"Sacraments are an initiation to a friendship with God."

This makes LaRon think about something that happened recently.

Beth Carr's grandmother had died. LaRon liked Noni. She would be at the Carrs' house at Christmas, sipping on vodka gimlets and telling stories. There were always a lot of people at the Carrs' house. LaRon liked being there when the grownups hung out. It made him feel safe.

He remembers it was senior week. Noni died on Wednesday. Carmel was playing St. Viator that Friday. Before the game, they introduced all the seniors and their parents. LaRon was on the field with Jim. Before the Carrs were announced, he wandered over to where they were standing. He had something to show them.

On his wrist, covered in tape, he had seven letters written in black. They read:

"RIP Noni"

∿

The funeral was Saturday in Grandville, Illinois, a two-hour drive. Mr. and Mrs. Carr said he didn't have to go. But LaRon insisted.

"Mrs. C, Matt was there for me when my mom died. I need to be there for him right now," he said.

At the cemetery, there was what seemed like a hundred balloons. All of the grandchildren and great-grandchildren—Noni was the matriarch of a large Italian family—were to release the balloons into the air at the end of the ceremony. The only grandchild not in attendance was Megan, Beth and Scott Carr's daughter and Matt's sister. She was in college at Michigan State and couldn't make it.

Beth approached LaRon with a request.

"Hey, can you let this balloon off for Megan?"

"Are you kidding?" LaRon responded.

"You are representing Megan today. When everyone lets out a balloon, could you be Megan for me today?"

While Beth was talking, all of the grandchildren and great-grandchildren were gathering in a circle on the grass of the cemetery grounds, clutching strings attached to balloons of many colors.

LaRon was still hesitant. "I don't belong here," he said to Beth.

"No, I am asking you to do this," Beth said, staring straight into his eyes. "Can you do this for me?"

"I'm in. I'll do anything for you," LaRon said.

And he joined the circle. The only black child in a large group of Italians, LaRon looked like a chocolate chip that had fallen into a bowl of King

Arthur Flour. As the balloons released simultaneously, an act of overwhelming unity and solidarity for a deceased matriarch, LaRon stared straight up, watching his red balloon drift higher into a dazzling blue sky.

If only I could reach up and pull her back down.

There was so much to say, so much left unsaid. It all happened so fast. Marion was here, and then she wasn't.

He remembers something he told Beth later.

"Mrs. C, what a different life I would have had if she hadn't taken me home. She did change my life."

~

Matt is at the lectern again. He seems so comfortable up there, so in control. But there's nothing comfortable about what he's talking about. His own life. Everyone is revealing so much of themselves. Jack about his brother. Tom about his father. Jon about his dad, too. And Luke. What a story. LaRon's never seen so many guys his age cry. He sees them every day, in the hallways, in class, the cafeteria. Before they were mostly human wallpaper, wearing the same school uniform—polo shirt, khaki pants—smiling that same white, dentistry-enhanced grin and sporting school-approved short haircuts (just above the ear, like Mrs. Gille insists). But now he understands it's all a façade. Just like Matt keeps saying. About how sometimes we all wear masks.

"I cannot live my life feeling sorry about past mistakes," Matt says.

~

LaRon had been there late the night before. At the hospital. Loyola Medical Center. Marion had checked back in a few days before. The cancer had spread to her liver. Chemo had worked a few months before, for her stomach. The doctors said she was in remission. But it came back.

He had been at the hospital all day. There were times he thought she wouldn't make it. So much medication. LaRon didn't know how she found the energy to keep her eyes open. But she did. And she spoke, although only

a few times. It was hard to understand, impossible to know if she even recognized a human face. The words so soft, as if an angel were on her pillow,
whispering into her ear. LaRon remembers what she told him over and over
again before he left that night.

"Love Jesus."

Marion was resting and it was getting late. Matt, Ricky, Brian and Ryan
came down and picked LaRon up and took him home. He would go back the
next day with Jim. That morning, they had hoped to arrive at the hospital by
9 a.m. But there was traffic.

Jim remembers her telling one of the children, *I'll let you know when I go.*

The clock on the radio read 9:03 a.m. On a bright, clear day, the sun
flickered through the dashboard. A thin breeze blew through the car. The
radio went static.

They got to her room by 9:10 a.m. Tom was there. He had spent the
night. No words were spoken. She was gone.

∼

*Two weeks before she died, I meant to call Marilyn [Jim's sister] and looked
at the wrong index card and it ended up I got Marion. I thought how wonderful that I had this chance to speak with her. She didn't moan and groan, poor
me. Nothing like that whatsoever. It was wanting to hang on and how her kids
had taken the bull by the horns and had gotten her into Loyola and how great
it was that the kids did that. Always on the positive side. She told me how much
she wanted to survive. Although she was in a lot of pain, she wanted to survive
to see LaRon graduate. I try to take the good she displayed and emphasize it
more in my life.*

– Joan Zupec

*She had a friend, Sister Elizabeth. Marion had met her in Florida. Sister
Elizabeth spent many hours in front of tabernacle and she prayed and prayed.
That was her ministry. She prayed lots and lots and lots for Marion. I assume
so that she'd be able to face death, live through the process of dying. It wasn't*

asking for prayers of petition. When you pray you aren't saying, 'Please God, give me this and that.' No, it's 'help me to be true. Give me strength to be true for what we are really here for.' I didn't feel she was asking for a miracle. She was too much of a realist. Miracles do happen, but other miracles are if we can die well.

    – Sister Joanne Wegener

With the chemo, they gave her three to five years. Fine, if she could have those years until LaRon gets out of Carmel and into college. I just feel so badly sometimes because she didn't get to see him finish at Carmel.

    – Marilyn Adams

My dad's OK. He internalizes a lot of things, doesn't like to show a lot of emotion. The rest of the family is OK. It's definitely been hard for me. I knew the impact, as I've seen some of that balance lost. My mom was the primary, and she took care of a lot of things, so I now take care of some of the responsibilities like financials. I do even the school stuff. It's funny. There was a creative writing course LaRon took at Carmel. I thought he had the book and he never told me he didn't. I went to a parent/teacher conference and they told me, 'You know he doesn't have the book' and I was like, 'He never told me,' and they were like, 'Well, if your mom were here she'd be on top of that.' It reminded me of how if she'd been here, she would have taken care of it right away. It's hard. I miss her.

    – Tom Biere, Marion's youngest son

CHAPTER TWENTY-FOUR

GET A GRIP

IT'S TUESDAY. Less than 48 hours earlier, Carmel won its 10th game of the season for the sixth time in a decade. The Corsairs are ranked in the top five for the first time all season, having dominated the first two rounds of the postseason like no one else in 7A. They appear to be peaking at the perfect time.

The DVD player in Coach Bitto's office doesn't care about the team's lofty heights. It keeps getting stuck, interrupting the Monday film session before it can start.

"Where's the plug-in? I've got too many wires," he says, poking behind the television stand. "I hate technology."

"Why do we always have technical difficulties?" Jordan Kos asks.

"I have technical difficulties with everything. My phone. My car has electrical problems," Coach Bitto says.

Brian Serio offers a helping hand to his coach. They are both leaning behind the television stand, staring at the perplexing machines, coach and quarterback wearing dual looks of bewilderment.

"Plug it in here," Coach Bitto says, pointing. "Put it closer to the edge so the wire will be long enough.

The untwisting of the cords works—at least temporarily—and Saturday's blowout of Rockton Hononegah appears on the screen. Also in the room is the newest member of the Monday film crew, running back Josh Walinski, who was the sophomore team's starting quarterback for most of the season. Because of injuries to Matt Maher, still out of action since suffering a knee injury in Week Five against Marist, and Michael Panico, Walinski was called up to the varsity. He's made the most of it, rushing 13 times for 144 yards and a touchdown in Carmel's two playoff victories.

It only takes a few plays to be shown on the screen before Coach Bitto is annoyed with the execution of blocks by his starting fullback.

"Now on 38, you want to ride the double-team. He's coming down. Why would you run into his ass?" Coach Bitto says to Kos. "You blocked the wrong guy."

"There's no one coming," Kos says.

"You didn't even block that guy! You should have chipped him. You get a zero."

"I don't agree with that," Kos says.

"You don't have to agree. I'm just telling you I'm right."

Coach Bitto sets down his Diet Pepsi while letting out a mild belch.

"That's disgusting," Walinski says.

"Come on, Wally. How many brothers did you have?" Coach Bitto asks.

"Zero. Just a sister."

"Well, I had nine brothers, and they all belched in my face until I was 10."

"My sister punches me in stomach."

"She does? Do you tell her you love her?" Coach Bitto says.

"Not when she does that."

"Be sure she knows you love her."

Coach Bitto's cell phone rings. It's Mrs. Bitto. "Hey gorgeous," he says using his favorite adjective to describe his better half. Kate Bitto wants to know when her husband will be dismissing the film crew and coming home.

"I'll be home in a little while. Thanks, sweetheart," he says, and then hangs up.

"*Hey, gorgeous!*" Kos says in a tone mocking his coach's greeting. Serio and Walinski laugh at their teammate's imitation. Coach Bitto lets out a mild chuckle.

He pauses for a moment. "Always tell your wife you love her and that she's skinny and gorgeous."

"So I guess we should just have a skinny wife?" Kos asks.

"Skinny and rich," Serio says.

"I like that," Walinski says with enthusiasm.

"My mother was overweight but she was one of the best people ever. My father loved her like anything," Coach Bitto says. "My mom had this big belly and we would just lay on it and listen to it gurgle. It was awesome."

The boys burst out laughing.

"What?" Coach Bitto says, feigning offense.

"I don't do that with my mom," Kos says.

"Yeah, that might be weird," Coach Bitto says.

He presses play again on the remote. It's back to work. The image on the screen moves.

"You have to get to the hip first, Jordan!" Coach Bitto says.

~

He's tired of hearing about it. Tired of hearing about the fumbling. So he's decided to do something about it.

Jordan doesn't agree with his coach about the pad level. Coach Bitto keeps telling him his shoulder pad level is too high. The higher the pad level, the more space there is between the ground and the ball. This makes it easier for a defender to gain leverage on a ball-carrier, to make a tackle or, more ambitiously, to rip the football from his hands. It does make sense. A lot of the stuff Coach Bitto says makes sense. Like benching him in the Elgin game, after the fumble on the first play. He had been talking all week about ball security and praising the job Timmy Serio was doing. And when Jordan put it on the turf, Coach Bitto took him out. Enough was enough. Jordan understood why his coach did what he did. Coach Bitto is a perfectionist. That's why he rides Jordan so much. Usually he's right. But not about this.

The fumbling has nothing to do with pad level. He just gets too amped up sometimes. Like before Hononegah. Listening to crazy music. He wanted to run over people in the halls at school. Football makes him that way, makes him forget about the details. It makes him angry. Defenders are the enemy. And enemies get punished. For Jordan, there is no physical experience known to man like lowering your shoulder and delivering a blow to a defender. Tackle him? You are going to pay for it. Any by pay, he means getting run over. That's what you do to your enemies. You hurt them and make them think twice before coming after you again. That split second of hesitation is all Jordan needs to put his foot in the ground and go.

He didn't tell anyone about the fumble against Hononegah.

OK, it wasn't exactly a fumble.

A defender reached over and put his hand on the ball. For less than a second, he lost control. Before it came out, Jordan was able to tuck it back in. But, boy, was it close. That's when he realized it's in his head. He's thinking too much about fumbling. He can hear Coach Bitto in his sleep.

Jordan's going to have to solve this puzzle on his own. He's not worried about being benched again. Not at this point in the season. He's heard Coach Bitto say he will, but he won't. He wants to win. Timmy Serio is a nice kid and a good player, but no way Carmel's beating St. Rita with a sophomore call-up. He's going to have to carry the load. Just like Marist.

He's at home. He cradles a football in his right arm, pressing it tightly against his chest. Jordan hasn't put it down all day. Even at school, he held it. He got a few funny looks, but people know. They know why. They know he knows why. He's tired of the looks. He's going to sleep with that football. Whatever it takes.

Jordan plays a video on his computer. There's a demonstration by a former running back at Stanford. He's talking about a way to grip the football to prevent fumbling. Jordan watches and listens. He likes that the Stanford player said you could still grip the football with one hand. That's good. Jordan doesn't like using two hands. He feels like he can't cut as well. He likes holding the ball with one hand and using the other to shoo away would-be tacklers.

The guy on the video has a name for the grip. He calls it the claw. He's saying how too many running backs put one finger on the tip of the ball.

That's Jordan. He likes to use his index finger, or the one next to the thumb. That will get you in trouble, he said. The best grip is to hold the tip of the football between your second and third fingers. This heightens the security within the pressure points of contact—finger, tips, palm, forearm, bicep and chest. When you use this grip, the ball feels that much tighter into your body.

He walks around the house that night, his leather pet tucked into his chest, trying out the new grip. Later, he falls into bed, exhausted after another long day. But the football stays with him. "I've got to figure this out," he whispers to himself. "I can't let my teammates down."

He falls asleep. His dreams are sweet dreams, of running over hapless defenders and holding a football that not even the Devil himself could wrestle from his clutch.

CHAPTER TWENTY-FIVE

SCOUT TEAM

THE PARADE OF THE SICK AND WOUNDED has slowed throughout the season.

Coach Bitto's office, once the pre-practice ward of ill refute, is now filled with healthy do-gooders. Winning 10 games, a conference championship and two playoff games has fermented the feverish and awakened the apathetic.

However, there are a few exceptions.

"I was sick yesterday and in bed all day. My mom wants me to come home and do my homework and get to sleep," Austin Zupec says to his coach while standing close to the door. Coach Bitto is sitting in his familiar spot in front of the television monitor, watching film on St. Rita.

"You have to do what your momma says. I never mess with mommas, wives, and grandmas," Coach Bitto says sliding over to behind his desk. "My mom's dead. I wish she were still yelling at me."

Zupec thanks his coach and leaves. The door opens, and in walk Jim and Eric Hessing. They are seniors and identical twins.

"Coach, we need to leave tomorrow at 5:30 p.m. because we're having our Eagle Scout board review," Jim says.

"What did you guys do for a project?" Coach Bitto asks. "You never told me."

"I made benches for Gurnee Park District," Jim says.

"How many?"

"Four."

"That's it? You make four and you get Eagle Scout for that?" Coach Bitto says, feigning outrage.

"They're hard," Jim says matter-of-factly.

"You should make 400." Coach Bitto turns to Eric Hessing. "What did you make?"

"Birdhouses," Eric says.

"Four?"

"No, 10 of them."

"OK, good luck. I didn't know this Scout thing was that easy," Coach Bitto says with a wide grin.

The Hessings are not only Scouts but scout-team players. They are the guys who mimic the other team's plays during team drills at practice. Bitto and the coaches recognize scout-team players at the end of each practice with a Player of the Day sticker. Those stickers are affixed to a player's helmet. They only see the field during blowout games, but neither Hessing boy has said a peep about a lack of playing time or has missed a practice or weightlifting session.

"You try to get those kids on the field if you can," Coach Bitto says. "It's easy to become disenfranchised if you are not willing to say, 'This is my role and this is how I can contribute to the wins we are getting.' That's pretty valuable."

From a pure football perspective, Carmel's 2010 success has much to do with its scout team, which includes several other seniors. All are most likely playing their last year of organized football, and all are taking hits in practice so the starters can be better prepared on Friday night.

"When we beat Marist, on the car ride home, I was really pumped because if the scout team guys hadn't been going 100 percent, we wouldn't have won," Eric Hessing says.

Chuck Hessing, the boys' father, said he asked Jim one night about his lack of playing time, about how he felt being on the scout team, most likely to never see the field in a competitive circumstance.

"I said, 'Do you feel like you are being cheated?' And he said, 'Dad, the best players are out there.'"

"Every night at 10:30, Jimmy comes down to tell me everything they have to do to beat the other team," said Sandy Hessing, their mother. "He's on MaxPreps and iHigh and figuring out what to do."

Those late-night conversations with her son are often about how he can improve his play so he can help his teammates.

"What Jim said to me was, 'I have to get better. [Tight end] Patrick Mulroy is not getting the right grade as I'm not getting him ready for the game,'" Sandy said. "'I've got to get back to practice and work harder.'"

This acceptance, this curtailment of one's self-interests, is counterintuitive for most teenagers. Yet this dynamic is critical to team chemistry. From his own experience as a player, Coach Bitto appreciates how challenging subjugating one's ego for the welfare of the team can be.

"When I was at Ball State, I was on the scout team, so I know exactly what they are going through. I went from zero money to full scholarship my senior year, which was awesome. When I became head coach here, we were crappy at first and now really good. That's what these guys are learning. You set your goals to a certain point, then you realize they are not going to get there. But how do you handle yourself to get as far as you can? That's what the Hessings have done.

"Jordan [Kos] has to put up with me yelling at him for scoring touchdowns the wrong way. That's tough. He's gifted. His ceiling is pretty high. The Hessings? They are not going to get much better. But they made a decision. They decided to give up any opportunity to play in a game to sacrifice themselves for the team. It takes a special guy to persevere through that stuff. So, in a lot of ways their job is way harder than Jordan's."

That's the job of a coach, to be sure every player on the roster feels valued. And rewarded. Those who see time on the field get the immediate gratification of making a catch or tackle or scoring a touchdown. But what's the reward for scout team players that do their best work in obscurity, in the shadows of Friday night lights?

"Well, at Ball State I wasn't going to quit. After freshman year, I was locked in. Sometimes you just make your decision even if it's not a good one. My sister was killed in college. I had to deal with that. There are other things that happen, other life things. I lean on those things," Coach Bitto says. "I would hope the Hessings would say being part of a winning team is an awesome experience. That they've bought into what the program can provide for them. I'm more proud when they are 30 and come back and say, 'Thank you for letting me play football—I learned a lot from it.' That's more important than winning a state title."

The phone rings in Coach Bitto's office, like it has about 11 times in the last 10 minutes. This time he needs to answer.

His hand on the receiver, he says: "So, each guy has their own little journey that they follow."

∾

Ben Berg is playing the "no respect" card.

An AP Psychology teacher at Carmel, the offensive coordinator has been scouring the Internet message boards. What he's finding is most fans don't give the Corsairs much of a chance against St. Rita on Saturday.

"If you listen to the Internet scuttlebutt, we're going to have to pass the ball 30 times or more to have a chance. There's no way we're going to be able to run the ball on them," Berg says, sitting in the coaches' office after Monday's practice.

One online post regionalized the argument, questioning whether Carmel, a suburban school, could handle the physicality of a team from the city, the Chicago Catholic League.

"Yeah, right," Berg says.

He pulls out a three-by-five card with quotations written on the back. He reads his notes, one by one.

"They are a bit small on defense to stop Jahwon Akui all night long w Rita's size on the offensive line."

"Carmel will have to pass more than they usually do to win"

"Carmel needs to bring their big boy pads for this one"

"There's nobody out there tougher than St. Rita"

"Rita's too physical for Carmel"

"Carmel may have to throw the ball 35 or more times. Rita just a little too big for them"

Wide receivers coach Tim Schrank listens to Berg read the love notes out loud. "Thirty-plus times? I don't think we've thrown it that much all year."

Close. Through 11 games, quarterback Brian Serio has thrown 53 times. Brian Brennan has two pass attempts. The most throws in a game were eight.

"We could throw the ball more," Berg says. "The problem with a game like Saturday against Hononegah is it got out of hand so quickly we couldn't throw it more. On three consecutive plays we scored."

He stands up and looks to the corner of the room where defensive coaches Dan Potempa and Jim Rejc huddle like mad scientists inventing crafty schemes to shut down St. Rita's offense. "Can you hold them to 17 Saturday night?" Berg asks.

Potempa looks up, removes his cap and scratches his head. "I think we'll be all right."

"If they stay on a long field, offenses are equal, both teams are playing well, yes," Rejc adds.

"Seventeen and under," Berg says. "That's all we need."

~

It's snowing inside Baker Stadium and no one is smiling brighter than Jerry Rejc.

Daylight savings was the previous Saturday. Clocks were moved back. By late afternoon, darkness falls over all of Illinois.

"Except in 64 football stadiums," Rejc says.

Carmel's longtime offensive line coach is referring to the eight classes of football in the state and the eight teams in each class still alive in the postseason in mid-November.

"When the first snow hits and you're still out here, that's when you know you are still playing. There's nothing better."

It's Wednesday and the Corsairs are in team drills. Scout-team quarterback Connor Greene is chucking the pigskin all over the field, simulating St. Rita's pass plays for the first-team defense. St. Rita likes to throw the ball to the tight end, specifically Tim Gorski, an all-conference player listed at 6-7, 245 pounds. Carmel hasn't played a team that uses their tight end all season and certainly hasn't seen a team with one as big and athletic as Gorski. As Greene throws, his former St. Mary's classmates reminiscence about his arm strength from their middle school days.

"Dude, he was able to throw back in the fifth grade," Chris Georgan says.

"He would throw bombs to (Ryan) Cappis," Matt Carr says. Carr has recovered from his broken left foot from earlier in the season and played in the second half of the Hononegah game. "Ryan would go from tight end and just streak. Connor would just throw it up. No one could catch Ryan. He was the quickest little kid."

Senior defensive lineman Jake Larson wanders over while on a water break. He's watched film on the Mustangs and said they are as big as advertised. "This is one of the better O-lines we've faced in terms of size. We just have to hold our gaps, clog it up so the linebackers can make plays."

Which is easier said than done. Although St. Rita features multi-talented skill-position players, at their core, the Mustangs are a downhill, power-running team. They want to get the football as often as possible to running back Jahwon Akui, a 5-7, 190-pound brawler.

"We can stop this kid but he's slippery. I saw film and he was breaking tackles all over the field. It will be a battle," Larson says. "Rita's a good program. I remember watching St. Rita-Mount Carmel games on TV and I always felt like, 'My God, that's high-class football.' I always thought Rita was this football powerhouse. Now we are playing them and we have a chance. A good chance."

It's a crowded practice field during the playoffs. The sophomores now practice with the varsity. At some practices late in the regular season, the number of players dressed was under 40. This made it hard to run scout team or "two-platoon" drills as there just weren't enough bodies. Now there are close to 70 players in uniform and practicing. Because the extra bodies need instruction, the sophomore coaches are also milling about, providing an extra set of eyes and ears. One of those coaches is Larry Whittier, the sophomore team head coach.

"Enzo!" he yells in the direction of the home bench.

The team videographer and resident prayer whisperer, Enzo Magrin, is on the field, a rare sight during the season. He stands near midfield just behind where the team is gathered for team drills. Whittier continues.

"Whenever I end up calling Enzo, he says, 'May God be with you.' That's his sign off. He's a dedicated prayer man!" Whittier says. "Don't forget I need help with the man upstairs."

"I do what I can," Magrin says, ginning from ear to ear.

Magrin walks off the field towards his devout perch above the press box. He needs to check on the camera that's filming practice.

∽

This is a special time for everyone around the program. For lifers like Magrin, it is the payoff after so many lamentable seasons that lapsed into decades.

"I've missed nine games since 1965," Magrin said earlier. Every day he films practice. He hasn't missed a day this season or since anybody can remember. "When I graduated we went through 15 years of one winning season. I was very frustrated, and every year I said I'm not coming back, but I would. This is where the good Lord wants me."

On this mid-November late afternoon, the view from Enzo's Prayer Cave is wondrous. Snowflakes glitter in the artificial light. The natural autumn shade mixes harmoniously with football's classic soundtrack—shouts, shoulder pads and whistles. The accumulation of snow makes it hard to stand. But when one strolls through the clouds, the ground beneath is often hard to feel.

∽

I know you pray up here and we've talked about that. About how it disciplines you. How do you know if it's working?

"I think about Elder. That affected me. We haven't had a lot of failure. But prayer helped me deal with that loss. And how do you keep success in perspective? If you get too full of yourself, you are going to end up failing, as you need a certain amount of humility. Football is good as it gives you that."

That is true. With sports there is always a winner and a loser. But isn't having faith the true answer? Believing that God will show us that he is listening?

"I'll tell you about somebody. There was one guy who was a real jerk out here. A good ballplayer but didn't get it. We really didn't think he would make it. The family came to me and I could see they were distraught. This is a junior playing now.

"So I kept praying. I started to pray for the family and they changed and they changed their son. I didn't realize it but God did. I think because they had prayer the entire situation changed. He's got a ways to go but he's getting it. Whoever the Lord used to change him, praise him. God already knew, but He wants us to pray."

Whom do you pray for? How do you know?

"We have to be open to Him and let Him touch our hearts. I remember the mother came to me distraught and I told her I was praying for her, that the Lord wanted me to do this for him. She was shocked. Why is everyone shocked about this?"

You took an interest in their child. You were looking out for that child. That's what we do.

"He's a kid God is not finished with yet. We are keeping him in prayer. Yes, that's what we do. That's why I'm still here."

~

Magrin leans over toward the camera. Through the viewfinder he sees snow-drenched bleacher steps behind an ivory-colored field. On that field, captured under a luminous, ornamental sky, the regimented yet joyful movements of the boys in brown are made.

CHAPTER TWENTY-SIX

LAST GOODBYE

THE SHADES ARE DRAWN WITHIN THE MODEST ROOM. Streaks of afternoon sunlight shimmer through. The ghostly electric beams shine against a translucent whiteboard on which a sentence is written in black marker.

I am who I am as a result of the sum of my experiences

LaRon certainly has had experiences in his young life.

He's thinking about the day she died. Marion. That awful morning when he and Jim had to wait for the valet to come and park the car at the hospital. They were a few minutes late.

He remembers her bed was by a window. He took a seat next to where she lay. It was bright that day, the dreary, cloudy January gray skies awash in diaphanous color. At first, LaRon's mind was blank, a solitude commanded by death. Gradually, as he remained by her side, thoughts of his life with Marion seeped back into his consciousness, like a projector playing scenes from a film. He scrutinized his life with the introspection of a sabbatical monk.

Is this the end of existence? Is she really somewhere else now? Where? With God? Who is God? What kind of God would take her away from me?

If I'd known I was going to lose her, things would have been different. I wouldn't have yelled. I wouldn't have done some of the stupid crap that I did. I wouldn't have gotten into trouble. I wouldn't have mouthed off. I would have buckled down. I would have tried harder not to be so angry.

When I got older I would ask her about it. About my real mom, about her giving me up. "Why did she do that?" Mom would respond, "She couldn't take care of you. She loved you but she just couldn't do it." There was the time she drove me to see her. I wish I could remember but I was so small. Three years old, maybe four. There's a picture. I'm in a booth at a restaurant. I'm sitting on her lap. Mom took it. I need to find that picture.

I was very calm and patient with her before she came back to the hospital, before she went to the place she is now. If there is a heaven, I hope that's where she is. That would be a good place for mom. It's a better place with her in it. But couldn't she have waited a little longer?

When she first got sick, I helped her around the house, driving her to the pharmacy to pick up her medication or to the grocery store. She was always in her robe, wearing that baseball cap to cover up her head from the chemo. She made a phone list for Dad to call about certain things around the house. Ann, Tom and a few of the others came over one night. She talked about her Will, how she wanted things settled. Oh, and she showed us the secret to her spinach and bacon salad. That was actually kind of fun. Mom was so desperate to keep traditions alive, as if she knew she'd be gone. Did she know? How? What's going to happen to those traditions now? Who's going to remember? She told me, "I just want you to know you have to try your best, continue to be a good person and you have to take care of your dad." That's the first time it hit me that, "wow, she's not going to live forever." And she was right. Why did she have to be right about that?

Mom was never good at keeping secrets. I was never good at keeping mine. She found some weed in the basement my sophomore year. She confronted me and I was defiant. Damn right I was. I told her, "I smoke pot. Deal with it." And you know how she dealt with it? By calling the school. She told them I was smoking pot. The woman flat ratted me out. The school made me see a counselor. We all went every Wednesday for six months. A Haitian lady. She was funny and sweet. But I hated it, leaving football workouts in the summer. I remember when she first said, "You don't have an issue smoking pot. Your problem is with your family, so we're going to deal with your family." She won my respect right away. And the sessions helped.

For the first time, my mom and I talked about things in a relaxed environment. We had real conversations, not shouting matches. I told her how I felt like she wasn't always on my side when she should have been fighting for me. Times when I got in playground fights and I'd say, "My friend was getting picked on and I stepped in to help him out." I expected her to say, "I understand. LaRon was trying to be a good friend." But Mom wouldn't do that. I'd try and explain it to her and she would say, "Well, you shouldn't have been doing that." That's all it is? That's all I heard. That was frustrating for me to hear. I did something out of my emotions, and you are not really accepting it? It was hard for me. But the sessions really helped me move on. I began to understand why she was on me so much, why she acted the way she did. She was so worried about the drugs. She had seen it at the clinic. She was terrified I'd end up like them. I explained to her how weed is not the same thing as heroin. The doctor said because of how I was born, I was more predisposed to addictions and how weed could be a gateway drug to harder substances. I said that would never happen. Thinking about it now, I'm not sure my mom was convinced. But I was grateful for the dialogue. Things got better after that. And then the stomach pains came.

LaRon remembers staring out that same hospital room window for what must have been hours, lost in reflection. He remembers how rapidly time slipped by that day, like raindrops off a flower pedal.

Now in the present, he lifts his head. The room is quiet.

Someone stands behind the podium. It's Tyler.

Behind him, three words are written on the whiteboard.

Love in Action.

"What is Christian love?" Tyler asks. "It's a gift freely given and expecting nothing in return. It's accepting others as they are and not as I would want them to be."

Love in action.

That was Marion. Every day of her life.

And although LaRon didn't completely understand his life story, he was starting to make sense of it all. He was starting to find peace.

∾

Later at the chapel, Matt calls his name. LaRon is ready to speak. He has never been clearer about what he wants to say.

"I'm LaRon and I'm reacting to Kairos. There are some things in life you can't explain. My Kairos brothers have taught me so much about myself and about each of you. I feel like I've gained so many new brothers I never knew I had. You all showed courage, honesty and so much heart. We shared some intimate things together, a lot of it about our parents, and how much we fought with them. I hope by sharing my story, they feel differently about themselves. I hope they have the courage to express themselves, to tell openly what is inside of them. I accept more now the importance of having people in my corner. I'm not afraid to fail. I have friends to fall back on. I didn't do all of this for me. I did it for others to see and think, 'OK, this is where this kid is coming from. He's being totally honest, and maybe I need to do that same thing.' I feel like I'm closer to knowing the real me and understanding what I have to do to get even closer to my true self."

He steps away from the lectern. He hugs Matt and the rest of the leaders. The last candle is blown out.

Outside, among the crowd of classmates and parents, LaRon seeks out Jim, his dad. He finds him. They hug. Jim reaches around his son with his right arm and gives him an extra pat on the right shoulder.

"I love you, son."

"I love you, dad," LaRon says back.

Above them is a statue of Jesus. A Biblical passage is written on the wall.

"Some are given to plant, others to water. But only God gives the growth."

CHAPTER TWENTY-SEVEN

ST. RITA

It's a cool, dry Saturday night at 7740 South Western Avenue in Chicago, the home field of the St. Rita Mustangs. The conditions—minimal wind, no rain—are ideal for a November football playoff game. This will be a game decided by the two crucibles of football—blocking and tackling—rather than an uncooperative weather pattern.

As it has been all season, Coach Bitto's pregame speech is short on Xs and Os. At this point, everyone knows the enormity of what lies ahead. Tonight, it's about execution and sacrifice.

"I don't have a whole lot to say," he says. The players are all on one knee inside St. Rita's congested visitors locker room, helmets on, their padded and taped bodies covered by the team's road uniform—white jerseys and brown pants. Coach Bitto's head moves slowly from side to side. He makes eye contact through the facemask bars obstructing the view of his players' zealous facial expressions. He continues after a few seconds pause.

"When does excellence ever end? When does getting better ever end? It never ends! Ever! We are always on a quest to get better. We are always on the quest to get close to one another. Turn to the guy next to you. Tell them you are going to play your ass off for him. Tell him the relationship never ends. Tell him how important this has been to you! Tell him how much Carmel means to you! Tell how much this team means to you! This is a lot of fun. You are special people for stepping out and caring for one another. And tonight you are going to get better. And we'll get better next week and the week after that.

"Tonight is our night. You've prepared for it, you've earned it, and you owe it to one another to do your very best without question on every single down, because every play is our last!"

∾

Carmel wins the toss and elects to receive. On its first play from scrimmage, Brian Serio takes the snap and stuffs the ball into the belly of his fullback, who falls forward for a two-yard gain. Just as important, Jordan Kos holds on to the ball. With that out of the way, the Corsairs can play football.

On third-and-eight from St. Rita's 22, Serio makes a good read. He keeps the ball and scampers for a first down. Two plays later, Brian Brennan takes a pitch from his quarterback and gets 10 more yards. Carmel is finding open running lanes over the left side of the Mustang defense. They might be wider if blocking back Matt Maher were playing. It's been seven weeks since Carmel's best blocker injured his knee against Marist. He tried to give it a go in practice this week, but went a bit too hard. Maher's in street clothes tonight.

The Corsairs march into St. Rita territory, converting another third down as Brennan takes a pitch from Serio and runs eight yards, this time over the right side, to the Mustangs' 43-yard line. Just over four minutes of clock has elapsed, an opening-drive touchdown appearing inevitable. But the next two plays yield only two yards and the Corsairs face a third and long from St. Rita's 41-yard line. For the third time on the drive, Ben Berg, calling the plays from the press box, says into his headset, "32 Pitch." And why not? The previous two calls yielded first- down runs. Only this time Rita is ready for it.

Serio runs to the right side of the field, and pitches the ball to Brennan, who appears to have an alley in front of the Mustangs' sideline. But safety Jake Pikowski fends off a block from Michael Panico and closes quickly and knocks Brennan out of bounds at the 39. It's fourth-and-six.

"Punt team!" Coach Bitto yells into the headset.

Matt Ryan's punt goes 22 yards, and Rita takes over on its 17-yard line. Although the opening drive does not yield points, it accomplishes an important directive: field position. Carmel's defense will be tested tonight, but no team has completed a multiple-play touchdown drive of more than 80 yards on the Corsairs all season long.

St. Rita manages four yards on three plays and punts back to the Corsairs. After two plays, the second a 16-yard run by Serio, Carmel again has the ball in Mustangs territory. It's first and 10 on the St. Rita 45-yard line. But the Corsairs get only four yards on three plays. Carmel kicks it back to St. Rita, and the Mustangs take over on their 21.

Earlier in the week, Berg asked the defensive coaches about St. Rita's offense. Jim Rejc said he had looked at every offensive play he could get his hands on.

"You don't think they can drive the length of the field doing what they do?" Berg asked him.

His reply: "I checked every one of their scoring drives on all their film, and every single one has had at least a 20-yard play. Four yards, five yards, three yards, seven yards—the length of the field, they can't do it. I don't know why, but they can't do it. They need 20-yard plays or more to score."

This proves to be a moment of clairvoyance.

On second down, Rita quarterback Brandon Johnson hits tight end Tim Gorski over the middle for a 20-yard completion. Johnson makes the throw running to his right, away from pressure. This was a concern leading up to the game. On film, Johnson showed he could throw with accuracy on the run, not a characteristic seen this season from any other opposing quarterback. After the completion, St. Rita has the ball on its 43. Jahwon Akui runs eight yards on first down (he'd only had six total yards before that) and the quarter runs out.

Two plays into the second quarter, St. Rita has the ball on Carmel's 46, second and 10. The Mustangs line up in a formation the Corsairs haven't seen—three receivers to the left (a "trips formation") and one to the right. Johnson is out of the game, replaced by senior running back Travis Starks.

Standing in a shotgun, the ball is snapped directly to Starks, who runs behind Akui through the left side of the line. Once across, he quickly turns it back right and gains 11 yards.

St. Rita runs the same play again, and if not for a Tyler Lees ankle tackle, Starks would have scored the first touchdown of the game. The six-yard run has the Mustangs on Carmel's 29.

Football at its core is a game of matchups. Where the Mustangs have begun to take over is in the trenches—their massive offensive line knocking back Carmel's undersized line with every snap. On St. Rita's one long passing play, the Corsairs had no one who could cover the 6-5 Gorski over the middle. Now, on second and four, the Mustangs exploit another mismatch. On the left side of the field, wide receiver Bobby Gallagher is lined up against Corsairs defensive back Sean Brennan. Gallagher stands 6-5. Brennan is 5-5. This is as close to David vs. Goliath as you'll see on a football field. Only tonight, Brennan isn't holding a slingshot.

The Mustangs quick-snap it and Johnson flings it over to Gallagher, who picks up 15 yards before Brennan—who despite his diminutive frame is one of the team's best tacklers—brings Gallagher down at the Carmel 14. Two plays later, St. Rita gets the same matchup and runs the same play. Michael Fitzgibbons, lined up at linebacker just off the left-side edge, recognizes the play and runs over to give Brennan help, but not before the completion to Gallagher picks up another eight yards. Akui gains five yards on the next play, and it's first- and-goal Mustangs from the Corsairs' two-yard line.

This close to scoring, St. Rita doesn't over-think it. The Mustangs give the ball to their bullhorn, Akui. On his second attempt, he leaps over the goal line for a touchdown. The 13-play, 79-yard drive eats up over nine minutes of clock and is just the type of punch-in-the-gut drive Carmel had hoped to get first. As St. Rita kicks off to Carmel, the sense of urgency from the offensive unit is palpable.

"Now it's our turn," Brian Brennan says before running onto the field.

～

Carmel takes over on its own 34-yard line with just over four minutes remaining in the half. Brian Serio is the team's only consistent offensive weapon, and on first down, the Corsairs' quarterback keeps it for no gain.

On the sidelines, there is mounting concern that Serio is running too much, that lanes are open and for whatever reason, he's not giving the ball to Kos inside, or pitching it to Panico or Brian Brennan on the perimeter. But in Carmel's decision-based option attack, the triggerman needs time to determine his read, and St. Rita is not cooperating. Mustangs defensive linemen are penetrating through every gap, and linebackers are reading Carmel's plays with ease, as if they know what is coming. What hasn't come yet is a Carmel pass.

On second and 10 from the Carmel 34-yard line, Serio voluntarily steps backward for the first time all game. He's looking to throw the football to Ryan Cappis, who has single coverage on the right side of the field. Cappis runs a curl route and moves his defender deep, creating a cushion for what should be an easy 10-yard completion. But the protection breaks down before Serio can set his feet and throw, so he takes off, running for a six-yard gain. He now has 38 yards on eight carries. The rest of the Carmel offense has totaled 22 yards.

It's third and four from Carmel's 40-yard line. It might still only be the first half, but there is a sense this third-down play is hugely important. Carmel needs to show it can be who it is—a prolific offensive team. A team that all season has moved the ball north and south with machine-like precision. A first down will go a long way toward reestablishing belief, even if the drive doesn't result in a touchdown.

The Corsairs line up in their base option formation. Brian Brennan goes in motion right to left. Serio takes the snap and puts the ball in the gut of Kos, but pulls it back, running to his left. It's the correct read as the defensive end crashes inside, leaving a running lane for Serio just off the edge. He should pick up the first down, but just as he crosses the line of scrimmage, Pat O'Connor, the end who first crashed inside, leaps back outside and trips up Serio two yards shy of a first down. Coach Bitto elects to line up as if his team will go for it, but it's nothing more than a ruse to try and draw the Mustangs offsides. They don't take the bait, and Ryan punts for the third time.

Carmel gets the ball back one more time before the end of the half. Three plays result in an incomplete pass, a one-yard run by Panico and a quarterback scramble of seven yards. St. Rita runs two plays on its ensuing possession before the first-half clock runs out. The score remains 7-0.

Carmel's offensive futility for the first 24 minutes is unparalleled in 2010. Four possessions yield four punts and over the last three possessions, just one first down. After Serio's 16-yard run on the opening drive, the team's longest play is six yards. The defense, however, has played well. Take out the one touchdown drive, and St. Rita has managed just 20 yards of total offense.

~

Carmel huddles just behind the south end zone. The atmosphere within the group anything but panicky. For an offense averaging 39 points a game, a one-touchdown deficit is more than manageable. "We have to take advantage of field position," Berg tells them. "We have to smash block when we get the opportunity. We have to read right and we have to play faster. We have to block the perimeter."

One reason for Carmel's offensive struggles is that St. Rita's defensive linemen are not taking on blocks by Carmel offensive linemen. They are simply falling to the ground. When this unusual tactic works, it closes gaps, making it hard for the fullback and quarterback to gain yards.

The risk with this "flop" strategy is it leaves a defense vulnerable to the pitch. Carmel rushing plays to the perimeter of the field should be wide open if St. Rita defensive backs are blocked. Against weaker playoff opponents, the Corsairs could get away with missed blocking assignments. But not against St. Rita. With each possession, the absence of Maher is magnified.

Berg ends halftime with verbal butt-kicking to the running backs ("Wing backs, do you even know what you're doing? Ain't blocking anybody, that's for damn sure! You're embarrassing yourselves!"), while Coach Bitto takes a calmer approach before the team heads back to the sidelines for the second half. He brings both offensive and defensive units together.

"A couple plays here a couple plays there, we're up 14-7. That's the way it is. Now we have to play our butts off to get back in this game. Score three times in second half, all right? We are going to kick off. Let's get field position and we can turn it on in the third quarter, get them on the run.

"Let's get a cheer—one, two, three, Corsairs!"

∾

St. Rita has the ball first to start the second half and, after O'Block's kick-off, takes over on its 20-yard line. As much as Carmel talked at halftime about being better at what it does, St. Rita's narrative is assuredly the same. And for the Mustangs, that's play power football better than their opponent. Four of the first five play calls are running plays out of the I-formation. Akui runs it each time, picking up 29 yards. The defense holds firm, not allowing Akui to break free for any long gains (as Rejc said, "They need 20-yard plays to score"). It's third and five for St. Rita from its own 49. In order to approach Coach Bitto's halftime directive of scoring three times, Carmel's offense needs the ball. The defense needs to stop the Mustangs right now.

St. Rita quarterback Brandon Johnson steps back to throw, he launches the ball at wide receiver Mitch Saffold. Cornerback Ricky Acosta breaks toward the ball and goes for an interception, but Saffold snatches it out of the air before Acosta can get his hands on it. He spins away at the Carmel 40 and sprints toward the end zone. Tyler Lees runs Saffold down from behind, but not before he picks up 29 yards. It's a huge play. A touchdown from the Mustangs on this drive could be devastating.

This scenario unfolds again as on fourth down from the Corsairs' 21. The Mustangs attempt a screen pass. It is read perfectly by the Carmel defense, and Johnson has no time to set up the play, so he throws the ball to the ground. Carmel takes over on downs. It's potentially a momentum-shifting play.

∾

Three plays later, Carmel once again faces fourth down. They are a yard short. There is 7:30 left in the third quarter, plenty of time to erase a single touchdown deficit, but Carmel's inability to move the chains, to show a glimmer of proficiency, becomes more alarming with each possession.

After another unsuccessful attempt to draw St. Rita offsides, Carmel punts. A 23-yard kick by O'Block gives the Mustangs the ball at midfield. St. Rita squanders the great field position, losing three yards on three plays, and kicks it right back to Carmel. The defense again does its job.

When Carmel takes over on its own 27, the possession is its sixth of the game. On a foggy November night in 2001, Richards shut out Carmel in the state semifinals, 10-0. That's the last time the Corsairs went without scoring an offensive touchdown.

A holding penalty on first down sets Carmel back 11 yards. On first and 21, Serio keeps the ball, gaining six yards. On second down, he drops back to pass. He quickly goes through his reads. With no one open, he scrambles for three yards. It's third and 12. This would be a perfect time for the team's first pass completion of the game. Cappis is split to the left, with single coverage on the outside. That's where Serio wants to throw the ball. The play begins and he drops back to pass. Cappis gets a step on Akui, the Mustangs running back who is in the game as a defensive back. Serio settles into a stable pocket, then fires. For a moment, as the ball spirals through the air, it appears Carmel will hit the big play it so desperately needs. But the ball is slightly underthrown, allowing Akui time to catch up and deflect the football. It bounces off the turf and skids away. Carmel yet again must punt.

St. Rita takes over on its 45 yard line and runs four plays before the quarter runs out. Two are from the Wildcat formation and gain 16 yards. The other two are power runs from Akui, resulting in nine yards. So, the fourth quarter begins with St. Rita on Carmel's 30-yard line, facing a third and 1. Akui plows over the right side for a gain of two and a fresh set of downs. On the next play, Johnson appears to give the ball to Akui again and the Carmel linebackers crash toward Akui. Only he doesn't have the ball. Lined up to the right side is Saffold, who sneaks through the confused Carmel defenders, running toward an open alley in the middle of the field. Johnson flings a pass in his direction and a wide- open Safford catches it at the five-yard line and easily scores. The extra point makes it 14-0 St. Rita.

There is 14:32 remaining in the game—ordinarily plenty of time for Carmel to rattle off two scores. But for anyone watching the game, a comeback scenario looks doubtful at best.

~

From his seat near the last row of bleachers, John Butler can sense it might be over. The thought of it has him feeling like he's falling off a cliff. He's felt this way for weeks. The stomach-churning dread. His son, Jack, is Carmel's starting left tackle. Skinny for an offensive lineman at 6-4, 190 pounds, Jack relies more on technique than brutality. He is the team's best downfield blocker, athletic enough to get to the second level and tie up back-heeled linebackers or safeties. Jack was the one Butler son (Brandon was the oldest) who always loved football, dragging his father and mother Kathy to games while at St. Francis grade school in Lake Zurich. The summer before his junior year, John would get up early to go to work and notice his son wasn't in his room, sleeping like a normal teenager.

"All of a sudden, out of the blue, Jack is gone. He sets his alarm in the morning and he gets up and he goes," John said. "He felt some innate responsibility to the football team and he developed a work habit that I'm sure he will live with the rest of his life. That's not something we taught him. Kathy and I are very thankful for that."

That school year, you know what Jack told his dad? He wanted to be a physician. John asked his son if he was sure he could do that. Jack replied that he believed he could if he worked hard enough. Just like football. If he worked hard, he'd win a spot. Life's a little like that, too.

Sitting in the visiting bleachers at St. Rita, watching the season slip away, John's wife, Kathy, is with a group of Carmel moms. She's wearing a gold down jacket. Around her neck is a Carmel scarf, the one she's worn diligently as the descending calendar turned the air of football evenings cool. Around her scarf rests a lanyard. At the end of the cord, a plastic sheet lies on the outside of Kathy's jacket. On the front is a picture of Jack in his uniform. On the back is Carmel's football roster. If before one of Jack's games this waxen sheet could not be found, Kathy would come close to filing a missing person's report. She would not leave the house without it. When the season ends, Kathy will put the object in a box, to be discovered someday. But for what's left of tonight, for her and the other moms, it represents everything that matters.

~

Standing up in the back row of the bleachers, leaning against the railing is Allan Acosta. Sitting down next to him is his wife, Irma. Their son, Ricky, is a senior cornerback for the Corsairs. He is the third Acosta to attend Carmel. Mark, their youngest, is a sophomore at the school. Allan and Irma are from Honduras, having immigrated in the early 1980s. They grew up impoverished, desirous for a better life in America. They made the decision to send their kids to private school when their oldest, daughter Nikita, was in first grade. It hasn't been easy. Allan is a construction worker. Irma works as an executive secretary. "We work two jobs to get the kids to come here," Irma said. "Because we work so hard, people think we are middle class. But we consider ourselves poor."

This fall there's been tension in the house between Ricky and Allan. Some of it is normal stuff between a father and teenage son—the attempt by son to accelerate 100 miles an hour into manhood, followed by the inevitable push by father back to boyhood. But as much as Ricky wants to be treated like an independent adult, he has the emotional intelligence to understand he needs his father to help him sort through the things he should be worried about and what he should just let go of. It's been hard. Allan's been working odd jobs, all hours. He has to work, to put food on the table and to pay his son's tuition. As a result, he's missed several of Ricky's games. They hardly see each other at home. And when they do, all they seem to do is argue.

"The only time we see each other is when we are addressing something that's wrong that I'm doing. I don't expect him to come to my games unless he can. I'd like to tell him to come to one of my games but ..." Ricky said. "In football, when I'm making plays, it's more for my parents, not for me. That's how I feel. I think of all the games over the years, games my dad's been to, my dad was happy if I made a play. I was making him proud. If he's not there, there's nothing I can do."

But tonight, he's here. And as Allan watches his son play so valiantly, he knows when it's over, that he will find his son and tell him how proud he is of him.

~

It started with a rickety old generator and one grill. Steve Lester would make pancakes. Bill Keller would make hash browns and sausage. Steve's wife, Tina, would bring hot chocolate and Dunkin' Donuts coffee. They could barely run the grill on the dilapidated power supply from the generator until later that season, 2006, when the Doolans showed up with a big generator. Then it was stuffed french toast for everyone!

By the time Lesters' oldest son, Steven, was a senior in 2009, a star defensive lineman, Steve Sr. would get off work at 2:30 p.m. Friday so he could stake out territory in the parking lot outside Baker Stadium. With the extra time, the once-minimal spread expanded to needing banquet-sized tables to fit all the food. There was everything from rib eyes to pulled pork to brownies the size of home entertainment speakers. And the Thursday-night pregame dinners at the Lesters' house on Route 45? Everyone would come. Coaches, parents, priests, brothers, sisters, aunts, uncles. So much food. So many laughs. The Lesters are a happy household. There's Steve, Tina, Steven—now a freshman at the Air Force Academy—senior offensive lineman Logan and youngest daughter Tess, a student athletic trainer and junior at Carmel. But the Carmel community is their family. The association is so much of whom they are and so much of how they want to be seen by others.

For years, Steve has been the team's unofficial photographer. Once the game kicks off, he swaps roles from master chef to camera chief. Steve, wearing his familiar Davy Crockett headpiece and Green Bay Packers jacket, casts an intimidating figure. He's a large man, the parent most responsible for Steven and Logan's hulking statures. But for years, he's roamed corners of Baker Stadium with his tiny digital camera and skinny tripod, shooting action pictures of Logan and the other boys.

Tonight, on the Carmel sidelines inside St. Rita's stadium, he checks his viewfinder to frame up another sequence of pictures. It's getting colder and his shooting finger is getting numb. But he doesn't care.

All he really wants is one more week.

~

Ed Kos has left his seat and is leaning over the bleachers' front railing. What he just saw worries him deeply.

After St. Rita's second touchdown, the ensuing kickoff was short and to the right. Michael Panico received the football and ran straight ahead. To his right was Ed's son, Jordan. As soon as Jordan saw the kick heading in Panico's direction, he streaked across the field in hopes of blocking a defender and creating a running lane for his teammate. At full speed, Kos collided with a Mustangs player and fell to the turf. After the play was over, Kos stood up, but wobbled. He then went down on one knee. It took several seconds for him to stand on both feet. Once upright, he had to be helped off the field. Tim Serio is now the Corsairs' starting fullback.

As Carmel begins its offensive series, Kos is off to the side, 30 or so yards away from where teammates and coaches are clustered on the sidelines. Trainer Dan Henrichs and Mike Kordecki, a well-known local physical therapist who volunteers at Carmel football games, are examining him. Henrichs is running through concussion-test protocol.

"Do you remember what happened?"

"No, I don't," Jordan says.

"On the kickoff, you got hit pretty hard."

Thirty seconds later, Henrichs repeats the same question.

"What happened Jordan? Do you remember how you got hurt?"

"No, I don't remember."

Henrichs and Kordecki repeat this question several times. They get the same answer. They ask Jordan to stand on one leg. He can't without almost falling over. Symptoms of a concussion. By now, Ed has made his way over to where they are.

"He doesn't remember the play, and he's starting to have headaches," Henrichs says to Ed. "We need to take him to the locker room so he can get his stuff. He needs to go to the hospital and get checked out."

"OK. Let's go," Ed says.

"What's going on in the game? Can I go back in?" Jordan asks in a desperate tone.

"No, Jordan. We have to leave the field and go into the locker room right now," Henrichs says.

Jordan gets up to head toward the room, turning his back away from where his teammates are still fighting to keep the season alive. As he walks across the track, his father and Henrichs at his side, his eyes moisten with tears. It wasn't supposed to end tonight, and certainly not like this.

～

After Kos's departure, Carmel runs off its best drive since the opening possession. Three toss sweeps to Panico produce 24 yards. Serio completes his first pass of the game, a 10-yard hitch to tight end Pat Doherty on third down. With just over nine minutes remaining in the game, Carmel has the ball with first and 10 on the St. Rita 35. But on the next four plays, old demons rear their ugly heads. Serio is sacked for a four-yard loss. After gaining five yards on an option keep, he overthrows an open Brian Brennan in the left flat on third down. Fourth down is a school-yard scramble, an intended pass that turns into a three-yard scamper. Serio runs for his life to evade the Mustangs' rush. He's tackled well short of the marker needed to keep the possession going.

When St. Rita scored its second touchdown, even the most sanguine Carmel fans were drained of optimism. But players still held hope, believing a team that had overcome so much in 2010—from skeptical preseason prognosticators to a rash of injuries—would assemble the collective fortitude needed to rally. But that belief is no longer palpable.

For the first time all night, the offensive unit appears reserved, placid, almost detached, as it returns to the sidelines. Carmel needs someone to make a big play, to seize some semblance of momentum. But that play hasn't come.

Logan Lester, the team's senior offensive guard, slowly removes his helmet with his right hand. He can barely move the left. It's been a problem since the Joliet Catholic game in September. A Hilltopper middle linebacker blitzed the "A" gap, and when he tried to push him back, he felt a pop in his shoulder. He played through it. Against Rockton Hononegah last week, Logan pulled out on a pitch play. He lost his footing and while falling to the turf, stuck his left arm out to break his fall. The shoulder popped again. It felt worse this time. An MRI confirmed what he suspected. The labrum was torn, surgery needed. But that could wait. His team had a state championship to win.

Sitting on the bench, Lester looks up at Coach Jerry Rejc.

"I can't move my arm anymore, coach."

"We need you in this game," Rejc says.

"I don't know if I can do it anymore."

"Logan, finish the game. You can do it."

"OK."

A loud ovation is heard from the opposite sidelines. Akui just ran into the end zone from 26-yards out. It's 21-0 Mustangs with just under four minutes left.

The game clock winds down, and Chicago feels like it's getting colder.

∿

Just a few blocks away is Holy Cross Hospital on 68th Street. Jordan sits in the passenger seat as his dad drives. His shoulder pads are off. A T-shirt covers his upper body.

"I hope we are winning," Jordan says.

Ed's phone beeps with text message updates. One comes over with these words written:

"21-0 Rita. It's over."

The car stops at a red light. Ed turns to his son.

"Sorry, buddy. You guys lost."

Jordan begins to cry.

He'll miss the locker room and a chance to say goodbye to his teammates. More than the game's result, this reality fills him with an overwhelming sorrow.

~

One of sport's harsh realities is its dichotomous outcome—there is always a winner and a loser. On this night, St. Rita was the winner, the better team. The final score of 21-0 is an appropriate result from the two and a half hours of football played. The upshot of the contest is its finality. There will be no more football in 2010 for the Carmel Corsairs.

"Coach, they just beat us on the line of scrimmage. There was nothing we could do," Berg says to Coach Bitto as they walk glumly toward the locker room. "I was pulling out straws."

"I thought our defense played awesome. If they had played just average, we should have won that game," Coach Bitto says, stupefied over the result.

Inside the locker room, emotions are a jumbled chorus. There's no hollering. No yelps. Just sobs of regret, smiles of remembrance, and actions of thankfulness.

Senior Michael Fitzgibbons sits on the floor in a corner, helmet still attached, tears glisten under sweat-stained eyelids. Through his own tears, Brian Serio bear hugs Logan Lester. There is no other way to hug Lester, a gentle giant. Coach Jim Rejc rests his hand on the right shoulder of Eric Hessing, whispering quietly to the senior. Luke Venegoni sits alone on a bench, still in full uniform. He's removed his helmet but clutches its facemask with the tension of a player ready for another series of football.

His coach stands in front of the group one last time in 2010.

"You did a great job. Ten wins is a great job. I just wish we had 13," Coach Bitto says. "I don't know what happened out there tonight. I do know this— I'm proud of each and every one of you. This season is not about one game. It's about how a group of young men came together, committed to one another, and achieved greatness. That's what I'll remember."

~

Everyone has said all there is to say. The bleary-eyed Corsairs scatter, some to a seat inside the school-sponsored bus for the ride back to campus. Others will ride home with their parents.

But before they can turn the lights out, there is still work to be done.

Andy, Tim, Tom, Jerry and Jim pick up scatterings of tape from the concrete floor. And there is Fitz, pushing a broom, sweeping up the last bit of dirt leftover from the boys.

Football is over at Carmel Catholic this season, but never its obligations. These men will always see to that.

CHAPTER TWENTY-EIGHT

SACRAMENTS

IT'S SUNDAY AFTERNOON. Less than 24 hours before, Andy Bitto's high school coaching season ended.

He's in the car with his sons, Jack and Peter, driving home. Earlier, his Stallions youth team lost in the league's Super Bowl. There will be no football championships this fall for the Bittos. In the passenger seat, Peter turns toward his father.

"Dad, thanks for coaching us. We learned a lot. I had a blast."

Jack, sitting in the back, reaches out, tapping his dad on the right shoulder. Today, Jack held a trophy for the first time in his young life.

"Don't worry, Dad. We tried our best."

As he stares straight into the road ahead, Andy manages a weary grin.

God. Family. Carmel. Football.

Sacraments are everywhere, he's thinking. You just have to open your heart and let them in.

EPILOGUE

On a warm July morning in 2015, Andy Bitto is roaming the practice fields at Carmel.

He isn't coaching teenagers on proper blocking technique, or on how to read a defender before galloping through a seam. No, Coach Bitto is lining the fields in advance of that afternoon's drills.

"A high school football coach has many jobs," he says. "Fortunately, I like to work."

In the five years since 2010, Coach Bitto has endured through a personal hardship—a torn Achilles tendon suffered in the summer of 2014—and before that, two losing seasons in 2012 and 2013.

The Achilles tear was a temporary inconvenience. It didn't prevent him from being on the sidelines—he rode around for part of the season with a walker on wheels—and the Corsairs finished 7-4, making it to the second round of the playoffs. It was the previous two seasons, the least successful in his long tenure as head coach, that forced him to look inward and re-evaluate how he leads and runs a program.

"My coaches thought I wasn't hard enough on the kids. I was getting more and more in my shell," Coach Bitto says of 2012 and 2013.

The reasons for him, and the program, losing their way are complicated. Carmel was not as talented as in previous years. There was a leadership void within the upper classes. The competition within the East Suburban Catholic Conference got better, the schedule tougher. But mostly, the decline happened due to an erosion of trust internally.

Coach Bitto said many times during our conversations over the years that for a program to be a consistent winner, it must have great kids, strong parental support and cooperation from the administration.

"Everyone must be on the same side, pulling in the same direction," he said.

By 2011, relations between Coach Bitto and the school president at the time, Dr. Judith Mucheck, were strained [she left the school in early 2014]. Over the next few years, there were a few incidents with players requiring discipline—"things that happens throughout the normal course of a season"—where he felt Mucheck did not back him.

"Because of the problems, I felt like I was looking over my shoulder," he says. "I was less demonstrative to the kids about being good guys. I didn't get on them if they didn't hustle. My coaches thought I was letting things go. I was very cautious."

This passivity was reflected in the results—Carmel went 3-6 in 2012 and 2-7 in 2013, its lowest win total since 1991. And while the defeats were hard, much tougher for Coach Bitto was the loss of identity.

$\approx$

At the center of his ability to relate to kids has always been his life experience.

"I was a star player and I got hurt. I had to fight through that. I have experience of being on the bench and working my way back from injuries. Then I go to college, and within 12 seconds I knew I wasn't as good as those guys. If there had been 13 running backs, I'd have been 13th. So I fight through that. Then my sister is killed in a car accident and I had to deal with that. I see my parents have to suffer and raise her kids, so I learn about resilience and hard work. Then I was an assistant for 13 years. I had to work hard at developing my craft before I became a head coach."

Those life experiences formed his hardscrabble Midwestern values, reflected in how he leads young men—that self-reliance over dependence is the fastest ticket to adulthood.

"Who is going to take care of your career? You. Who's going to take care of your education? You. If you are second team, figure out a way to be first team. OK, you may not be first team on this team but what about the next team? What about the next job you have? Part of it is telling a kid you are powerful and you can do this. I always tell the kids they don't know how powerful they are. You are in control of everything you do. They don't hear that enough. They don't hear 'yes you can.' Football is the perfect model for that scenario."

Before the 2014 season, Coach Bitto vowed to get back to his core principles. "If the kids get out of line, they are going to hear about it. They know there are expectations and consequences. I've gotten back to being more of a taskmaster. It's back to where it was and it's worked out better for our program." He says he does more one-on-one coaching, when before, those interactions might be tasked to an assistant coach.

This evolution has Coach Bitto excited about the future. The program has regained its footing, and 2015, his 18th as head coach, could be the team's strongest since 2010. His oldest son, Peter, is a senior on the team. And as he has since that day in October of 1984, when, under the back drop of tragedy Fitz found him in the Carmel gymnasium, and like a whisper from God, helped guide him on a path towards his life's mission, he's right where he wants to be, teaching, coaching, and mentoring young men.

"We have so many kids who are willing to do a million things. I'm always excited as most of them get the work ethic. And parents do want them to get it. That's why people come to Carmel. There's the faith part, yes. The other part is work ethic.

"We are going to push them father than the public school. No, you earn that 'A', you earn that 'B', you earn that playing time. You earn being on a team. Then you and the team will be successful."

∾

Jordan Kos finished his career at Carmel as the school's all-time leading rusher. His senior year, 2011, he earned his third all-conference award while scoring 18 touchdowns. As of the fall of 2015, he is a junior running back at Winona State University on track to graduate with a degree in Business Administration.

Luke Venegoni played four years of college football at Western Illinois University. His senior year, he finished second on the team in tackles. In September of 2014, he totaled seven tackles against the University of Wisconsin in Madison and the Badgers Heisman Trophy-finalist running back Melvin Gordon III. He graduated in May of 2015 with a degree in Economics. He lives in the Chicago area and works in private business.

Mike Fitzgibbons is a senior at Culver-Stockton College in Canton, Missouri. He plays linebacker and safety for the Wildcats and is on track to graduate in the spring of 2016.

Brian Serio did not play college football. He attended Purdue University and graduated in May of 2015 with a degree in mechanical engineering. He lives and works in the Chicago area.

LaRon Biere spent one year at Illinois State University before moving to Lansing, Michigan. He works in the hospitality industry, writing music and helping to produce songs for friends. He remains close friends with Carmel teammate Matt Carr, who graduated from Michigan State University in May of 2015.

And Jim Biere is still living in the same home where he and Marion raised their family.

ACKNOWLEDGMENTS

THERE ARE A LOT OF SIMILARITIES between writing a book and playing football at Carmel. Success is not achieved without everyone doing their job.

From our first meeting, I knew Andy Bitto had a story to tell. And he let me tell it, and for his trust I will be forever grateful. Michael Fitzgibbons sat with me for many long interviews, remaining patient with my repetitive questions. His ceaseless dedication to Carmel has my lifelong admiration. I am especially thankful to Ben Berg, Joe May, Jerry Rejc, Tim Schrank, Tom Young, Dan Potempa, Enzo Magrin, Kevin Nylen, and Tom Kelly, who were more than generous with their time. This book would not be possible without them.

To the players, I can never thank you enough. Your passion for the game, for Carmel, and for each other is for me, still a daily inspiration. I want to particularly thank Jordan Kos, Luke Venegoni, Mike Fitzgibbons, Brian Serio, Sean Wolf-Lewis, Jake Larson, Matt Carr, Chris Georgan, and LaRon Biere for being so truthful at what can be, a very vulnerable time in the lives of teenagers.

Heartfelt thanks to Scott and Beth Carr, Jeff and Sara Klahs, Steve and Tina Lester, Paul and Mary Serio, John and Claudia Venegoni, Mark and Michelle Reimer, and Scott and Terese Greene, for generously inviting me into their homes, sharing their perspectives, and lucky for me, their tasty meals. To so many others associated with Carmel—teachers, faculty members and support staff, your assistance was invaluable.

It's not easy writing about someone no longer on this earth. Without the hours of interviews with Jim, Tom and Ann Biere as well as Joanne and Ron Wegener, I could not have brought Marion's story to life. And to Nadine Sedar, Marilyn Adams, Joan Zupec and Ed Ravine, thank you for sharing your memories.

Without the contributions of my cousin Carl Nerup, John Butler and Pete Wifler, this project never would have gotten off the ground. Thank you for your support.

A book is not in finished form until it is edited thoroughly. The conscientious work of Peter Meyer, Mindy Werner, Phil Hagen, Jim Powers and John Borneman made the book immeasurably better. I can't thank Neil Hayes enough for being so giving of his time. And to Clayton Smith and Steven Luna of Dapper Press and Kelley Jensen, for adding their creative visions to the project.

Most important, I have to thank my family. My parents, Howard and Patricia, my three siblings, and eight nieces and nephews. Your encouragement gave me much-needed energy at the beginning, during, and end of the project. Now that it's finished, you will never have to ask, 'how is the book coming?' ever again.

ABOUT THE AUTHOR

Jon J. Kerr is a sportswriter for Chicago Tribune Media Group. He has contributed to *Sports Illustrated* and *Catholic New World*. In 2014, Kerr won an Associated Press Sports Editors award. He lives in Chicago. For more information, visit his website at jonjkerr.com.